African Narratives of Slavery and Abolition

African Narratives of Slavery and Abolition

Testimonies from the Nineteenth Century

RICHARD ANDERSON

BLOOMSBURY ACADEMIC
LONDON • NEW YORK • OXFORD • NEW DELHI • SYDNEY

BLOOMSBURY ACADEMIC
Bloomsbury Publishing Plc
50 Bedford Square, London, WC1B 3DP, UK
1385 Broadway, New York, NY 10018, USA
29 Earlsfort Terrace, Dublin 2, Ireland

BLOOMSBURY, BLOOMSBURY ACADEMIC and the Diana
logo are trademarks of Bloomsbury Publishing Plc

First published in Great Britain 2025

Copyright © Richard Anderson, 2025

Richard Anderson has asserted his right under the Copyright,
Designs and Patents Act, 1988, to be identified as Author of this work.

For legal purposes the Acknowledgements on pp. xiii–xiv constitute
an extension of this copyright page.

Cover design by Grace Ridge
Cover image © Nastasic via Getty Images

All rights reserved. No part of this publication may be reproduced or
transmitted in any form or by any means, electronic or mechanical,
including photocopying, recording, or any information storage or retrieval system,
without prior permission in writing from the publishers.

Bloomsbury Publishing Plc does not have any control over, or responsibility for,
any third-party websites referred to or in this book. All internet addresses given
in this book were correct at the time of going to press. The author and publisher
regret any inconvenience caused if addresses have changed or sites have ceased
to exist, but can accept no responsibility for any such changes.

A catalogue record for this book is available from the British Library.

A catalog record for this book is available from the Library of Congress.

ISBN: HB: 978-1-3504-5965-6
PB: 978-1-3504-5964-9
ePDF: 978-1-3504-5967-0
eBook: 978-1-3504-5966-3

Typeset by Integra Software Services Pvt. Ltd.

To find out more about our authors and books visit www.bloomsbury.com
and sign up for our newsletters.

*To Robert Harms
and Clare Anderson*

CONTENTS

List of Figures ix
List of Tables x
List of Maps xi
Preface xii
Acknowledgements xiii
Note on Orthography xv

Introduction: African Voices in Missionary Archives 1

PART ONE West Africa

1. Josiah Yamsey 27
2. David Noah 35
3. Matthew Thomas Harding 39
4. John Attarra 43
5. John Campbell 49
6. Charles Harding 53
7. George Thompson 57
8. James Will 63
9. Joseph Boston May 75
10. Joseph Wright 81
11. Joseph Right 91
12. James Gerber 95
13. Thomas King 99
14. James Barber 103
15. Peter Wilson 107

16 Susannah Bola 113
17 William Doherty 117

PART TWO Enslavement in Africa

18 Awa 125
19 Daniel Dopemu 129
20 Jack Macumba 133
21 John Cupidon 137
22 Mary Ann Gay 143
23 John Gum 147

PART THREE East Africa

24 George David 155
25 William Henry Jones 161
26 Ishmael Semler 167
27 James Deimler 170
28 Paul Deimler 171
29 Lewis Brenn 172
30 David Rebmann 172
31 Cecil Mabruki 173
32 Duiah William 173

Notes 175
Bibliography 203
Index 214

FIGURES

1 'How Thomas King Became a Slave', *Church Missionary Gleaner*, March 1851, 139. Courtesy of the Church Missionary Society Archives 5
2 Joseph Boston May. Courtesy of The John Rylands Research Institute and Library 79
3 William Jones. Courtesy of The John Rylands Research Institute and Library 165

TABLES

1 Narratives in this volume 23

MAPS

1 Birthplace of narrators in Bight of Benin interior 14
2 Regional origins of East African narrators 22

PREFACE

This edited collection of primary sources brings together testimonies of slavery and the slave trade found in the archives and contemporary publications of British Protestant missions in Africa. As studies of the slave trade and the African diaspora are witnessing a 'biographical turn', historians are seeking out testimonies of enslavement by individuals born free in Africa. While historians have generally considered there to be few first-hand accounts by Africans who experienced enslavement and the middle passage, recent research has greatly expanded the number of known testimonies. Many of these accounts are found in mission archives and publications, composed in the context of the missionary encounter in West and East Africa. This volume comprises some of the most substantial, previously unpublished accounts of the slave trade in the archives of the Church Missionary and Methodist Missionary Societies. While most compiled accounts of slave narratives have focused on West Africa and the Atlantic, this book places accounts from the transatlantic trade alongside narratives from the Indian Ocean slave trade, as well as accounts of enslaved people who never left the African continent. The compendium is intended for both research and undergraduate classroom use.

ACKNOWLEDGEMENTS

The idea for this collection emerged in a classroom. Working with my mentor, Robert Harms, I was introduced to Philip Curtin's pioneering *Africa Remembered: Narratives by West Africans from the Era of the Slave Trade*. A half century after publication, *Africa Remembered* remains an essential research and teaching tool, and students and scholars alike obtain used and bent copies of this now out-of-print book. Recognizing the importance of first-hand accounts in both undergraduate teaching and my own research, I have spent the last several years seeking out more such narratives.

I undertook much of the research and transcription for this volume during an SSHRC postdoctoral fellowship at the Harriet Tubman Institute, York University. At York, I was fortunate enough to participate in the institute's Studies in the History of the African Diaspora – Documents (SHADD) project, a digital initiative focused on uncovering narratives of individuals born free in West Africa who experienced enslavement and the middle passage. Project members including Sean Kelley and Kyle Prochnow have been great supporters in finding and analysing the sources presented in this volume. Olatunji Ojo has been a fount of knowledge of the history and human geography of Ilẹ̀ Yorùbá. Robin Law, Leo Spitzer, Kristin Mann, Matthew Hopper, Maeve Ryan, David Perfect and Fred Morton generously assisted with additional sources and interpretation.

The introduction to this volume is revised and expanded from my 2017 article in the journal *Slavery & Abolition*, 'Uncovering Testimonies of Slavery and the Slave Trade in Missionary Sources'.[1] I am very grateful to *Slavery & Abolition* editor Gad Heuman for permission to republish an expanded version of this essay. Earlier versions of the introduction were presented at the SHADD Biography Project Conference, Museu Vivo do São Bento, Rio de Janeiro, 3–6 November 2015, and on the panel '*Africa Remembered* at 50: New Perspectives on Biography and the Middle Passage' at the 2017 African Studies Association Annual Meeting.

A Commonwealth Rutherford Fellowship at the University of Leicester facilitated further research on narratives from East Africa. Thanks to members of Leicester's Global, Colonial, and Postcolonial research cluster, especially Clare Anderson, John Coffey, Zoe Groves, Prashant Kidambi, Svenja Bethke, Deborah Toner and Kate Boehme. The staff of the Cadbury Library, University of Birmingham – the home of the Church Missionary Society Archives – have helped me navigate a vast archive. Ken Osborne,

CMS archivist, has graciously provided permission to reproduce CMS archival materials. Thanks also to the staff of the John Rylands Research Institute and Library, The University of Manchester, for providing images for this volume. I am greatly indebted to Maddie Smith, Megan Harris and Paige Harris at Bloomsbury Publishing, Shamli Priya Vijayan at Integra Software Services and to the anonymous peer reviewers for such engaged and insightful comments on this volume.

Last but not least to Christine, Rosa, my parents David and Lorraine, and the Johnson, Garrahan and Whyte families.

NOTE ON ORTHOGRAPHY

The texts in this collection are verbatim transcriptions of primary sources. Apart from the addition of minor punctuation and paragraphing, I have not edited the texts for spelling and grammar, preferring to present the primary sources as originally written. I have not utilized the condescending '[*sic*]' as in almost all instances the meaning is clear. In cases where words are unclear – or if the quality of the original primary source or its microfilm copy is illegible – I have added explanatory notes. Wherever possible, I have also added explanatory notes regarding historic places. In certain instances, I have been unable to positively identify locations mentioned in the sources.

Introduction: African Voices in Missionary Archives

Narratives written by enslaved Africans are the most invaluable sources for historians of both the transatlantic and Indian Ocean slave trades, and slavery in Africa, Asia and the Americas. Such narratives help uncover the means by which Africans came to be enslaved, the trade routes over which they were forcibly moved and the factors that determined whether they would be held in slavery in Africa or sold into the trans-oceanic trade. Equally importantly, these narratives elucidate the experience of enslavement, separation from family and kin, and the anguish of uncertainty in alien surroundings. Often, these very personal tales also provide insights into larger historical forces of politics and warfare, offering unique glimpses into the broader history of pre-colonial Africa. Yet these autobiographical accounts are as scarce as they are valuable. While multiple compendiums and edited volumes of slave narratives exist, most of their protagonists were born in the Americas.[1] By contrast, we have far fewer accounts by individuals who were once free in Africa.[2] Philip Curtin's pioneering edited collection of narratives, *Africa Remembered*, contained the voices of eight enslaved Africans.[3] Subsequent findings have added to this number, most especially in the work of Sandra E. Greene, Alice Bellagamba and Martin Klein.[4] The imperative of identifying and disseminating such unique sources remains a central concern of scholars of slavery and the slave trade.[5]

Since Curtin published *Africa Remembered* in 1967, historians have recognized missionary archives as an important repository of narrative accounts from Africans who experienced enslavement in Africa and sale to Europeans on the African coast.[6] The Church Missionary Society (CMS) and Methodist Missionary Society (MMS) archives hold some of the most famous narratives of enslavement in West Africa, including those of Samuel

Crowther, Joseph Wright and Ali Eisami Gazirmabe, all of which were recorded in Sierra Leone and all of which appeared in Curtin's volume.[7] Similarly well-known are the brief biographical sketches that CMS missionary Sigismund Wilhelm Koelle wrote of his linguistic informants while composing his monumental *Polyglotta Africana* (1854).[8]

While these accounts are the best-known narratives in the CMS and MMS collections and publications, they are only a fraction of the life histories recorded in these archives. Mission stations in West and East Africa drew in formerly enslaved people, many of whom subsequently wrote or dictated accounts of their experiences of enslavement, liberation, and eventual conversion. Twenty-six of the thirty-two accounts in this volume were written by so-called Liberated Africans, a legal designation for Africans emancipated in Vice-Admiralty Courts and Courts of Mixed Commission from slave ships intercepted by the Royal Navy off the African coast after 1807. This volume focuses in particular on Liberated Africans transported to Sierra Leone, The Gambia, India, or mission stations in present-day Kenya.[9] Like enslaved people disembarked in the Americas or Asian destinations including the Arabian Peninsula, Persian Gulf and India, Liberated Africans were torn from families, commoditized, placed in deadly conditions and transported to unfamiliar settings. Though their own middle passages were diverted to courts around the Atlantic and Indian Oceans, all Liberated Africans had experienced capture in Africa. They were subjected to weeks of disease, cramped conditions and uncertainty as they were forcibly moved to the coast, held in barracoons, and sold to European traders.

Many Liberated African converts, at various points in their life, wrote accounts of their enslavement, liberation and eventual conversion. In many other cases, missionaries also recorded accounts spoken to them. The policy of educating young Liberated Africans in missionary schools in Sierra Leone (the epicentre of Britain's naval campaign), The Gambia (where several thousand Liberated Africans were sent from Freetown) and India (where Liberated Africans intercepted in the Indian Ocean were often placed with CMS schools) and the high level of literacy that many of these formerly enslaved Africans attained mean that these African diasporic communities composed more first-hand accounts of enslavement than most regions of disembarkation in the Atlantic and Indian Oceans. As missions spread within West Africa – particularly what later became Nigeria – mission agents began to recount both their own experiences of enslavement in the region while recording the testimonies of enslaved and formerly enslaved people in the Bight of Benin hinterland. At the same time, mission stations in the Bight of Benin interior were outposts for enslaved Africans seeking refuge as well as sites of contention when Africans held in slavery by Christian converts sought to affect their freedom by appealing to missionaries or British officials on the coast at Lagos.[10]

Methodologies: Uncovering narratives, reading narratives

The CMS archive, held at the University of Birmingham, is a vast collection. The CMS Original Papers (CA1/O) for the Sierra Leone mission alone comprises 5,115 letters and journals written by 210 individuals between 1820 and 1880. In addition are 2,867 documents written by eighty-six individuals involved in the Yoruba mission (CA2/O) from 1844 to 1880 and a smaller collection of 664 incoming original documents by twenty-five individuals in the East Africa (Kenya) Mission (CA5/0) from 1841 to 1880. Yet the great strength of these sources, compared to British colonial sources or travel narratives, is that Africans wrote a large percentage of the material in the archive. African mission agents wrote perhaps 30 per cent of the Sierra Leone CMS archive; most of these writers were Liberated Africans who had experienced enslavement and British naval interdiction. For the Yoruba mission, forty-seven of the eighty-six authors who produced documents were Africans, including many Liberated African 'returnees' who travelled with the mission from Freetown. Though African authors produced only 47 per cent of the individual documents in the CMS Yoruba mission archive, J. D. Y. Peel estimates that over 60 per cent of journals (as opposed to short business letters) were written by African agents of the mission.[11] In East Africa, many of the first mission agents in what would later become Kenya were Liberated Africans from East Africa, emancipated in the Persian Gulf and educated in India before returning with the CMS to East Africa.

The large number of African authors means that the prospect of uncovering life histories recorded by Africans is therefore much greater. Moreover, accounts appear often in the papers of these missions since CMS mission agents were encouraged to keep daily journals. For most of the nineteenth century, agents were expected to keep journals or 'journal extracts' for dispatch to headquarters in London to inform policy decisions and provide excerpts for publication in CMS periodicals such as the CMS *Gleaner*, *Intelligencer*, *Record*, and *Missionary Register*.[12]

The journal extract system came into being by the 1830s and was further elaborated upon during the years when the Rev. Henry Venn was clerical secretary (1841–73).[13] The prosaic quality of these journals and their sheer abundance make them rich sources for uncovering the biographies and autobiographies of formerly enslaved men and women. The journals reflect aspects of diaries as personal reflections. But they were always intended as an information-gathering and propaganda-disseminating tool. As such, these 'journals' were composed with the knowledge that they would serve as the basis for extracts that would be edited and censored for potential publication. As the mission instructed the missionary W. A. B. Johnson in 1817, 'Send us particular narratives of what takes place that you think will interest our friends.'[14]

The MMS did not have the sophisticated information system and journaling policy of the CMS and did not require their mission agents to compose journals. The MMS archive is nevertheless an equally rich source of biographical accounts. An even greater percentage of the mission's staff was African-born, owing to their lack of funds and European staff compared to their CMS counterparts. As we will see below, a large percentage of the African MMS missionaries and preachers – particularly those of Yoruba birth – left accounts of their enslavement in the MMS archive.

Historians have known of some of these accounts for some time, though they have often used the sources for different purposes. Robin Law used the accounts of Samuel Crowther, James Barber and Thomas King in order to establish a basic chronology of the fall of the Oyo Empire and the subsequent Yoruba wars.[15] Leo Spitzer employed the narrative of Joseph Boston May – one of the lengthiest accounts in the MMS archive – to explore experiences of assimilation and marginality of colonized people in the era of emancipation.[16] Fred Morton has utilized many of the accounts from East Africa presented herein, especially to illuminate the experiences of children caught up in the Indian Ocean trade.[17] This volume re-evaluates several of the previously identified testimonies from mission archives alongside less-known but equally significant sources.

In many cases, the testimonies of Africans regarding their enslavement were subsequently printed in missionary propaganda, which was sold to fund the mission, though this is more the case for those associated with the CMS rather than the Wesleyan Methodists. Eleven of the thirty-two accounts in this volume were published in Britain at some point in the nineteenth century (Table 1). Many times published accounts were accompanied by dramatic wood-block engravings depicting the moment of enslavement or the deprivation of the barracoon. Images such as that which accompanied the article 'How Thomas King Became a Slave' (Figure 1) were designed to amplify the emotional impact of the testimony. Their perceived effectiveness was such that the images were often recycled and used to accompany multiple accounts across CMS publications.[18]

Missionary publications can help us uncover more narratives and identify the original manuscript.[19] Whenever possible, it is important to transcribe the original archival document. Published accounts were often heavily edited, with details omitted. In many cases, the author was left anonymous, and their accounts reduced to a few paragraphs. In other cases, CMS editors cut out details they deemed too unseemly for a Victorian audience; the missionary censor cut out a graphic portion of Samuel Crowther's description of a barracoon, in which he recalled the squalor of chained men needing to defecate in the night. The transcriptions include strikethroughs and marginal comments showing the workings of editorial interventions in rewordings and deletions.

This is not a full anthology of accounts of enslavement from within the vast CMS archive or its Methodist counterpart. The CMS's uniquely

FIGURE 1 'How Thomas King Became a Slave', *Church Missionary Gleaner*, New Series, No. 12, March 1851, 139. Courtesy of the Church Missionary Society Archives.

sophisticated information system led to the production of copious letters, journals and reports, resulting in a monumental archival collection. References to slavery within the archive span reports on nineteenth-century mission fields from Sierra Leone; to western, eastern and (later) northern Nigeria; South Africa; to present-day Uganda, Kenya, Tanzania, Egypt and the Sudan.[20] This book is an annotated collection of the richest testimonies of enslavement held within the archives of two missionary societies working in various parts of Africa in the nineteenth century.

A volume on African narratives of enslavement requires a workable definition of 'narrative' and a rationale of which narratives have been included. Autobiographical narratives are simultaneously unique productions – autobiography as unique tales of a unique life – and often invariant works marked by common themes and conventions. This work takes narrative to mean a memory exercise or recollective act in which the writer or narrator reflects on past events of their life in a way that shows how their past history reflects on their present state of being.[21] Narrative also implies a certain structure and arc, which in turn requires basic chronological details and, therefore, a certain length. The narratives herein share certain basic details of regions of birth, circumstances of enslavement and a span of years between enslavement, liberation and date of writing or dictation. While it is difficult to establish a threshold for what constitutes a testimony or biography, I have included only accounts of at least 300 words, ranging up to 4,000 words.[22]

The contents of this volume are lopsided in two key respects. First, the majority (twenty-three of thirty-two) of accounts originate from British West Africa. Second, the overwhelmingly majority of accounts (twenty-nine of thirty-two) are written by men. This latter shortcoming is perhaps not surprising given the nature of missionary training, the attitudes of the mission towards women and their emphasis on domesticity in educating females.[23] The preponderance of male voices in this collection is reflective of missionary gender biases and policies which sought to identify young, male African candidates to serve as mission agents. Only one of the three accounts by women in this volume – that of Mary Ann Gay – is in the first person, while the testimonies of Awa and Susannah Bola clearly show the significance of the male European missionary as amanuensis. The imbalance of female-to-male voices in this volume is not reflective of the ratio of males-to-females in the transatlantic slave trade or Indian Ocean trade, let alone enslavement within West and East Africa where women often predominated.[24] Though lopsided towards male experiences, the thirty-two accounts in this volume nevertheless comprise a unique collection of female and male voices from the Atlantic and Indian Oceans.

The texts herein were produced during a particular era of the slave trade in the nineteenth century, when the Danish, British and United States had abolished the trade and when the trade was under attack by abolitionists, including state and non-state British actors. These changes in the external trade were concomitant with momentous ruptures within many African societies. In West Africa, the collapse of Oyo after 1817 and the jihād led by 'Uthmān dan Fodio brought a fundamental change in the relationship of Yoruba speakers with the slave trade.[25] Oyo's collapse and the ensuing Yoruba wars instigated a sharp increase in the number of Yoruba-speaking captives sold to the coast. At least fifteen of the accounts in this volume relate to the history of imperial collapse, jihād and warfare in the Yoruba-speaking regions of the Bight of Benin interior.

The expansion of the East African slave trade in the nineteenth century brought with it an extension of the slaving frontier inland and long-distance caravans taking enslaved Africans from the interior to the East

African coast.²⁶ At the same time as the suppression of the external slave trade from African shores, slavery expanded in many parts of the continent. Meanwhile, slavery within European colonial enclaves experienced a slow death as colonial officials were hesitant to intervene in what they viewed as a 'domestic' system of slavery.²⁷ The narrators in many of the accounts, especially in sections two and three, describe the tension between slave trade suppression at sea and colonial slaveholding on land.

Circumstances of writing

The documents in this collection date from 1820 to 1880. Many of the accounts from West Africa were written within a few years of one another and are particularly concentrated in the late 1830s. The October 1837 edition of the *Church Missionary Record* featured a lead article on the 'Narratives of Three Liberated Negroes'. The article did not name the authors, but it included the account written by Samuel Crowther, as well as Liberated African catechists Thomas Harding and John Attarra.²⁸ These were among the first publications of such accounts from the pens of Liberated Africans.²⁹ These articles are also significant in that they may have influenced the Wesleyans' decision to solicit Liberated African narratives in Sierra Leone and The Gambia in 1838 and 1839.

The narratives of Joseph Wright, James Will, Joseph Boston May, Charles Harding and James Campbell – all Wesleyan Methodists from various Yoruba-speaking regions – are dated between October 1838 and June 1839.³⁰ This close concentration of dates suggests that converts were prompted to record their experiences, most likely for the purposes of missionary publications in Britain. Joseph May, the first of these five men to write an account, introduced his narrative by telling how the Wesleyan missionary Thomas Dove had 'read one of his little books to us and give two or three away he then told us that it will be very good if we can make or write something like this of our conversion or our Experience'. As May's introductory remarks make clear, these written statements were first and foremost intended as narratives of conversion rather than narratives of enslavement and liberation. In other instances, converts wrote these accounts on their own accord, whether they felt a personal need to do so or because they thought it might be of interest to the mission and its publications. The resulting text often asserted the embrace of a new Christian identity.

These were documents written with a particular form and for a particular purpose. They were often labelled as 'conversion statements' rather than slave narratives, though their titles also often read simply 'The Life of …'; William Henry Jones (no. XXV in this volume) titled his account as a 'self history'. Though these are biographies of formerly enslaved people, they are as much a part of the long-standing and widespread literary tradition of spiritual biography in which the convert documents the trials of their life and their spiritual conversion. These documents must, of course, be used with some caution, as Christian converts wrote them several years after the fact and likely shaped their narrative for publication for a Christian audience in Britain.[31] Many authors interpreted the arc of their life narrative as reflecting 'the dealings of Providence', as the Liberated African John Attarra described his enslavement. Josiah Yamsey, an early convert to the Anglican mission at Regent in the 1810s, was convinced of the design by which 'God bring me out from my country people & when I live on slave ship, God send English ships & God give me favour before that Englishman'.[32]

Twenty-two of the accounts in this volume are presented in the first person while ten are clearly the product of dictation to European missionaries who rendered testimony into the third person, possibly also via translation.[33] This process is perhaps most evident in the first account by Josiah Yamsey, which takes the form of a question-and-answer dialogue with the missionary W. A. B. Johnson, himself a German-born working-class immigrant to London from Hanover. In some cases, the process of composition is less clear and accounts can shift from first to third person (see, for example, V 'Statement of John Campbell'). The most obvious interventions by white missionaries are those than amplify the suffering and violence inflicted upon their subjects in order to elicit spectatorial sympathy in the reader.[34]

Sandra E. Greene's work on narratives from southern Ghana dictated to German missionaries has broached the question of whether it is 'possible to separate the voice of the enslaved from that of his or her amanuensis? Or does this unravelling in some instances undermine the shared effort that was at the very heart of the collaborative production of the narrative?'[35] Greene observes that while enslaved and formerly enslaved individuals may have shared their experiences with the interested listener 'it was the amanuensis, the person who recorded the words, who then selected extracts and shaped the resulting fragments into a narrative'.[36] Beyond mediation, dictated accounts also raise questions as to whether oral accounts differ from written accounts in terms of composition (dictated in one sitting or multiple retellings), narrative rhythm and candidness.[37]

Scholars utilizing narratives of enslaved and formerly enslaved people in sub-Saharan Africa have placed increased attention to the circumstances of their production, considering the complexities of memory, amanuensis, editorial interventions and audience, especially as many accounts were the product of either or both missionary propaganda and abolitionist movements. Gareth Griffiths points out the paradoxical nature of these texts as they 'reveal how narrative conventions operated to contain the "native voice" they claimed to express, while, paradoxically, that very act of containment inscribed a record of its presence and even its actual operation in the choices and narrative strategies of the texts themselves'.[38]

The narratives in this volume are replete with improbable and poetic stories. Many of these reflect common religious tropes: divine providence, redemption and reunion. The narrative conclusions of some of these stories are unlikely reunions with family members. Missionary tropes should not mask the fact that these unlikely reverse middle passages actually occurred.[39] At least three of the individuals in this volume – Joseph Wright, Thomas King and Susannah Bola – were able to reunite with family members, making them among the few of the 10.7 million survivors of the middle passages to ever see kin in Africa again.

Many of the narratives in this volume evince a complex relationship between homeland and diaspora. First and most obviously, most authors present themselves with Anglicized names denoting their proximity to the missionary establishment and the colonial project. The thirty-two narrators include four James, three Johns, and three Josephs, and surnames include Gerber, Deimler and Rebmann which were shared with white European missionaries.[40] Few authors mention an African birth name and in only a few instances has it been possible to identify (at times tentatively) an African name from other archival sources. Descriptions of homelands are generally infused with notions of civilization and atavism ingrained through missionary education. Joseph May began his narrative by stating that he 'was born in Aku Country, a heathen nation, a country full of idolatry'.[41] May, Wright and Will all identified themselves as 'Aku' – a colonial Sierra Leonean term for Yoruba speakers – at the beginning of their statements but were often critical and even derogatory towards their places of birth. This, of course, came from their own personal disapproval of 'paganism', as well as what they felt would be the expectations of the mission's publishers and their audience.

Reminiscences of homelands were also shaped by the young age at which many Liberated African narrators left their homeland. Paul Lovejoy has noted that 'while the ability of individuals to remember is particular and specific, the corresponding aptitude of children is clouded by a partial perspective on the adult world and the politics and economics that may have accounted for their enslavement'.[42] The nineteenth-century slave trade was to an unprecedented degree a trade in children, while in the Indian Ocean children were always a large percentage of captives taken from East Africa.[43] Though it is not possible to establish the age at which all of our Liberated African narrators were enslaved, many of them do list their approximate age when they were captured. John Campbell, a Yoruba Liberated African, recounted 'that he was at the age of twelve years old when War fell to his Country', while Joseph Boston May arrived in Sierra Leone 'in the year 1826, when I supposed to be about nine or ten years age'. Ishmael Semler described being taken when 'a very little boy' and spent at least eight years enslaved within East Africa. Most of our authors therefore arrived in Sierra Leone or India as adolescents, which is not surprising in that they were the most likely to become literate through missionary schooling. Nor is it surprising that some of their accounts lack specific place names, approximate dates, or a full comprehension of the political and military events that often affected their enslavement.

The ambiguities of memory and the prism of subsequent experiences are clear in the content of narratives. In some cases, though, the events recorded in these testimonies were not only remembered; some narrators researched aspects of their own history using the archival data from British records made in the suppression of the slave trade. Peter Wilson, an Owu Liberated African, 'endeavoured to gain and collect the facts of the events ... even the minutest particulars respecting his liberation from the bondage of slavery'.[44] Wilson was uniquely well positioned to do so, working for many years as a domestic servant to M. L. Melville, then registrar of Freetown's Mixed Commission Court. He may therefore have gained permission to access the court's records to uncover details of his arrival in the colony. These details were recorded in a posthumous account written by Peter's wife Eliza in 1860, based on what her late husband had uncovered. Published locally in the Liberated African village of Kissy, Wilson's life history recounts in tremendous detail that he was

> a native of the Aku Tribe, born in the Town of Owu; and was early sold into slavery to Portuguese slave dealers. His country name *Lai-guan-dai*, signifying, his being deprived of his father during infancy, may in some measure have led to his so easily falling a prey into the hands of the slave hunters. By the good Providence of God, he was however rescued from the holds of a Portuguese Brig called the 'Anizo' which was captured while on her destination for the Brazils, by H.M.S. Maidstone; Commodore Charles Buller, on the 26th of September 1824; and after a lengthened passage of 43 days, he, together with his fellow captives were safely landed and emancipated in the Colony, on the 8th November.

Wilson was able to identify the slave ship (actually the *Avizo*), the circumstances of their interception at sea and the exact date of their arrival, despite forty-six years in the colony. At least some Liberated African narrators therefore consulted colonial documents in order to reconstruct the details of their improbable journeys to Sierra Leone.[45]

Enslavement: Geographies and chronologies

Many of the individuals in this volume, victims of the transatlantic or Indian Ocean slave trades, were born within relatively concentrated regions of west and east Africa. Most narratives recorded from Sierra Leone are from individuals born in what would later become Nigeria. There are several reasons for this. First was the scale of the movement of Liberated Africans from the coast of present-day Nigeria, at the time better known as the eastern Bight of Benin and western Bight of Biafra. In total, 38,360 Liberated Africans reached Sierra Leone from the Bight of Benin and 31,471 from the Bight of Biafra, embarking primarily at the ports of Lagos, Bonny, Ouidah and Old Calabar.[46] The collapse of the Oyo Empire

(c. 1817–36), the ensuing Yoruba wars and the large number of captured vessels from the Bight of Benin in the decades after 1817 also coincided with the most concerted attempts to educate Liberated Africans in mission schools. In 1816, Governor Charles MacCarthy reached an agreement with the CMS to greatly expand the mission presence and schooling within the colony. Thereafter, emancipated youths were sent to one of a number of Liberated African villages outside of Freetown and placed in their newly founded mission schools.[47] Many of the accounts we have are from those educated by the missions in this period of church-state symbiosis.

The establishment of CMS and MMS missions in Yoruba territory and the Niger also led to several forms of life histories being recorded. Interpreters and CMS 'native agents' travelled from Sierra Leone with the Niger Expedition and subsequent Yoruba Mission. During their travels, many told of their experience of enslavement, particularly if they were travelling through or near their place of birth.[48] The first of these were the testimonies of translators who accompanied the 1841 Niger Expedition. James Frederick Schön, who participated on the expedition on behalf of the CMS, wrote in his journal upon their arrival at Anya near the mouth of the Niger River how

> our Brass [i.e. Ijo] interpreter was peculiarly anxious that one of the large number of persons who surrounded our vessel this evening should come on board, because he thought he recognised him. Though many years had lapsed since our interpreter was sold, and the other had, in the meantime, become an old man, they instantly recognized each other; and I cannot describe the astonishment manifested by the Ibo man at seeing one whom he verily believed had long since been killed and eaten by the White People ... The Interpreter then found out that Anya was the very place to which he had first been sold as a slave, and at which he had spent nine years of his early life; and that the very person with whom he was speaking had been his doctor and nurse in a severe illness, on which account he had retained a thankful remembrance of him.[49]

From 1841 on, missionaries recorded the accounts of Liberated Africans who accompanied the CMS mission as it attempted to establish itself in Yoruba-speaking territory. James Barber, a Liberated African born in the Egba town of Ijemo, returned with the CMS mission to become native catechist at Ibadan. In 1854, Barber told the missionary Edward G. Irving the story of his enslavement and the capture of Ijemo. Irving recorded Barber's account in his 'Journal of a visit to the Ijebu country', which was subsequently published in the *Church Missionary Intelligencer*.[50] Irving learned that Barber '[a] native of Ijemo ... was taken captive at the destruction of that place, and followed his new master into the Ijebu country'. Barber was forced to serve as a slave soldier with the allied Ife, Ijebu and refugee Oyo forces that destroyed the Egba settlements. Irving added that Barber 'was with the army which besieged Ikreku [Ikereku]' before being sold to the coast and intercepted at sea.

The influx of CMS 'native agents' into Yoruba-speaking districts led many to write their own reminiscences. Thomas King, a CMS pastor and repatriated Egba Liberated African from the town of Ẹmẹrẹ, travelled inland from Badagry to Abeokuta in early 1850 as part of the inchoate Yoruba mission.[51] King observed how everything he saw 'bespoke cheerfulness as well as reminding me of the pleasant sight and diversified prospect of trees and plants on which in my childhood I used to take a fond delight'. These reminders prompted King to reflect on

> the morning of that unhappy day that I was separated from my parents about the year 1825 in the beginning of November. I left home about eight o'clock for farm about three miles distance from home, in order to get some corn. My mother and elder sister, about a fortnight previous, went to Ishaga, a town about fourteen or fifteen miles distance from hence for trade ... My niece and I, my sister's daughter, were the little ones that were left at home. I stayed with my father, but my niece was left to the care of her father. No sooner had I got to the farm, and just cut sufficient corn for my load, than the repeated reports of muskets at the town gate acquainted me of my dangerous situation. All my endeavour to escape had utterly proved a failure, as I was surrounded by a number of men, who were very eager, as to whose lot my capture should fall. At last, as a kid among many chasing wolfs, I was caught by one of them.

King was taken to Lagos and sold to a Havana slave trader, and 'a few days later, with heavy hearts and sad countenances, we took leave of our shores without the slightest hope of visiting it any more'. Or so the young man thought.

The Egba youth who would later be named Thomas King was likely on board the Havana slave ship *Iberia* which departed Lagos in December 1825. The Royal Navy's interception of the vessel and its arrival in Freetown in January 1826 set in motion an improbable return. Legally emancipated by Freetown's Mixed Commission Courts, King was subsequently educated in CMS schools and graduated from Fourah Bay Institution in 1849.[52] A year later, he returned to Abeokuta via Badagry, where he was improbably reunited with his mother, whom Samuel Crowther had redeemed from slavery.

For some Liberated African missionaries, pastors and catechists, spreading the Gospel meant traversing the slave route in reverse. William Allen, a CMS pastor at Abeokuta and Liberated African of Iporo and Egba origin, recorded in his journal for 9 February 1865 that he 'started from Lagos by the river route as I could not return [to Abeokuta] by land'. Much like Thomas King before him, his familiar surroundings led him to contemplate 'a retrospect views of former years' and

> [h]ow I passed Lagos as a slave, not knowing where would my destination be, and what would become of me ... When at Lagos for some time in

the slave barracoon, I was then shipped together with several of my age in a slave ship; some months passed away in sailing here and there in order to avoid the English man of war, during which time several of my companions died only three of us survived. We afterwards fell into the hands of the man of war, and taken to Sierra Leone, where I was placed in school and taught to read and write, and all other instructions suitable for a Christian.[53]

His retrospective concluded with the emphatic assertion of his return to Lagos and how, '[i]n 1855 I landed again not as a slave, but as a freed man, and a teacher to my own land'.

Many of the testimonies recounted by Liberated Africans about Yorubaland – whether composed in Sierra Leone, The Gambia, or upon return to their region of birth – provide the only first-hand accounts of the revolutionary changes that swept this region of West Africa in the first decades of the nineteenth century. Several of these sources have helped historians determine the basic chronology of particular battles and campaigns in relation to the collapse of the Oyo Empire, the ascendance of the Sokoto Caliphate and the subsequent Yoruba wars. Robin Law's analysis of the chronology of the Yoruba wars draws heavily upon the details provided by Samuel Crowther, Joseph Wright, Thomas King and James Barber (the latter as recorded by Edward George Irving).[54] Barber's experience as an enslaved soldier in the destruction of Ikereku Idan is central to this reconstruction since 'the town, he states, was destroyed in 1826, as it was the year previously to his being liberated at Sierra Leone, which he knows to have been 1827'. Thomas King's recollection that his home town, Ẹmẹrẹ, was destroyed 'about the year 1825 in the beginning of November', is equally significant in dating the chronology of warfare in southern Yoruba-speaking regions in the 1820s. The recently uncovered narrative by Charles Harding (no. VI in this volume), a Liberated African at The Gambia, may provide the only first-hand account of the Owu War (c. 1816/17–1821/22), a catalytic event in the expansion of warfare in Yoruba territories.[55]

With the advent of the Yoruba and Niger Missions, other forms of testimonies began to emerge, namely those of Africans held in slavery, pawnship or other positions of servility who were often drawn to the mission due to their vulnerability. Though these Africans had not experienced sale into the European-led oceanic trade, the circumstances of their enslavement often mirrored those who had. Two of the accounts, those of Awa and Daniel Dopemu in Part Two of this collection, exist specifically because the deponents claimed to have been enslaved by a CMS convert at Abeokuta and had sought refuge at Lagos.

Map 1 demarcates the place of birth of narrators in this volume from the Bight of Benin, when known. It shows the close concentration of birthplaces among Yoruba speakers in what would later become southwestern Nigeria.

Indeed, almost half of the accounts in this volume come from individuals born within 100 kilometres of one another in a region that corresponds with the southern edges of the former Oyo Empire and the Egba territories to its south. The expansion of the Yoruba wars over an ever-greater area in the 1820s brought with it a moving and fluctuating frontier of violence and enslavement.[56] This expansion of violence has led David Eltis to conclude that 'it is highly likely that the Yoruba sub-groups ... entered the slave trade sequentially, as war and civil disturbance moved through or broke out in their area'.[57]

The concentration of these narratives means that these missionary sources contain fewer personal narratives from many regions caught up in the transatlantic slave trade, such as West Central Africa. However, these sources do provide a rich corpus of narratives among Africans who were drawn from many contiguous societies and who entered the slave trade along some three hundred miles of African coastline in present-day Nigeria and the Republic of Benin. Even then these narratives are not exclusively written by Liberated Africans from the Bight of Benin. Two of the lengthiest Liberated African

MAP 1 Birthplaces of narrators in the Bight of Benin interior, marked by asterisk (map by author).

accounts come from the above-mentioned David Noah from present-day Liberia and Josiah Yamsey, who was born in the Cameroon grasslands and sold to Portuguese slave traders at the Cameroon River *c*. 1815–16.

While these accounts are composed by individuals about their own lives, they often recount the enslavement of several others, usually family members who were simultaneously captured. Many evince the gender dynamics of the African and transatlantic trades, with men and boys separated from women and girls. In many instances, the male members of the family were sold into the transatlantic trade while the female members were retained and enslaved in African societies.[58] Thomas King's mother, Ije, was captured along with her family during the destruction of the Egba town of Ẹmẹrẹ in late 1825. She was sold to Ijebu and then Lagos where she remained 'in hard servitude under six or seven different owners, and would probably have died under the same, had it not been for the arrival of the missionaries here a few years ago'. As the narratives uncovered within the CMS and MMS archives to date are written overwhelmingly by men, the recorded fates of female family members provide glimpses of their own experiences of enslavement.

A number of these testimonies also describe the experience of re-enslavement, a common prospect for many Liberated Africans in Sierra Leone. Matthew Thomas Harding, a CMS catechist, recounted that he

> was born in a town 6 days journey to the sea, we were seven born of one father and mother, four sons and three daughters: I was at present when my father died, after the death of my father, behold war came upon us. I only was taken away from the family by the same war into the hand of a stranger, carring [*sic*] me from place to place untill to a slave vessel; but by the providence of God I was taken to Sierra Leone by the English vessel at governor Maxwell's time.[59]

Harding was apprenticed to Nancy Smith, a widow in the colony. Harding experienced enslavement for the second time when his master 'was enticed by her country man to go with him up to the country'. There they stayed for two months until

> the king order his 6 men to lift me up and carry me away the same night into other village, after two days the King came there and call for me and said to me now you are become one of my slave ... after that he order his man to lain a strips on me he said to me now this to make you believe that I am your master, he deliver me to one of his concubine who I lives 6 years, not openly but secretly for fear of the strangers that comes there often from Sierra Leone.

Harding was eventually redeemed from slavery by a Sierra Leonean trader, with charges brought against his former master for her complicity in his re-enslavement.

Liberated Africans also faced re-enslavement in their journeys beyond Sierra Leone. James Gerber, a Liberated African who lived fifteen years in Sierra Leone, returned to Badagry in 1843 to become a trader. In 1848, while on a trading excursion inland to Ijaye, he was enslaved for the second time in his life. Gerber told the CMS's John Christian Müller how he 'was taken, with many other Egbas, to a town called Ibatang [Ibadan], and sold there'.[60] The treatment he faced meant that 'when his new master wished to sell him, there was no purchaser', though eventually 'an Ibu man, pitying his wretched condition, bought him for six heads of cowries'. Gerber was carried through Ijebu to Lagos, where he was sold to Portuguese slave traders. Eventually, Gerber's relatives were able to intercede and ransom his freedom. Accounts such as those of James Gerber and Matthew Thomas Harding show that being a 'liberated' African was often a precarious designation and status, especially for those who sought employment outside of the Sierra Leone colony.

Enslavement in West Africa: Gambia and the Bight of Benin

The narratives in this volume are divided into three groups: West Africa (Sierra Leone and The Gambia); Enslavement in Africa (The Gambia and Bight of Benin); and East Africa. The first section has the largest number of accounts – seventeen – owing to the large number of Liberated Africans landed at Freetown and the scale of the missionary enterprise in the Sierra Leone colony after 1807. Five of the narratives in this volume were composed at The Gambia. Charles Harding, John Campbell, Joseph Right and Jack Macumba all wrote or dictated their accounts at St. Mary's Island in 1839. Also in 1839, John Cupidon wrote his account at MacCarthy's Island in the middle of the River Gambia some two hundred miles upstream from the coast.

The British took possession of St. Mary's, known today as Banjul Island, following the 1814 Treaty of Paris. The treaty returned to the French the settlements of Gorée and St. Louis that had been part of the British Senegambia Colony. In return the British retained James Island, a small trading outpost on the River Gambia, and the French recognized exclusive British rights to trade on the river. In 1816, Sierra Leone Governor Sir Charles MacCarthy ordered British army officer Alexander Grant to proceed from Gorée to the River Gambia to search for a place that 'afforded a facility of preventing vessels for slaves from entering the river and would at the same time be advantageous as a commercial establishment'.[61] Grant signed a treaty with the Mansa of Combo to station a garrison at Banjoul, a small, mangrove-covered island in the River Gambia estuary. Grant proceeded to establish the settlement of Bathurst on the renamed St. Mary's Island. In 1823, the British established a military post at Lemain Island, also known as

Janjanbureh and renamed by the British to MacCarthy's Island. The upriver outpost was intended to consolidate British military and mercantile influence on the river.[62] The Methodists – encouraged by Charles MacCarthy during a return visit to Britain – established mission outposts at St. Mary's and MacCarthy's. In the early years of the mission most of the congregations were either Liberated Africans or enslaved Wolof, the latter having primarily been brought from Gorée and St. Louis.[63]

There were two types of narratives composed in British territory along the River Gambia. The first was by Liberated African converts who were sent to The Gambia with the Wesleyan mission. The second were those of former 'domestic slaves' or enslaved Africans working on St. Mary's. The legal status of slavery within the colony was ambiguous. British occupation of the island was predicated on slave trade suppression. Once occupied, British officials relied upon the persistence of slave labour to grow the fledgling colonial economy. Domestic slavery may well have experienced an expansion in the region in response to demand for British exports.[64] The Methodist William Fox recorded in his journal seven months after the enactment of the Act for the Abolition of Slavery throughout the British Colonies, 'Today have had another interview with the Governor and a long conversation about the slaves he wishes me to tell my congregation that while they are on the Island they are not slaves. Why does His Excellency not tell the whole colony this?'[65] Fox was the most vocal of several resident missionaries, including Richard Marshall, William Moister, Thomas Dove, William Swallow, Henry Wilkinson and Robert MacBrair, who advocated and at times directly intervened against slaveholding.[66]

The accounts in this volume from The Gambia speak to the ambiguous legal status of slavery in a nascent British colony, especially among colonists who had recently migrated from the restored French territories of Gorée and Saint-Louis. British forces held Gorée from 1800 to 1817, during which time an Anglo-African trading community formed and worked with existing Goréen trade networks to The Gambia and rivers to the south.[67] By this time, enslaved people formed a large majority of the population of Gorée. When the British left Gorée to occupy St. Mary's and then MacCarthy's Island, a significant group of Gorée's population followed. This group included *habitant* merchants, artisans, the formerly enslaved and *laptots* (enslaved sailors whose skills were vital to the river fleet trade system).[68] All four of the narratives from The Gambia in this section – Jack Macumba, John Cupidon, Mary Ann Gay and John Gum – are from Africans brought unwillingly to The Gambia. Two of the accounts, those of Macumba and Cupidon, recall instances of self-purchase by enslaved men brought from Gorée to Bathurst.[69] In other instances, the Methodist Church engaged in a practice of redemption, by seeking funds to purchase the freedom of their members. This practice led disgruntled enslavers in the colony to bring court cases against missionaries including Fox and Swallow, accusing them of participating in slave trading through their transactions.[70]

The Gambia-Gorée accounts highlight the possibilities and challenges of manumission in this trans-imperial context as well as some of the tensions between missionaries and colonial officials on the subject. The Rev. William Fox reported on a conversation with Lieutenant-Governor George Rendall, in which the latter allegedly stated, 'They are not slaves, strictly speaking while they are on this island; but immediately when they leave, they are and. may be taken.' Rendall told Fox his preference was that he 'wished them to continue with their masters, but at the same time said he should feel a pleasure in doing what he could to get the freedom of any who wished it, at a moderate price'.[71] Wesleyan missionaries did not agree with Rendall's emphasis on the status quo and intervened in the freedom suits of enslaved converts. Missionaries such as William Fox put pressure to bear on the local government to accelerate and facilitate manumission. As Florence Mahoney explains, missionaries were motivated by a desire both to secure full social rights for members of their congregations and also to absorb them as evangelists.[72] John Gum, whose account features in Part Two, was one of a group of 'slaves, I could recommend in a short time', William Fox told Methodist readers 'were it not that they are tied in the same way'.[73]

The 1839 accounts of Jack Macumba, John Cupidon, Mary Ann Gay and John Gum from The Gambia are four of six accounts – the other two being from Lagos in 1865 – which feature in Part Two, Enslavement in Africa. The six accounts in this section are from individuals born free in West Africa who were enslaved and taken from their societies of birth. Unlike the other narrators in this volume, however, they remained enslaved within Africa, rather than being sold to European or Arab slave traders on the coast. They are the only narrators in this volume who were not Liberated Africans; though all four regained their freedom, this was not at the behest of the Royal Navy. The two accounts from Lagos are, rather, from refugees from slavery and part of a larger pattern of flight into Lagos from Abeokuta and other settlements to the north. These accounts – the testimonies of Awa and Daniel Dopemu – both assert that they were seeking refuge from Henry Robbin, a prominent trader and member of the CMS congregation at Abeokuta who they claimed had purchased and held them in slavery. Their accounts are thus quite different from the others which appear in this volume.

While most accounts in the missionary archive were consciously constructed tales of emancipation and salvation designed for potential publication and dissemination to British sponsors, the accounts of Awa and Daniel reflected the uncomfortable fact that many converts continued to hold Africans in slavery. As J. F. Ade Ajayi and E. A. Ayandele long ago pointed out, the CMS was often accommodating in looking past slaveholders in their congregations even as they condemned 'domestic slavery' in Africa as anathema to Christian values.[74] It was only in 1879 that a Lagos meeting of the CMS reached the decision that 'no Christian should purchase or sell a slave, and those who possessed slaves before their conversion, should afford them time and opportunity to buy out their freedom, and in the meantime should provide for their Christian instruction'. The temperate resolution – which prohibited converts from slave trading without confronting slaveholding – was unevenly enforced by missionaries.[75] Taken together, the accounts in Part Two involve themes of free soil and the status of slavery in Britain's West African empire during the central decades of British anti-slavery in West Africa. The individual accounts also reveal how missionaries could pressure colonial officials to intervene against local slaveholding while in other instances were much more ambivalent about the relationship between slaveholding and their congregations.

Enslavement in East Africa

Part Three focuses on East Africa and the Indian Ocean. The nine accounts in this section come from Liberated Africans intercepted on vessels crossing the Indian Ocean and brought to Bombay (today Mumbai) where they were placed with CMS missionaries. They are nine of approximately 22,000 Africans captured by the Royal Navy in the Indian Ocean who were subsequently landed at one of ten port cities stretching between Bombay and Cape Town.[76]

Until the 1850s most of the slave ships captured in the Indian Ocean were European vessels transporting enslaved Africans to Brazil and Cuba as well as sugar-producing islands in the Indian Ocean, especially Mauritius and Réunion. In the second half of the nineteenth century, most of the slave ships captured were Arab dhows bound for destinations in Arabia, the Persian Gulf or East Africa.[77] All of the accounts from this section are recorded from Africans taken from captured dhows.

The legal basis for these captures was an 1845 treaty which the British consul Atkins Hamerton forced upon the sultan of Zanzibar, which restricted the legal trade from Zanzibar to the sultan's dominions between Lamu to the north and Kilwa to the south, encompassing roughly five hundred miles of the coastline of present-day Kenya and Tanzania.[78] The treaty meant that dhows were only liable to seizure beyond this protected coastline. Given the inability to intercept ships in East African waters and the small size of the Navy's East Africa Squadron, the British sought to intercept vessels as they approached the Persian Gulf.

Most Africans on board intercepted vessels in the Indian Ocean were taken to Mauritius or the Seychelles. But several hundred Africans liberated by British interdiction in the Indian Ocean were turned over to the British municipality of Bombay. The first Liberated Africans taken to British India arrived in the 1830s. In 1835, two hundred Liberated African children were taken to Karachi and forwarded to the police commissioner in Bombay.[79] British policy in India at the time focused on the religious impartiality of the government. As such, Liberated Africans were distributed to European, Hindu and Muslim homes. Some Liberated Africans were placed at the 'Indo-British

Institution', an agricultural and trade school. This included William Jones, Ishmael Semler and George David, whose testimonies appear in Part Three.[80] All three were later relocated into the African Asylum, founded in 1860 at the CMS Industrial Mission in Sharanpur, near the city of Nashik.[81]

CMS missionaries W. S. Price and C. W. Isenberg founded the Asylum at Sharanpur, with the intention that pupils might return to East Africa with the mission. From 1860 to 1874 some two hundred young Liberated Africans arrived at Nashik.[82] Many graduates of the African Asylum joined the expanding East Africa mission, where they became known as 'Bombay Africans' or simply 'Bombays'. The origins of Bombay Africans covered a wide area from Ethiopia in the north and southwards to present-day Zimbabwe, Malawi and Mozambique.[83] Three accounts in Part Three are by the Bombay Africans Jones, Semler and David, who returned to what would later become Kenya in 1864.

Jones, Semler and David were taken from slave vessels in the 1850s as the British began a more consistent campaign to suppress the East African slave trade. From 1858 a specific anti-slavery squadron was deployed to operate as part of the East Indies Station.[84] With the expanded campaign to suppress the dhow trade from East Africa to Arabia, the CMS and Sir Bartle Frere (governor of the Bombay Presidency since 1867) saw the need for an East African equivalent to Sierra Leone. In 1873–74, the CMS expanded their mission presence in East Africa by setting up stations with the assistance of formerly enslaved converts. The CMS instructed W. S. Price, the superintendent at Sharanpur, to travel to East Africa and select a location for a new mission station on the mainland. The mission was established specifically for the reception of Liberated Africans. Founded in 1875, the settlement was called Frere Town after Sir Bartle Frere, who in 1873 had negotiated a treaty with the Sultan of Zanzibar legally abolishing the seaborne traffic in enslaved Africans. The final six accounts in this volume are from Liberated Africans taken from dhows in this period and taken to the CMS mission station at Frere Town where they composed life histories as part of a school exam. The narratives of James Deimler, Paul Deimler, Lewis Brenn, David Rebmann, Cecil Mabruki and Duiah William were written at Frere Town in 1880 and are the latest testimonies in this volume.

Fred Morton has previously analysed the CMS accounts from India and Frere Town, focusing in particular on the experiences of enslaved children in the nineteenth-century Indian Ocean.[85] The accounts appear here in publication for the first time. Morton, Marcia Wright, Edward A. Alpers and Matthew S. Hopper have contributed to uncovering accounts of enslaved Africans in the Indian Ocean world, principally from missionary sources as well as British Admiralty and consular records.[86] They conclude that, compared to testimonies from the Atlantic, 'those from Africans whose enslavement drew them into the Indian Ocean trade are for the most part quite brief and were not generated by the enslaved themselves'.[87] Two of the following accounts – those of William Jones and George David – are exceptions to this general rule. The concluding grouping of six accounts recorded at Frere Town reflects the terse nature of many Indian Ocean accounts in comparison with the earlier West African accounts in this volume.

Other published missionary accounts of enslavement from East Africa are well known. The Universities' Mission to Central Africa (UMCA) published fourteen well-known accounts between the 1880s and 1930s.[88] As published accounts intended to inspire metropolitan support for the UMCA mission, these accounts amplify physical abuse and violence. Further missionary accounts from East Africa include the testimony of Swema, an enslaved Yao girl from north-western Mozambique, which Edward Alpers has analysed in detail.[89] Morgan J. Robinson has analysed a broader collection of UMCA narratives found in volumes of the missionary publication *African Tidings*.[90] The advantage of the CMS narratives compared to their UMCA equivalents is their comparatively early date – the CMS was the first missionary society to operate in East Africa – and the less interventionist role of an amanuensis focused on publishing missionary propaganda.

Thus far, the CMS narratives from West and East Africa have been largely read in isolation by historians of the Atlantic and Indian Oceans, respectively. Presenting and analysing accounts from West and East Africa consecutively provides insights into the continuity and evolution of missionary depictions of enslavement and liberation. The accounts from East Africa are equally dominated by male voices as the mission continued to pursue a male ministry literate in English. As with West Africa, a noticeable feature of these accounts is the young age at which these Bombay Africans were enslaved. The demand for servants in urban homes around the Indian Ocean littoral meant that prepubescent boys and girls were a significant proportion of the traffic in enslaved Africans from Zanzibar, Pemba and the Kenya coast to Arabia, the Persian Gulf and India.[91] The narratives below also speak to the multiple transactions that enslaved children were subject to along long-distance caravan routes.

The geographic origins of the narrators in Part Three are not as easy to trace as those enslaved during the Yoruba wars, though there are some similarities in geographic concentration. Most originated in the region of Lake Malawi (Lake Nyasa), the principal catchment area of the East African slave trade in the nineteenth century (see Map 2). These accounts do not describe the large-scale violence and enslavement in warfare that mark the Yoruba narratives in Part One. Rather, many of the narrators in this section were pawned or sold by family members often due to a parent's or relative's debt. William Jones and George David were both enslaved on account of family debts. Jones was enslaved during a family dispute involving his stepfather and his brother's debt; David was taken in retaliation after his grandfather had seized an enslaved woman to settle an unpaid debt. The death of parents was also often a precarious moment. James Deimler was sold by his elder brother from the Makua country following the killing of his father and death of his mother.

While war captives could be quickly escorted to the coast, the accounts of youths from the East African interior generally record weeks or months

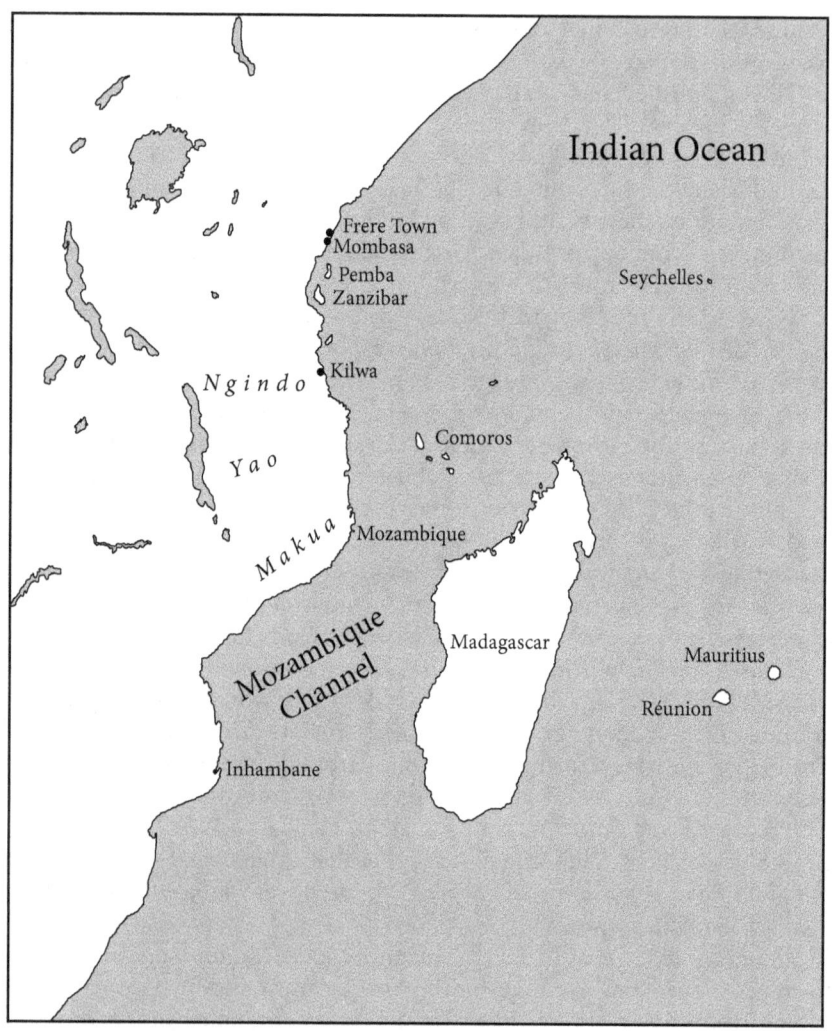

MAP 2 Regional origins of East African narrators (map by author).

between capture and reaching the coast. Captives coming from the area west of Lake Nyasa passed through a number of hands and could be the subject of three or four transactions before reaching the coast at or near Kilwa.[92] Echoing West African accounts from Samuel Crowther, Ali Eisami Gazirmabe and others, the CMS narrators from East Africa were often enslaved in households for extended periods, and their eventual sale into the external oceanic trade was never a foregone conclusion. As the missionary Charles Isenberg noted tersely after questioning Ismael Semler, 'Ishmael [was] captured and sold by Nyassa [Nyanja]. Sold back to Yao. Stayed a year with man who bought him. Man died. Man's people sold him to a Makuba. With him 3 years.'[93]

The production and publication of these accounts occurred at a different historical juncture than those in Part One in terms of both the chronologies of empire and British anti-slavery. The accounts in Part Three date from 1861 to 1880, a period in which British anti-slavery advocacy was in decline before the death of David Livingstone in 1873 revived metropolitan interest in supressing the 'Arab' slave trade.[94]

Conclusion

The CMS and MMS archives contain a rich corpus of testimonies from those who experienced enslavement in Africa. These sources are of relevance not only to scholars of the colonial and missionary histories of Sierra Leone, Nigeria, The Gambia and Kenya. Together, these accounts help illuminate the experience of the slave route in West and East Africa in the nineteenth century. Spared the vicissitudes of slavery in the Americas or Arabia, the life histories of Liberated Africans recount these journeys to the coast in vivid detail. The narrative speaks not only to missionary and colonial histories but to the global history of slavery, emancipation and the cultural history of the African diaspora within and beyond the continent.

TABLE 1 **Narratives in this volume**

Individual	Year	Author	Region of birth	Where written	Published
Josiah Yamsey (CMS)	1820	Dictated	Cameroon	Sierra Leone	Y
David Noah (CMS)	1824	Self	Bassa (Liberia)	Sierra Leone	N
Matthew Thomas Harding (CMS)	1837	Self	?	Sierra Leone	Y
John Attarra (CMS)	1837; 1845	Self	?	Sierra Leone	Y
John Campbell (MMS)	1839	Dictated	Yoruba	The Gambia	N
Charles Harding (MMS)	1839	Self	Yoruba	The Gambia	N
George Thompson (MMS)	?	Self	Yoruba	Sierra Leone	N
James Will (MMS)	1839	Self	Yoruba	Sierra Leone	N
Joseph Boston May (MMS)	1838	Self	Yoruba	Sierra Leone	N
Joseph Wright (MMS)	1839	Self	Yoruba	Sierra Leone	Y

Individual	Year	Author	Region of birth	Where written	Published
Joseph Right (MMS)	1839	Dictated	Yoruba	The Gambia	N
James Gerber (CMS)	1849	Dictated	Yoruba	Abeokuta	Y
Thomas King (CMS)	1850	Self	Yoruba	Igbein	Y
James Barber (CMS)	1854–5	Dictated	Yoruba	Abeokuta	Y
Peter Wilson (CMS)	1860	Wife	Yoruba	Sierra Leone	Locally
Susannah Bola (CMS)	c. 1873	Dictated	Yoruba	Ebute Metta	N
William Doherty (CMS)	c. 1873	Dictated	Yoruba	Ebute Metta	N
Awa (CMS)	1865	Dictated	Yoruba	Lagos	Y
Daniel Dopemu (CMS)	1865	Dictated	Yoruba	Lagos	Y
Jack Macumba (MMS)	1839	Self	Kajoor	The Gambia	N
John Cupidon (MMS)	1839	Self	Wolof	The Gambia	N
Mary Ann Gay (MMS)	1839	Self	?	The Gambia	N
John Gum (MMS)	1839	Self	?	The Gambia	N
George David (CMS)	1876	Self	Ngindo	Frere Town	N
William Henry Jones (CMS)	1861	Self	Yao	Sharanpur, India	Y
Ishmael Semler (CMS)	1861	Dictated	Yao	Sharanpur, India	Y
James Deimler (CMS)	1880	Self	Makua	Frere Town	N
Paul Deimler (CMS)	1880	Self	Mozambique	Frere Town	N
Lewis Brenn (CMS)	1880	Self	Makua	Frere Town	N
David Rebmann (CMS)	1880	Self	Makua	Frere Town	N
Cecil Mabruki (CMS)	1880	Self	Mozambique	Frere Town	N
Duiah William (CMS)	1880	Self	?	Frere Town	N

PART ONE

West Africa

CASE ONE

Josiah Yamsey

Author: William Augustin Bernard Johnson
Region of birth: Cameroon grasslands
Date of birth: c. 1800
Year of enslavement: c. 1815–16
Place of writing: Regent, Sierra Leone
Date of account: 24 March 1820
Year of death/last known year of activity: Unknown
Published: 'Account of a Liberated Negro: Illustrative of the Oppressive Influence of the Slave Trade', in *Proceedings of the Church Missionary Society for Africa and the East, Twenty-First Year, 1820–1821* (London: R. Watts, 1821), 236–41.

Source: W. A. B. Johnson, 24 March 1820, CA1/O126/121

Introduction

This is one of the earliest testimonies provided by a Liberated African and was possibly the first to be published, appearing in the *Proceedings of the Church Missionary Society for Africa and the East* in 1821. The document is written by W. A. B. Johnson, the charismatic CMS missionary based at the Liberated African village of Regent from 1816 until his death in 1823. Johnson's published accounts of his success at Regent drew widespread attention in Britain. Johnson produced a large body of written correspondence and journal extracts which he dispatched to mission headquarters in London. This document takes the form of questions posed to Josiah Yamsey, a convert at Regent, and was composed in March of 1820, four years after Johnson's arrival in the colony.[1] Yamsey recounted that 'when I come on shore in Free Town I stayed there about 3 months then we got all Clothing and were send here to Regents Town I had been here a few days then you came too Massah'. This suggests that Josiah arrived in Freetown in late 1815 or early 1816, since Johnson first arrived at Regent in March of 1816.[2]

Yamsey allegedly told Johnson that his 'country' was called Bambah. He also mentions that once on the slave ship he encountered 'a Bacumcum man & I understand a little of that language'. Though the term 'Bacumcum' is not an unambiguous reference to any African polity or ethnic group, it is most likely a reference to Lundu/Mbo.[3] Our narrator was on a Portuguese vessel (as he specifies) which arrived in late 1815 or early 1816 (as we can calculate). Yamsey was therefore most likely on the slave ship *Dido* (Voyages ID 7645), a Rio de Janeiro-based vessel whose crew purchased 364 enslaved people at the Cameroons River and departed the coast on 12 May 1815.[4]

HMS *Brisk* intercepted the *Dido* and escorted it to Freetown, where the vessels arrived on 6 July 1815. The case was adjudicated and the enslaved on board liberated on 25 August.[5] The Liberated African Registers for the *Dido* record one fifteen-year-old boy named Yamsay (Liberated African no. 7169), described as having a 'scar on top of chest', 'several small scars on belly', and a 'large scar [on] right elbow'.[6] Yamsey states that 'when I come on shore in Free Town I stayed there about 3 months'. This was in keeping with the policy of then Governor Charles Maxwell to have Liberated Africans above fourteen years of age serve on public works in Freetown before being distributed to villages around the capital.

Text

Life of Josiah Yamsey

What is the name of your country?
Bambah

What is the country next to yours?
Bamfat we walk about 10 mile before we get to that other country.

Tell me now Josiah about all what has happened to you as well as you can remember?
My father was king of Bambah my mother died when I was very young, I was about 3 years old when my father died too, my father I think had about 200 wifes one of the my Brothers who was by another woman was made King and he took care of me untill I was about as big as the Taylor Boy Young /about 16 years/ Then I used to go with my Brother in the bush to catch wild cattle, we catched them with a long rope.

About that time another King of Bamgot made war with my Brother, because one of his wifes had come to my Brother and he took her and would not return her again then the king of Bamgot hired some ~~of the~~ people of the other country to help him fight against my brother, and when they came we were not able to fight against them, but ran away as well as we could to another country which is called Bandoo, my brother then made peace. I was afraid to go with my Brother again thinking that he was not able to keep me as he had plenty children of his own, I went therefore to another Place called Banjum because one of my Brothers lived there & I went to stay with him. But soon after the King of that Country sent some people to catch me and he sold me to a man who kept me in his farm to drive the Elephants out of the farms which came every night and troubled me very much.

I was so much troubled that I at last tried to run to my Brother again who was King in Bambah but when I got about half way I was caught again by another headman who send me back again to my old master they then try one woman with read water[7] another headman made my master Palaver for that; then he took me and paid me for that palaver to that headman.

I stayed there a little then that Headman sold me for a Hoe to a country which is called Bamum, that man which buy me for a Hoe was a trader he go all about to Buy & sell slaves. He took me to another Place which is called Lo and there sold me in the market for sold[8]; I saw plenty people there in the market they were all tied together like beasts and I was put amongst them.

That man which bought for about 1/2 Bushel of salt took me to a country which is called Sobembeh to a place called Bacam from that place me and plenty more slaves were taken to a large River which the people in that country call Ning it was as wide I think as from here to the other side of Leicester Mountain[9] / about 2 miles / They put us into Canoes which were made of Bamboo sticks not like the Canoes here but the were flat the sticks were tied together and so on the water we were about 6 Hours before we got across. I thought then that they people who carried us were going to eat us I was fraid to myself wanted to cry but I was so fraid I could not; they killed some people and eat them but God help me he kept me he wanted to bring me in this place to hear his word; and saved me.

When we come from the water they took me to another place into the market were they sold me again for salt & those people which bought me took me to another market close by and sold me again for a piece of cloth and the people which bought me took me to a large grass field; when I came to that place I was quite faint for I had been without food for some time I began to weep & fell to the ground; my master took his hand and knocked me about the head saying that he would kill me and eat me I thought then that all was over I expected that a dagger would be driven in my bowels every moment.

I remembered that some people prayed in my country to a being which they call Jeecob or God who is supposed to live in the woods. I prayed and said Jeecob help me, but I had no rest I cried much; they took me & dragged me away till night came on & they took me into a wood were market is kept by night & I had again to stand amongst many more to be sold I was so hungry that I thought I should have died.

Many people came to buy us & those who were strong and fat were bought first, at last a short man came & bought me for some salt & then took me to a high hill to his house, and gave me some Cou Cou[10] to eat, & took me again to another town & sold me in the marked for salt, I saw there a great many slaves it was the largest marked I ever had seen. The man who bought me carried me a long way into the woods at last we came to his home which was surrounded with Bush nothing grew there but Palm nuts which was all I had to eat. The man kept me one day and then carried me a long way to a large Town There I found one of my Brothers sons who had been sold many times & was now with a Blacksmith as a slave I was very glad to see him; He told me that the people there did not eat slaves, this made me glad too much. My master did not sell me in that place but carried me to another Town a long way off I do not know the names of any of those Towns as I could not understand the people My master did not pretend to sell me but kept me & pretended to be fond of me, did use me better than others had done; gave me plenty to eat. One day he said to me let us go walking I thought he would have gone back to his home but he took me to a very bad place where the people eat slaves & there he sold me for what I cannot tell.

I was afraid again that the people would eat me & I was fraid too much but the man who buy me took me the next day a long way to another Town when we came there I saw the people dancing having a feast & they had mens heads on long sticks & thus danced & walked about the Town, the had eaten the flesh & the heads they played with; I cried I thought they will kill me now, there is no help for me. O massah I cannot tell you what I feel that time, I think by & bye they will dance with my head in the same fashion.

I heard a big drum at a short distance & my master took me to the place & a great number of people where dancing. We stayed there that day the dance was soon over and they did not pretend to buy me nor eat me, in the morning my master took me to another place where my master sold me for a piece of cloth, another slave was there he was very poor & he died. Then they people tied his hands & feet like a dog & hanged him on a stick and carried him in the bush threw him down for the wild beat to eat him. I stayed at that place a few days then the man carried me away again to another place; & there sold me for a piece of cloth and a little salt to a Trader a Black man who goes long way to buy & sell slaves; he was very kind to me carried me to his farm a long way & made me understand that he would not sell me again.

I was glad of this & worked very hard in my masters farm But one day he take me again & carried me to another town & sold me for Gunpowder. The man who bought me made me a fool again he made me understand that I should be like one of his children to which he pointed I thought I was at length come to rest; He send me to cut farm for him and I was so pleased & worked very hard, he kept me about 2 weeks. I came home one day from the farm having worked very hard all day & I thought my master was well pleased with me, but when I came into the home I saw a stranger sitting & my master was preparing something to eat for that man; & I saw that that man gave my master a piece of blue cloth. When he had dined he went away but the next morning he sent for me & I was carried away to his place. I said I don't want to go but my master gave me some salt to carry & said that I was to come back. but when the other man saw me he kept me & I belonged to him.

One of my masters wifes used me very good & I was carried soon after my arrival to the farm to work. I had been there a few days; then the people make their country feast they come with a large drum and plenty people to my masters house & I did not understand what they wanted but soon found by their motions that they wanted to buy me to kill me & eat me on the feast day; but my master would not sell me then they wanted to take me by force; they had hold of my legs & wanted to pull me out the door but my master was strong he got me clear, then they got cross with my master & went away I cannot tell whether they did kill another person instead of me they did eat Plantains and some meat but what meat I cannot tell. I stayed with my master who liked me much & I went & worked in his farm every day one day I did cut my foot with the cutlass with which I was working then my master did not like me anymore but took me one day to another place to fetch salt; I walked all the day & my foot was very bad at last we came to a large town & he took me to a home & gave me something to eat; I wanted to rest myself but my master would not let me, but sold me immediately to another man, what he got for me I cannot tell. The man who bought me would not let me sit down but made me walk and carried me to another place, my foot was very bad but he had no pity. I do not know the name of that country; I saw plenty Pigs there, also plenty cows & then I saw the sea for the first time; plenty fish were there and plenty canoes; & they made salt at that place. But I forgot Massah to tell you one thing which live in my heart very much that was when I live in my own Country a very bad sickness came the people were hungry to much the eat & eat and they never have enough, the more they eat the more they want to eat. & then the got so poor & die, allmost all the people die at that time. This I see now Massah & it live in my head very much. I suppose God no keep me that time what place me live now. but blessed be the Lord Jesus Christ that he has brought me here, O I thank Him for he has kept me he has brought me here.

But now I tell you when I get to that place where I see the sea my master kept me there one night & then put me into a canoe to carry me to the Portugse people. 3 more slaves were in the Canoes. They kept us all day in the Canoe & gave us nothing to eat, towards the evening we arrived at the place were the Portugse people lived I had never seen white people before & I was fraid too much; now I have come to the people who will surly eat me. The Portugse people bought me for an Iron bar and took me into the Canoe & I was so fraid I could not look at them I think they will kill me bye.

When I see the big ship I see non but white men I think that they buy black man to eat because I see no black man, but they was all below, I don't know that time how a house can live upon the water. I think me get into a big house. When I get on deck two white men came with a Razor to shave my head. They give me first something to eat and I think that be the last time I eat. They make me sit down & get the Razor I tremble I think now all done. I cannot tell what I feel then. But they shave my head. When they done shaving me they open a big hole, & when I look down I see plenty black people & I find one of my country people there. I glad too much. I ask him, what people the white people he said he did not know where they did come from. He thought that they come out of the water. I ask him if they eat people he said he thought so for what place could they put all the people which they bought, I begin to be afraid again I thought they kept us there to get fat and then to eat us. One man lived there he made us understand that he had been to Portugee Country that they did not eat the people but made them work. That make me a little easy. But again them white people came and put Irons on all the men feet that make me fraid again, I say suppose they no want to kill what for do they put Irons on our feet?

O Massah I was fraid too much. One man understood the whiteman that man who had been in their Country before was a Bacumcum man & I understand a little of that language then the white man tell this man to tell us that Caraambango /. That means English people./ were no good he says suppose English ships come & see us in the sea they have big fire & burn the ship & kill us all. That make us all afraid. One morning we was on Deck. One white man look through the glass & he shake his head and stamp with his foot; they send us all down in the hole & put Iron very fast on our feet. About 2 hours after we hear great noise on Deck, and all at once somebody open the hole & we see plenty white man standing on the hole some come down & shake hands with us, and say 'good!' 'good!' Then they make us loose take us on Deck & take the Iron from our feet and put them on the Portugee people feet and make them go into the boat to the other ship. I say oh that them people that do us bad? As they tell us before? Look they tell us lie. English people glad to see us they give us plenty to eat, and give us plenty water to drink O Massah we was so glad one English man take his hand and stroke my cheek, and said 'you good.' he take me then and make me cook for all the black people. You see Massah God look him people before thi know Him – God bring me out from my country people & when I live on slave ship, God send English ships, & God give me favour before that Englishman he did very good to me. God did all them things to save me from Hell by Jesus Christ.

Then they bring us to Sierra Leone and they make me Cook again when I come on shore in Free Town I stayed there about 3 months then we got all Clothing and were send here to Regents Town I had been here a few days then you came too Massah. When I come here Mr. Hirst was here he keep prayer sometimes, but me no go 2 or 3 people go but we all laugh them people ..."

Revd. and Dear Sirs

The above is indeed a narrative which passes all I have yet heard. I have as much as possible kept to his own words; sometimes I have changed a word as you would not have been able to understand its meaning. I was much struck with what he said at the missionary meeting which we had last week at Charlote Town where I took him to address his Country people; from that time I wished to spend a day with him in order to get his life by questioning him; which I have so far now accomplished. That he has stated the fact I firmly believe I believe him to be an Israelite in whom is no guile. He has been above 3 years Housekeeper & nearly 3 years Converter and ever since walked worthy of his high calling which is known by, not all by missionaries, some call him 'honest Yamsey.'

I remain,
Yours most affecting
W. Johnson

Regents Town
March 24 1820

CASE TWO

David Noah

Author: David Noah
Region of birth: Bassa (present-day Liberia)
Date of birth: Unknown
Year of enslavement: *c.* 1813
Place of writing: Kissy, Sierra Leone
Date of account: 1824
Year of death/last known year of activity: Unknown. Journals and quarterly reports end in 1829.
Published: No/unknown

> Source: 'David Noah's Speech at the Anniversary of the Church Missionary Association, Written by Himself', CA1/O165/3

Introduction

David Noah was a Liberated African from present-day Liberia and a Church Missionary Society schoolmaster. Noah did not experience the slave ship but was, rather, taken by British forces in an early coastal raid on slaving operations on the West African mainland. In late June 1813, the crews of HMS *Thais* and the Sierra Leone colonial schooner *Princess Charlotte* raided the slave-trading factory of Charles Mason and Robert Bostock on the St. Paul River (present-day Liberia) slightly upriver from Cape Mesurado.[1] During this early period of suppression, British officials often operated beyond the parameters of the 1807 Abolition Act and used the colonial schooner and members of the Royal African Corps – including Liberated African recruits – to undertake anti-slave-trading raids on shore.[2] Mason and Bostock attempted to hide their captives, taking as many as possible to the nearby factory of John Sterling Mill. Mill, son of an English father and an African mother, operated a factory on the Mesurado River in close proximity to modern-day Monrovia.

The crew of the *Princess Charlotte* landed at Mill's factory and demanded the recovery of those who had fled Mason and Bostock's factory. Mill delivered over an equal number of Africans. This included the boy who would later be known as David Noah, though he had never been enslaved to Mason or Bostock. Noah, who at this point was only a young child, had reached Mill's slave factory after being enslaved in the Bassa country. Noah's father (we do not know their birth names) had directed the young boy and his older brother to undertake a trading mission with a group of men at the behest of the 'headman of their country'. The expedition was a ploy and the boys were separated. David Noah was marched for fourteen days and sold to Mill. He was imprisoned for some three weeks prior to the navy's raid of Mill's compound. In total, the naval men rounded up 233 Africans – whom they took to be the prisoners of Mason and Bostock's barracoons – and proceeded to Freetown.[3]

Of his arrival in Sierra Leone, Noah recounts that

> we were send to Regent's then called Hog Brook. At the first, when we were at Regent's, which was then a desert, Mr. Macaulay and one Capt. William were there, we were surrounded with nothing but bushes and we did not like to stop there but we were forced to do so. I believe we were at Regent's a whole year without a white man.

Noah was an early inhabitant of this Liberated African village (founded in 1812) and arrived about three years prior to the CMS taking over superintendence of the village. Originally named Hog Brook after the stream that traversed its hillside, the village of Regent was one of several Liberated African settlements placed under missionary control in 1816. John Peterson notes that the origins of Regent are unclear, despite its subsequent importance in the history of West African Christianity. The village was formed independently by Liberated Africans and was officially recognized by the government in 1812.[4] The arrival of Noah and his shipmates at Regent was significant enough that observers soon after credited their arrival as having 'formed' the village 'in July 1813, chiefly by people brought by a slave ship from [Cape] Mesurado, principally Foy people, but it contains some of almost all the neighbouring nations'.[5]

In February of 1829 David Noah undertook a 'visit to his Native Country Bassa', during which he kept an extensive journal (CA1/O165/19). Noah sailed to colony of Liberia and received a passport from governor before proceeding inland. His journal entry for 25 February 1829 records how 'we were at Picaminy Bassa and landed immediately. I was surrounded with many of my country men, I was appeared to them just as one who arose from the dead'.[6]

Text

Christian Friends,

With pleasure I stand up to tell you what great cause I have to thank God for the unspeakable merriness he has bestowed upon me.

I am a native of the Bassah Country from which it pleased our gracious God to bring me, through the horrid slave trade.

My mother died when I was an infant, and after that I had stayed with my father a few years, he send me with an elder brother of mine, to one of the chiefs of the country, with whom I stayed about 2 weeks when he send some people to another country to go trading with whom he also sent me; I did not know that they were going to sell me. We walked about 3 days before we reached the place, still ignorant of their intention.

The next day I was called for, and when I came I heard by their conversation, that they had sold me. I cried very much, but alas as there was no Christian religion then, there was no pitty, so I became a slave and looked about me and saw none but strangers, my country people had all withdrawn; whilst I was crying, one came and told me that I was only put in pound for one month, and that I should return to my friends again. But this proved all false, no pitty, no mercy, was shown to me, like a best they began to treat me although I was free born.

Soon after they took me to an island to a white man named John Mills to him they sold me.

I had been about three weeks a slave to this white man, when it blessed God to send English men to deliver me & many more.

About 5 O'clock in the morning 5 boats full of soldiers and sailors were landed, we were taken by the headman into the bush, I and another boy tried to run away but they soon caught us and brought us back again and John Mills delivered us to the English, who took us off on board the schooner, Mr. Cooper commanded her this time.

We stayed about one week at anchor, and then sailed for Sierra Leone where we were landed immediately.

After we had stayed about one month in Freetown, we were send to Regent's then called Hog Brook.

At the first, when we were at Regent's, which was then a desert, Mr. Macaulay and one Capt. William were there, we were surrounded with nothing but bushes and we did not like to stop there but we were forced to do so.

I believe we were at Regent's a whole year without a white man, and we lived in a most wretched way, without God, and without hope in the world.

After that Mr. Hirst came and he took the trouble of teaching me the Lord's prayer, but my heart did not delight in it. Mr. Hirst also kept meeting but I only went to make game.

In this awful state I continued untill Mr. Johnson came who caused me to stay with him, but I did not like to stop with him at this point, so when he had gone down to Freetown to bring up Mrs. Johnson I went down to stay with Mr. Reffell.

However Mr. Reffell soon found out that I was good for nothing and he send me back again to Regent's and was glad when he got rid of me.

So I went and stayed again with Mr. Johnson who put me to keep the rice store.

I then with rest of the people attended divine service in the Church regular; and it pleased God soon after, through the instrumentality of Mr. Johnson to call me out of natures darkness into His marvelous light.

CASE THREE

Matthew Thomas Harding

Author: Matthew Thomas Harding
Region of birth: Unknown
Date of birth: Unknown
Year of enslavement: Unknown (*c*. 1810–15)
Place of writing: Gloucester, Sierra Leone
Date of account: 1 March 1837
Year of death/last known year of activity: Unknown. Journals and letters from Banana Islands, Sierra Leone, end in 1858.
Published: 'Narratives of Three Liberated Negroes', *Church Missionary Record*, No. 10, Vol. VIII, October 1837.

Source: Matthew Thomas Harding, Letter to Mission, 1 March 1837, CA1/O112/12

Introduction

Matthew Thomas Harding was a Liberated African and 'native catechist' with the Church Missionary Society. Harding's account states that he 'was taken to Sierra Leone by the English vessel at governor Maxwell's time'. Governor Charles Maxwell served as governor from July 1811 to July 1815, though he returned to England in July 1814, leaving in charge Charles MacCarthy, the Lieutenant-Governor at Senegal. This chronology suggests that Harding reached Freetown between 1811 and 1814. Harding's narrative is also an account of re-enslavement, a common prospect for many Liberated Africans in Sierra Leone.

His account was one of the first testimonies by a Liberated African published by the Church Missionary Society. The October 1837 edition of the *Church Missionary Record* featured a lead article on the 'Narratives of Three Liberated Negroes'. The article did not name the authors, but it included the account written by Samuel Crowther, as well as Liberated African catechists Matthew Thomas Harding and John Attarra.[1]

Text

Gloucester, March 1st 1837

Sir, as our Minister the Rev. J.W. Weeks told me that you desire to know of what man I am, therefore I take the opportunity to tell you as far as I can, Sir I am one of the poor Africans, was born in a town 6 days journey to the sea, we were seven born of one father and mother, four sons and three daughters: I was at present when my father died, after the death of my father, behold war came upon us. I only was taken away from the family by the same war into the hand of a stranger, carring me from place to place untill to a slave vessel; but by the providence of God I was taken to Sierra Leone by the English vessel at governor Maxwell's time. I was then apprenticed[2] to a widow, her name's Nancy Smith who I live a month, after the end of the month, I was taken fever which carry me two month in bed by the mercy of God I was recover six month after my recovery she was enticed by her country man to go with him up to the country for she never be there before so she was afraid to go, but after word she agreed to go so I and her went both the man by boat three days journey. We was there two month, at the end, this morning Thos. Chamber told my mis. that today we shall start for Sierra Leone, after that about 9 o'clock we saw many many men with goods from the King's house king of that country or town to the wharf. at six o clock in the night I and my mis. take our things to boat and to be there untill the time, as soon as we get in Thomas Chamber came to call us to come shore, that there are something in the water will hurt person in the night, we do not believe him because we were many, so he continues call till 5 times at last she and I went to shore. we know not that he is try to get me from her and pay the king for his goods which he took. So I and her went to our lodging place, again about 8 o'clock, Thos. Chamber send me to call one of the sailor, as he usily to me, the man whom he send me to call was in the Kings house, as I got there the king order his 6 men to lift me up and carry me away the same night into other village, after two days the King came there and call for me and said to me now you are become one of my slave, who sold me to you he said Chamber after that he order his man to lain a strips on me he said to me now this to make you believe that I am your master, he deliver me to one of his concubine who I lives 6 years, not openly but secretly for fear of the strangers that comes there often from Sierra Leone. One day I was then met with a man which was sent by my Ms. to find me, he then took his own goods and paid the king, and brought me to my mis. then she and Thos. Chambers was appear before the magistrates Chambers was guilty and was transported, I was taken away from my Mis to Thos. Harding to be with him for some times: at the end I was part from him, I went to the Manager that if he should please to recommend to the Governor, to take me up to one of his village; I was then brought up under the car of Rev. Henry Düring at Lester because there was no house at Gloucester; only one hut in which I and some men was to prepare a place for him; after he came he begin to teach us how to pray, after some years I was then baptized by Mr. Johnson at Regent in the year of our Lord 1818. I took a wife on April 16 1819. She conceive and pare William Dec. 1 1820. James Harding born Nov. 10 1823 Hannah she was born August 6 1826 Thomas on Sept. 2 1830 Betsy on the 15 of May 1832, after Betsy she died on Apr. 27 1833 soon after that, Betsy she die on Janur. 24 1834. There are with me in the house the first that is William Harding is in the Institution Fourah Bay who I hope to be a faithful soldier of Christ, and I hope my Father in the Lord, when you pray remember him for me in your prayers. Sir this year will make 18 since I enter into the mission. All the Brothers and Sisters said their Christian reposes.

Sir I remain your affectionately
Son in the Lord
M. Thos. Harding

CASE FOUR

John Attarra

Author: John Attarra
Region of birth: possibly Mende
Date of birth: Unknown
Year of enslavement: *c.* 1816–19
Place of writing: Hastings, Sierra Leone; Wellington, Sierra Leone
Date of account: 3 March 1837; 1845
Year of death/last known year of activity: Died Freetown, Sierra Leone, 25 February 1866[1]
Published: 'Narratives of Three Liberated Negroes', *Church Missionary Record*, No. 10, Vol. VIII, October 1837; 'A Liberated African's Account of His Slavery, and Subsequent Course', *Church Missionary Gleaner*, No. 2, Vol. VI, February 1846, 16–18 and No. 3, Vol. VI, March 1846, 27–8.

Source: CA1/O33/3 and CA1/O33/4[2]

Introduction

John Attarra was a Liberated African schoolmaster and catechist in Sierra Leone. His account, along with Samuel Crowther and Matthew Thomas Harding (Case 3), was one of the first testimonies by a Liberated African published in the October 1837 edition of the *Church Missionary Record*. The article's content is based on a letter sent by Attarra to mission headquarters on 3 March 1837.

John Attarra's narrative does not specify his place of birth or mention any geographic locations before his arrival in Sierra Leone. Another letter in his personal papers comments upon the Yoruba mission, stating that '[m]y heart indeed rejoices to see the prospects opening for my country through the Abbeokuta mission & also that the Lord has raised up those noble missionaries & sent them, on the Eastern side of my county'.[3] Yet in another journal entry from Hastings in 1836, he recounts an encounter with the 'chief drummer' of the village in which the man retorted to Attarra 'that I disbelieved him because I am not belong to the Aku nation, or else I would not deny the fact concerning his country fashion'.[4] Christopher Fyfe refers to him as the 'Mende John Attarra' but cites only the totality of his personal papers (CA1/O33) rather than any specific document.[5]

Attarra arrived in Sierra Leone at some point between 1816 and 1819. We know this from his recollection that 'we were landed at Freetown. And the next day we were located at Regent, under the care of our dearly beloved Father the late W.B. Johnson'. Johnson first arrived at Regent in 1816 and travelled back to England for a visit from 22 April 1819. Attarra mentions Johnson's departure and return, signifying that he had been in Sierra Leone for some time before April of 1819.

Attarra is one of the few individuals who composed multiple versions of his life history at different moments in time: the first in 1837 and the second (which exists in duplicate) in 1845. This later version was published anonymously in two parts as 'A Liberated African's Account of His Slavery, and Subsequent Course' in the *Church Missionary Gleaner*.

Text

CA1/O33/3

Hastings March 3rd 1837

Rev. & Dear Sir

I have gladly received your excellent note, and kind present of a very delightful manual since the arrival of our long expected teacher the Rev. Mr. Weeks, in the Colony of Sierra Leone. The style of your excellent manual is such and one, which is very suitable to our weak capacity in this country, who are weak in understanding. I doubt not but that it will prove, a useful book to me, when I am better acquainted by repeated perusal.

I think it necessary to acquaint you of a something concerning myself; how the Lord has wonderfully brought me from my native land, to this Colony of Sierra Leone; and where I am now set at liberty, & also am enjoying many privileges. The first trial that I had, in my own native land, was that I deprived of both parents by death. And thus became an orphan. After this, I was taken into the care of my name sake. But, he was a bad man, he treated me badly. It happened in a day, as I came from the farm, I saw some foreigners with him. As soon as he saw me, he called for me & desired me to offer him some water. This he did, on purpose, to have me, to appear before the men. Some times, after this, he called men again, and one, of his servants, & told both of us to go with those strangers, to bring some palm oil. As soon as we had left the town, & were gone about a space of a mile, the young man, that came with me, told me, to proceed on, & that he would directly overtake us. He then made his way into the bush; (when I was looking at him as if he was going there, for a particular thing.) When we had gone a little way off, I told the stranger, that I would not go further with them, until I had seeing him, who came with me. But my proprietors, soon openly showed it to me, that it was in vain for me to expect to see him, because I cannot see him anymore for he had bought me for his slave. When I heard that, I burst out into a lamentable cry. But the men did not pay attention to my crying, only were continually hasted me on to proceed to their place; which was from the place of my nativity, a distance of about, 13, or 14 miles off. My master, had a wife. But she was barren. Both took me, therefore, almost as instead of a dear child. And they were very fond of me. But whilest, I had been there, for a few months, a heavy sickness prevailed upon me. My master tried all he could, but nothing was effected, to the cure of the disease I had. When I appeared a little better, my master was obliged to part with me. And during that time I was in slavery; I was never well. In consequence of that, I was then sold to different persons. Till at last, I was sold into the hands of the Portuguese, who took me, & put me on board a ship. And from that time, I was in the ship, until we landed in Sierra Leone I was perfectly well, without using any means. And since that time, I never had such a sickness again.

CA1/O33/4 [Undated. Reached mission headquarters in London 23 July 1845]

Sierra Leone
Wellington

Rev. and dear Sir
   ... As I think, you will be interested to hear me state to you an account of the dealings of Providence towards me, in bringing me to this colony, where I am, now, so richly made to be, in the enjoyment of the privileges of the Gospel of peace.
   I shall now give you a brief account of it.
   To notice, that man is born to trouble, is not a thing to be admitted or denied. The first bitter cup of trial which Providence so wisely caused me to drink quite up, in my own Country, was that, I was, first deprived of both parents by death. And thus, I became an orphan. Oh what a painful thing it was then to me! After that, I was sent to live with one, who was of the relation of my late parents. He at first treated me, with kindness. But afterward, he used me cruelly. His ill treatment made me to become very unhappy and was frequently found to weep and mourn my great loss. It was so happened, on a day, as some of his servants and myself, returned from farm, we met him with some strangers. He immediately called me, to bring him some water. After which he presented the cup again to me. During that time, he had already agreed with the men about me. About an hour after this, he called one of his servants, and afterwards myself. He then ordered both of

us to go with the men and they will give us palm oil, at our return. But I was quite insensible that I could not tell that, that evening would soon prove an unhappy one to me. Nor yet, that those in the family, as well as the place of my nativity, would from that time know me no more forever. But without the least hesitation; I followed them. I was still cheerful, went on with them for a while, and then stopped, determined to see my fellow, whom I thought was obliged to turn to the bush. But while I was thus refusing to go with the men, they immediately began to use their influence over me, and what was secret to me, was now plainly revealed to me by their declaration to me, that I had become their property. Ah, sir, I cannot sufficiently describe to you, my feelings, my groans, and tears in that, very unfortunate evening as I then thought it was. But now, I see, that it was indeed, a happy evening, and why? because, that on it, the Lord began to lead me, as he did with his ancient people – the Children of Israel – as he delivered them, from the Egyptian's bondage, superstition, and idolatry, so did he also for me. After that, I went on with the men, all the way weeping. At length we arrived at our expected habitation. His wife was very glad to see me. She did all she could, at that night to make me happy, but, oh! there was no such happiness to be found in me. But through the kind treatment of both my master and mistress, in a few days, I became very happy. And now, I did think but very little about my country. They had no children; so I was in both sight, as a son with his tender parents. Here, Providence, as it were spoke to me, by a voice of heavy affliction, that, this was not the place which he had purposed to bring me into. My master, after he had used various means for my recovering – and found that I was not better – but rather grew worse, he determined to sell me. And so it fell out on a day, that he told me to accompany him for rope.

When we had gone a distance of two, or three miles off, we met with some men. My master then delivered me into their hands. It appeared, that they did not buy me, but that they were only hired to sell me. The next morning, I was sold to another master. Here, it was also, so providentially allotted to me, that they also had no children. And thus I was to them instead of a son. But even here also, the Lord was still saying to me, that I was yet in my way to where he had intended for me. So it was, that when my master saw that I was a sickly person, he also made up his mind to sell me. But he could not do so on that year. Every thing being in that year devoted to their Country God, whose practice was then carrying on, in that year. But after the time was completely expired, and all things, went on as usual my master then spared no more time, but sent me off directly to be sold. Thus I was again sold to a third master who took me the same day and returned to his place, where we arrived at night. The following day, his wife sent me with her servants for water. But I escaped from them, and got into the bush. Here I thought it better for me, to put an end, to my existence. I then made up my mind, to hang myself. I got me a rope, and fixed it around my neck and fixed it up, on a branch of a tree. But was not courage enough to perform such a dreadful act. But I owned it, that through mercy, I was thus preserved from so great a sin. The moment I left the spot, I was caught, by the pursuers, whom my master had sent after me. After they brought me home, my master's wife persuaded him, not to give me any food. To this, he did not consent – but he did it in this manner. He sent me away from her into an island. Here, I first had sight of Europeans. I found here, many Africans, who were already bought before me. But, here, I could not find any with whom I might converse. I remained here, only for a couple of weeks, and then we were conveyed into the open sea, where I had with trembling, to behold the faces of many of the Portuguese. After they had bought us, we were all taken on board ship. Here we met with many, who were already in before us. And thus, was the end of my bondage under my own colour. Now, the Lord, Jehovah, as it were, spoke to me, that his purpose concerning me, was nearly to be fully accomplished. And that, within a few days more, he would bring me to where he had appointed for me – viz – Sierra Leone. Here, without the application of any medicine, I was perfectly recovered. And in a few weeks, we were landed at Freetown. And the next day we were located at Regent, under the care of our dearly beloved Father the late W. B. Johnson. I remember him very much still. Because it was through his instrumentality, that I was first, brought to a knowledge of myself as a great sinner, – and of my beloved Lord and Saviour, as a sufficient and willing Saviour. At our first arrival at Regent, we were obliged to dwell with the inhabitants, for want of school houses. And we daily attended the school and then returned home. But this lasted only, for a short time. When the two houses were quickly erected, and then we were gathered together. Sometime after, our master, left us, to pay a visit to England, for the first. But before he left, he particularly ordered me, to remain at school till his return. But afterward I acted foolishly, and did not wait till he returned, but left to be employed as a sailor. When he came back, he was grieved, because I did not wait. He kindly reproved me for my conduct; and then ordered me to return to school, After that, I was put into the Christian Institution at Regent. Here he left me in the year 1823 to visit England a second time.[6] At this time, he promised me and five other youths that after his return he would send us also to visit England, to get a higher education. But a short time after his departure, alas! a sad and painful tidings reached us, that our faithful and beloved Shepherd, had finished his course here below; away from his numerous sheep.

I must here beg, to remark, that the inhabitants of Regent, as long as they are still in existence, shall never forget their beloved master, – the Rev. W. B. Johnson. They had also much attachment, to the Rev. J. Weeks, – who had been obliged to part with them. And who had been also very useful among them. Since his removal, to England. I have heard many a one, spoke very favourably both of Mr. & Mrs. Weeks. And many have often expressed their wishes, that if it were for their return to Africa. For instance, once I made a visit to a family, here I happened to meet a stranger, who had come from Freetown. While I continued there, I heard her spoke so highly of Mrs. Weeks', labour in the colony, and said thus – ah! Mrs. Weeks – that good lady – has done very great good, for young women in this colony, – so that, they are now, very useful n the colony.

A report was raised abroad in the colony, when the Rev. E. Jones was yet in England, that he would come out as a colonial chaplain – This effected great many people, because, we were then going to be deprived of so useful a man, of his service, in our mission. It grieved the students of the Christian Institution much more; when they observed, that they were going to lose, their kind and useful master. But at his arrival, it gave us much joy, to find it to be, to the contrary. And now, it gives great pleasure to the students, at Fourah Bay, to see, him come again to be their teacher.

On the 29 September 1823. I was united in marriage with a young woman, whose name was then, Jane Davis, – but now Jane Attarra. We have great reason to be very thankful to our heavenly Father – that he has since preserving us both to the present day. And has also blessed us, by given us, children. Although it had pleased him, wisely to take four away from us by death, – yet he is still preserving to us, a son and four daughters. In the year 1825. – When that valuable and laborious servant of Christ, the Rev. Mr. Brooks, came and took charge at Regent; it was then at his time that I was appointed a schoolmaster at Regent.

In the year, 1826. The local committee, saw it proper to remove me to Charlotte. Here I continued to labour, till in the year, 1828. When I was made a Native teacher, and then changed my residence to that of Bathurst, under the late Rev. T. Davey. Since that time, I had been removed to labour in several other stations connected with our happy mission. And in 1840, I was appointed for this station, where now, I am laboring.

In my time of ignorance, I used to think, very hard of that man, who sold me from my native land. And I used also to say, that if I were to see him in this country, and he so happened to be under my power, that I would certainly deal very hard with him. But now, that is far from my thought. I would rather entreat the Lord, to give me a mind that was in Joseph of old, who instead of revenging himself on his Brethren, spoke so kindly to them.

When I review from the time I first placed my feet, upon this land, and observed, how the Lord has in various ways directing me in all my ways, I am often, by such reflections, lost in wonder – and frequently exclaimed, 'Not unto me O Lord, not unto me, – but unto thee he all the praise.'

CASE FIVE

John Campbell

Author: Dictated by John Campbell. Transcriber unknown.
Region of birth: Yoruba
Date of birth: Unknown
Year of enslavement: Unknown
Place of writing: St. Mary's Island, The Gambia
Date of account: 20 May 1839
Year of death/last known year of activity: Unknown
Published: No/unknown

Source: MMS Sierra Leone, Sierra Leone Correspondence, Fiche Box 25, Box No. 280, 'Sierra Leone Odds Papers', Fiche No. 1880 and 1884, #7[1]

Introduction

John Campbell was a Yoruba Liberated African who was sent to The Gambia following his emancipation in Sierra Leone. From 1818 onwards, some 3,478 Liberated Africans were forcibly transported on a second oceanic journey to The Gambia.[2] John Campbell recounts being part of a group of nineteen Liberated Africans. He may well have been part of the first two small groups of Liberated Africans transported in 1818 or 1825. It is possible that he was one of twenty boys sent to St. Mary's from the Brazilian vessel *Bom Jesus dos Navegantes*, intercepted off Lagos in 1825.[3]

The transcription below is the first of two different renditions of Campbell's life history, contained in the papers of the Wesleyan Methodist Missionary Society archive. The first appears to be a corrected version of the latter. The narrative begins in the third person with an unknown author transcribing Campbell's verbal account, though it quickly switches to the first person.

Text

Statement of John Campbell

The above named person John Campbell being one of the Ackoo Tribes born in the West Coast of Africa States that he was at the age of twelve years old when War fell to his Country and from whence he was brought to a state of Bondage. The said person John Campbell Continued with his statement and says that the day in which the War Broke out to his Country it found that his elder Brother were gone to the Bush to fetch them something to eat, having return from Bush came on Crying immediately given information to my father + mother that the War people would come in town today, Drakie the father of the above named person having Rose up and took his sword + gun with much people who went out of the town to meet the Enemy in the Bush, having went a little further and returned. Not knowing what to do with such Lots of people. So he Came home and took away both the Mother of the above named person with Sister and the younger Brother of the said John Campbell their father then took them away and went and Hide them in the Bush to see what the Consequence of the War would be, the father of the named person John Campbell on the Return from the Bush where he went to hid us, was coming home it is said that before he reached the town the War people set fire on all the houses so unfortunately I could not see my father any more, the people then Killing both men + Women in town after destroyed the whole City they then hastened to the bush in order to see if they might find any more to destroy. Coming to the bush they then found us where our father was hid us, our Mother then began to cry we also began to cry when I saw them coming in. I fled Myself from them then I could not see my Mother any more, so I went and hid myself from them, where they could not discover me, I still Kept myself secret until the Pursuers were gone then I appeared where I had been hiden myself from them and Returned to the town where I found only dead Bodies of human beings and so I could not bear to stand looking at them.

I returned back to the bush and where I stop 10 days and came to a little town where I found some people and talk to them but they could not talk my Language I could not tell what sort of beings they are. I was in great fear + wonder whether these are the devils of human beings. I then went again to another town where I found the people who made fool of me that my mother was before, so having consented with them, they took and sell me to a King's servant who having sold me to a Portuguese Merchant where we all wer Loaden to a Vessel having stop three days at sea we fortunately meet a Man of War who came along side of us who ordered the Captain of the slave Vessel to be Killed both him and the Mate also, after Killing the captain + the mate they then took out all the sailors and bound them on Board the Man of War and take them down to Sierra Leone – where I staid five days.[4] Several of the Merchants of that Colony took some of us to servants. Nineteen of us Liberated Africans were then brought down to The Gambia –

While we nineteen of us were brought to The Gambia we found Captain Fraser[5] who was a governor here at that time, we then Landed from on Board and was taken to the Soldier's Barracks on the preceeding morning he the said governor sent to all the Merchants to come and Look at us, and returned home, we then was taken at the Government House at Breakfast time. Mr John Grant then took me to his choose, where I was a servant to him for 3 months and then he turn me to be a cook about one year's time having relieved me from Cooking I was taken on Board the Cutter Highlander as a sailor till Mr Charles Grant then arrived from England and John Grant tell him all about me, who ordered me to be call on Board the Vessel and asked me what sort of work I may wish to Engage in. I told him at any Capacity which he himself may think proper to put me in, I am consent to it.[6]

He then sent me back on Board the ship where I were Engaged as a Seaman, having stop on Board the Vessel for 2 months time. Mr Charles Grant took me from thence and brought me to learn the Carpenter work, and then I have little chance to pray to God sometimes but not frequently. I used to go to church but never understand what the Minister says My heart felt no glad for I was altogether Blind to what I always heard him says until Mr Fox came out from England and the first time I heard him preach affect my heart very much indeed and then I began to love God then I was formerly to what I heard until now at present, and thanks be unto God for what he has already done, and still thank him for what he would still continue to do yet.

John Campbell

St. Mary's
    20 May 1839

CASE SIX

Charles Harding

Author: Charles Harding
Region of birth: Owu, Yoruba
Date of birth: Unknown
Year of enslavement: 1822 or before
Place of writing: St. Mary's Island, The Gambia
Date of account: 15 April 1839
Year of death/last known year of activity: Unknown
Published: No/unknown

Source: MMS Sierra Leone, Sierra Leone Correspondence, Fiche Box 25, Box No. 280, 'Sierra Leone Odds Papers,' Fiche No. 1880, #6

Introduction

Charles Harding's account begins with the author, a Liberated African, stating that he 'was born in Western Coast of Africa ockue nation particularly native owoo City'. The Owu kingdom was one of the principal Yoruba states in the nineteenth century prior to its destruction in the 1820s. The disintegration of Oyo Empire after 1817 was followed soon after by a series of wars in southern Yorubaland, of which Owu was the first polity to be affected.

The dates of the Owu War are debated within the literature. Samuel Johnson suggested Owu fell in 1823 after a siege of about five years, a chronology accepted by Robert Smith.[1] J. F. A. Ajayi suggests dates of roughly 1820–25, while Robin Law places the onset of the siege as *c.* 1816/7, and the fall of Owu as late 1821 or early 1822.[2] While the start and end dates of the conflict are debated, it is generally agreed that the siege of Owu lasted about five years. Charles Harding recalled that for '6 or 7 years they fight day and night', which, given his young age at the time of his enslavement, is a reasonable estimate.

As Robin Law points out, there have heretofore been no contemporary written accounts of the Owu War and its immediate aftermath.[3] Several sources written in and outside of Yorubaland between the 1830s and 1850s do derive testimonies from eyewitnesses.[4] Previously, the earliest known account of the Owu War was recorded from Osifekunde, a formerly enslaved man of Ijebu origin, in Paris in 1839/40.[5] Charles Harding's account is therefore significant as perhaps the only first-hand account by an observer of the war and Owu's demise.[6]

The destruction of Owu produced a wave of captives who reached Freetown in the middle years of the 1820s. The drawn-out conflict provided abundant opportunities for skirmishing and kidnapping, while the fall of the town left those who did not escape open to capture. Charles Harding reached Freetown in 1822. The Liberated African Department assigned him to be settled on the Banana Islands, a Liberated African settlement off the southwestern tip of the Sierra Leone peninsula, where he also attended school. He was then taken as a servant by an unnamed doctor who brought Harding to The Gambia in 1824.

Harding does not specify whether he was sent to St. Mary's or MacCarthy's Island, though he mentions being summoned by the Wesleyan missionary R. Marshall who was based at the former. His account also mentions William Fox who was based at St. Mary's in the 1830s and 1840s. The narrative is one of several testimonies recorded in The Gambia in 1839 by members of the Wesleyan Methodist Missionary Society.

Text

I Charles Harding was born in Western Coast of Africa ockue nation particularly native owoo City and when I was in my country and what ingratitude wicked child I was when I quit young boy and I was constantly to fight course and swear day and night no peace no raece at all because I was point upon that my mother her so very rich in western side and her could not able to number many slave her get and I was so very insolent boy and Owoo city was very larger and greater city and if any was able to interning my country good walk about 3 days and our market a long about half mile and six gate what go through in and owoo was very larger and greater city and some time when I went at the market I fight I broken the market because when I was to my country I never hearing any Gospel preach we only all one prayer not but Mahomting until when war come to my country speacely 6 or 7 years they fight day and night and all that I was save and Afterward my own mother her take me to given her own brother that he make take careful of me and her said because I was so wicked child & my mother her was not get much child on this life and the day that war was broken my country they catch my mother and my father he was save and they take my mother her to the another country and myself other part and when my mother her hear that I was another coast and her crying out that her may see me or else she Die before she Hired one good man that he may go after me quickly and bring me unto her and After when I saw this man he that come after me and he say I am very glad to saw you and you yet Life and I answered I say I myself I also quite glad to see you and the man call my name he say my son your mother and father they sent me to you that I may fetch you to them and I answer the man I say that I would not Gone with you and so the man began to begged of me that I may go with him and I say I shall not go with you and the man say him no because I too insolent boy that reason but he say he shall not leave me a long he say my son except you would go with me and if you would remember that that you mother her was so very rich and she did not get much child on this life and since war catch your mother all her slave they all one go to your mother and so you must go with me to my father and mother and say man I tell you what will you go to my father and mother and you willing Endeavouring told them I would not come I say and after when years over speace about Eight months only my own brother he Come to call me that we may go after own mother perhaps we will meet our father then and I say yes Sir, I will go with you also and about six days we are ready and when we are walk speacely about 5 days or 6 we arrived one large country we called Gye and many people round after us and they ask we wer you goin to and we answered them we say our mother she have lost from us and we hear that her leave one Country and we which go to our own mother and so they catch we there and when the king of that country hear that we are pass in the Country and they catch we there he riest up quickly sent messenger that they may Deliver us and the people refusing and king say that 2 people shall not be to sell because this people I hear they father and mother they are second to the king of greater City and if we Do sell them After when war over great trouble will come upon us and the people say if its occasion we willing endeavouring sold then and so I come to be slave and they sell me to were portugueses used to make slave trade I stay there about one month and number of us 400 something another we are sailed away ten days the merciful Lord having watch over us and when English man of war come and took our ship to Sierra Leone land and before we all little boys sent to the villages and I transposed sent to the bananas near to the York over the Kent in the years of our Lord 1822 and who the chief over us his most excellency generall Charles MaCarthy shine is divine favour and affection kindly for Each of us ....[7]

CASE SEVEN

George Thompson

Author: George Thompson
Region of birth: Yoruba
Date of birth: *c.* 1804
Year of enslavement: *c.* 1822–23
Place of writing: Sierra Leone
Date of account: Unknown
Year of death/last known year of activity: Unknown
Published: No/unknown

Source: Sierra Leone Correspondence, Fiche Box 25, Box No. 280, 'Sierra Leone Odds Papers,' Fiche No. 1884–85, #34

Introduction

George Thompson was a Yoruba Liberated African and Methodist. Thompson had reached Freetown in 1823 at about eighteen years of age and was immediately sent to the British colony of The Gambia where he became an apprentice to a sailor at Bathurst. He later returned to Sierra Leone and in 1830 took a job on a ship bound for Liverpool.

In a remarkable account of misfortune and bravery, Thompson successfully staved off an attempt by two Spanish crew members to re-enslave him while at sea. The ship was the *Maggie Lauder*, formerly the Cuban slave ship *Loreto*, purchased by British merchant John Martin at a public auction in Freetown in May 1830.[1] Unable to find British seamen, Martin hired four Liberated Africans, including George Thompson, and 'two Spaniards, who had been brought here in some of the slave vessels'.[2] On their voyage to Liverpool, the Spaniards stabbed and killed Martin and his mate in an attempt to take over the ship and direct it to the Cape Verde Islands. George Thompson and the three other Liberated Africans were able to subdue the two attackers, killing one of them. They navigated the vessel back to Freetown where the surviving Spaniard – Gabriel Morillo – was tried and hanged for the murders of the captain and mate.

Text

The Journal of G. Thompson

I George Thompson, was born in the west africa, in acoo nation, 18 years old was I when the Bad people Rose up to make war, in our country, and when they begin this war, in some country or town about us, they Shut us up in the house, about three months, from going to our farm, and if any Big man do go out, and if the war people find him, they sure kill him, and if they find any Boy, they catch him and sell him until one morning about seven o-clock, they all fall upon us in our Town, and kill all the Big men, and caugh all the Boys, and I flee in to a Bush, and I was in the Bush from the morning till 3 o-clock in the afternoon, Before I escaped into another country about us, But it all was in vain, as soon as I arrive, they caugh me, and sold me into the place these the portugaiss use to make slaves trade and I was there about three months Before they sell me to portugas, and when they make all the trade they want then load they all theire slaves in the vessel, and they get on the way, and sailed four days in the sea, Before an English man war press theire vessel, and the slaves, then they Brought us to Sierra leone, and they sent some Boys & girls to the school at the vilage and some boys was taken apprentice at Sierra Leone, and about 19 of us Boys were Brought to Saint Mary's Gambia in the year 1823,[3] and I was taken apprentice by one gentleman at Gambia, to serve for seven years, in a Board ship, I was there about one year, and the vessel is now going to Sierra leone, when I heard that I was very glad to go, Because I have/get many country people there, But some person perseve that if I do go, that shall not come Back, But I don't mean to go stop there myself But when the vessel arrive there, and land all the thing what she carry, I was on Boad Cooking, about four days Before I went to Shore, and when I have land shore, there I have found my country man which told me that I must not go back any more, and I told him that I shall not be able to stay there, what the Reason says he and told him that I have left all my clothes at The Gambia, But you soon get more than what you have leave there, he says, I will look my head says I, till one night I parck up my clothes in a Bag and get it Ready, till about five oclock in the morning I took my Bag and jump in the Boat and went to shore, & I go to one vilage about forty miles destence from Sierra leone, I was there three full years, Before I Return Back to Sierra leone, in all these three years which I stop in the vilage, I have get no more clothe than two shirts and two pairs trousers which I have Brought with me from The Gambia, now when I came to sierra Leone I get one employment, 4 shillings pre month, there now I use to go with my company boys to church on every sunday, and some time go to meeting in week day, in that time, I know not whether hell is to scape or heaven is to gain, neither have I know that I have a soul to save use to pray that God may give me money to live good and get every thing which I want, and when I go to meeting I use to go laugh at those people which cannot speak good english when they are praying, and when I came home use to mocking at them now when my four shillings month work are end, I fall sick and spend all my four shillings Before I get Better, and when I get Better I get nothing and get no other work, and my sloth are wearout, now one quarter master sergent were call me in the Tower, for servant, I went to him and ask him what will he give me for a month, two dollars says he, and he refuse to give me agreement paper, I live with him two months, till one day he get drunk and Kick me away without given me any thing, and I live Kicking about in the Town, till he call me again to mind for him the horse, and I mind the horse two months again for him, without pay me any thing he turn me a way, and I went to labourers work, for one merchant, two dollars in the month, and carrying the stone for the masson, and from there I went to the River to Burning lime, two dollars in the month, and when I have Received that pay I Buy pain Shift and Trousers, I now I carried down from the River, and went to a Boad ship for eight dollars in the month, ninth months I have work there, and I Received all my pay, now am happy, and when I come Back to sierra leone Build little hut and married, and after I have married, about three months Before I shiped in one vessel which going to Liverpole, which sailed in the 19 June 1830, with two spanish sailors Board, and after we have sailed ninth days in the sea, fierce wind day and night, and in that very nine night, there two spanish sailors Rose up with theire Knif and went down in the Cabin to meet captain and mate, and they cut captain's throat and mate, and they slew them Both there down in the cabin, and the mate was sing out Before they Kill him, he was howling O Lord o Lord, save me soul, Before he fell down and died, I was in the fore head ship, and when I heard it, I awake my country man which Both of us can speak one language, and run after them to see what is matter, But meet Both of them are died and Blood flow down in the cabin, when I saw this I was greatly afraid, and run back fore head ship again, I was astonish and know not what to do, then one of them came and told us to go down Below But I don't please to go at all, for if we do go, they will shut us up in the hole, therefore we refuse, till the other one came and call me, and says Captain is dead, I asked him how come the dead of capt and mete at once, they too Bad ways he, then they ask me now if am afriaid, I told them no, then they told me that they are going to carry the vessel to cape verds' Island, and they says if we go there, they well run the vessel shore at once, and say the vessel is Break, then they will look for passinger to their country, and we to Sierra Leone, then I speak to my country man, to let us fight with them, if we are able to catch or tie them, then we will return Back to Sierra leone, or els if they able to Kill us, then we die, we was four Black men, and those two Spanish only, But there three men more fraid than I, now they cast capt and mete into the sea, and when day light, they washed cabin and opened capt trunk & charge all things + in that day I prey very much, that god may deliver me from these Bad people, in that day I think about many things to do, some time I think to fall in the sea and die, But am afraid till one time Both of them are go down in the cabin, and all of us got stick Ready on the deck, waiting for them, Just one of them coming up, I give him Knock in his head with stick, he faint, But just the other one saw that, he Rose up with Knife in his left hand sword in his right hand, coming up after us, But as soon as his head came out, three sticks meet together on his head, his head Brok and he die we cast him into the sea, & tie the other one and carried him to sierra leone, And when they Brought him Before the magistrates, and they asked him of the consequences, he deny them not But confess that he did slew the Captain and the other his country man slew the mate, and when the curt was over, he hanged at Sierra Leone, from that I don't whish to be a sailor any more, I stay at Sierra Leone learning taylor, and I use to go to one meeting every Sunday and every evening, But I don't join to any class, till one evening I went to meeting and I meet with one my country boy which asked me if I ever join in to class, I told him no, then he tole me to come go to their meeting then I went with him, in that night so I continue go in that meeting, until I go to pray, I remember the words which been read in my ears, then I Begin to repent of my sin, while I learning to read I learning to writ also, till I can read Testament, so I continue in reading and pray till I feel the pardon of my sin, in 22 December 1830, then our preacher ask me if I love God now I told him yes, he told to go and call my friends and neighbours come and see what the Lord hath done for me, and I did so, And now my master which had been taken me for apprentice he is come to Sierra Leone and fine there, and take me to governor Finden, and tell him I was his apprentice and run away from him about six years ago, and now I have found him and which to carry him, yes says governor, you must carry him and make him to serve you seven ful years again, I told him that I get yard and house, and I was lawful married, But the governor says he don't care whether I be commissary I must go, then I took my wife and go with him my lader was cam to me Before I go, and speak very Kind words, and he says that you are now to go this day I and you can not tell whether we shall see one and another in this life or no, But god can see Both you and I at all times, whether you live in the sea or land let the fear of god be found in your heart, and remember that we shall see one and another again, whether in this life or in the life to come, we shall see one and another again, he repeat this same word again, and again, that we shall see one and another again and while he spoke these words, am Bust crying, and he told me go, the god Abraham, Isaac, and Jacob, I who was been with Joseph in the land of Egypt, he is some God until now, he will Be with you, now we sailed in the 15 September 1831, from Sierra Leone, and when we sail from Sierra Leone we call to some River to buy wax and Hides, there are nearly drown, when we are returning Back from the river, we towing the vessel with Boat and long rope, there strong wind and rain fell right stern of the ship, which made her to sail over the Boat, and sunk her under the ship, four was of is in the Boat, two men swim shore and one man drowned with the Boat, and by the help of god I was escaped by the small cage anchor been hang over the stern of the ship, this was done in the 25th of Sept, the owner he is captain himself, next morning he return to the factory instrument of war, and the next morning being the 12th day of november 1831 and the vessel was very far from shore now we drawing her more close to the shore, there and fell over Boat with the anchor, which sunk me to the Bottom, with Blanket frock & trouser and by the help of God, I was able to swim up, and after we draw the vessel more close to the shore, now we Begun to land the soldiers, and while we pulling near to the shore the enemies are shouting at us very Bad, there am wounded, which cut the part of my ear and past through my cheek, there I was fell in the water Before one sailor drew me up, I was in that sickness about three months Before I get Better, and return to me master, and he put me in a Board ship, while I was in sailor I never forget my prayers to God at all times, although sailor was very wicked, But still I try to close my God all I can, that thou God sent me, I was desire nothing, But that I may dwell in the house of the Lord, I was got my Bible and my prayer Book with me, every sunday I use to read prayer and pray over it, I whish to learn write But get no paper nor ink neither slate, I use to learn write with chok upon the piece plank, and wash it out and write it again, till By and by one man give me one small slate, which am very glad of it about four years Before my master know that I can write, and when he Known that I can write he sent me in the River to the factory trade, there I was taken captive by two harlots, in commit do great sins against light and love, and when my wife came up there to see me, told her to pray from me for am sined God, she was very sorry indid, and said if my man would tell me that you stay with him I told him yes then he ask me if like to go and make trade in the River, that he will pay me I told him no that am Rather go to my sailor ship than to go trade again, then he told me to stop in the shop But his wife don't whish to see me there at all, then I go about my Business, But while am go our, he think that I shall not get any situation, But God was so good, to cloth the smiling field with corn, and to feed young ravens when the cry, when Mr. H. Wilkinson saw that I get nothing then he call me to be assistant teacher in the Wesleyan Missionary School, not by my Known any thing nor by my understand, only by his love to poor people and the Goodness of God, there am continue until now, and he told me that he want me for local preacher, and I trust to the same God, which preserve me from my youth until now, he will save me to end.

CASE EIGHT

James Will

Author: James Will
Region of birth: Yoruba (likely western)
Date of birth: *c.* 1821
Year of enslavement: *c.* 1829–30
Place of writing: Sierra Leone
Date of account: 9 March 1839
Year of death/last known year of activity: Unknown
Published: No/unknown[1]

Source: Reference: MMS, Special Series, Biographical, Various Papers, Anti-Slavery Papers 1774–1891, Fiche Box 44, Box 662(1); and Special Series, Biographical, West Africa, Fiche Box 4, Box No. 593(1), Fiche No. 123[2]

Introduction

James Will was an MMS preacher and Liberated African who recorded an account of his enslavement dated Freetown, 19 March 1839. His begins by stating that he was 'born in the land of Akue', adding that 'the place where I was born undoubtedly is about seven days journey to the sea shore'. Beyond this, Will's narrative between capture and sale into the Atlantic trade is devoid of specific places people.

Will's account delineates a period of at least ten months between his capture and sale at the coast. Will's slave vessel departed the port of Jakin in early September 1830, suggesting Will was enslaved in the latter months of 1829. Will describes the surrounding country as ravaged by internecine warfare but also notes that war had not reached his particular town until around the time of his enslavement. That warfare came to Will's birthplace in the late 1820s would suggest a location, to the west of Owu and south of Oyo.

Will recounts that following the destruction of his town he was part of a group which fled and met a 'large body of army', possibly the joint Ijebu/Ife/Oyo refugee force which was currently devastating Egbaland. The picture of anarchy Will paints suggests Egbaland in the aftermath of the Owu War. Alternatively, the three days' journey between his own town and where he encountered this army may suggest his birthplace was further north in the Onko, Ibarpa or Epo provinces.

Wills observes that he landed at Freetown in October 1830 and that he was apprenticed to a prominent Liberated African merchant, Thomas Will. The record of apprenticeships inside the Liberated African registers indicates that Will was on board the Havana-based *Veloz Pasajera*, the only vessel captured from the Bight of Benin and adjudicated at Freetown's Mixed Commission Court during that month.[3] Of the *Veloz Pasajera*'s male captives whose names and details are recorded in the register, one – receptive number 37,732, with the name of 'Kealoo' – was apprenticed to Thomas Will.[4]

British court officials rendered phonetically the African names given by the landed captives, via interpreters. Kealoo may be their rendering of the Yoruba names Akinlu or Akinyalu, though this is certainly open to interpretation.[5] Kealoo is listed as 4'8", with cuts on his cheeks and forehead, and estimated to be nine years of age.[6]

The voyage of the *Veloz Pasajera* has a uniquely rich documentary record among ships tried before Freetown's mixed court. This is due to a subsequent court case arising from the killing of three British seamen as the slaver's crew attempted to avoid interception. A mate and gunner of the *Veloz Pasajera* both testified at Freetown's police court that 'the present cargo of slaves were all purchased from Chacha (de Souza) and shipped from Jackin, a place near Whydah'.[7] This testimony suggests that Will and his shipmates on board the *Veloz Pasajera* were sold into the Atlantic trade by the notorious Brazilian slave trader, Francisco Félix de Souza.

Kealoo and his fellow captives 'were on board about four days' when the crew of HMS *Primrose* spotted the *Veloz Pasajera* on the evening of 6 September 1830 while on patrol between Principe and Badagry.[8] A battle of twenty to thirty minutes aboard the *Veloz Pasajera* left five of the enslaved and fifty-two of the crew dead; three British seamen lost their lives.[9] The *Veloz Pasajera* and *Primrose* arrived in Freetown harbour on 8 October 1830.

Following his arrival in Freetown, James was apprenticed to Thomas Will. Thomas was a Liberated African, though it is not known exactly when he landed in the colony. By 1830 Thomas was a highly successful trader located on Freetown's Pademba Road. For four years prior he had profited from the resale of goods purchased at auction from captured slave ships.

Such business acumen had earned Thomas Will the title of 'Aku King'. By the early 1840s and the completion of his apprenticeship, James Will had established himself as a successful shopkeeper and Wesleyan preacher. After 1848, the only mention of James Will is in the Methodist's annual lists of preachers in the colony and in references to his presence by other missionaries.

Text

1st
I James Will, was born in the land of Akue. The place where I was born undoubtedly is about seven days journey to the sea shore. My father and my mother have not known the salt waters. This land is very fruitful, corn bear twice in a year, yams, cocoa[10], plantains, guinea corn and various other fruits, and many grow in bushes sweet to the taste and pleasant to the eyes. These are the fruits and vegetables which we live upon for the sustenance of our lives from age to age. Rice and flour is not in my country where I was born, and many other things which we eat in this country. In that country our clothes were made of cotton. The women made the cotton into thread and dyed it, some of it either black or blue or as they may want it, then men bought it of the, and made clothes of it, made white, check, stripe and other different cloth.

Silk, velvet, woollen and scarlet they hardly been seen in that country though is often carried there to buy slaves yet it can hardly be seen and you may know by this, in that country no person to wear taffety beside our sovereign, the king of the heathen country &c.

And if person or persons should have that cloth in their possession the king would immediately sent [sic] for he or them to be brought before him and he will take it from them, and also umbrella is not allowed to be worn unless the king of that country who use it once a year.

A crown in my country is made of coral and other beads, these stringed up and made up like a small basket and the king wear it as a crown. In my country beef and fishes are not our daily food, there are not much bullocks and goos [?] as they are in this country, and we can hardly get fish except in dry season when all the rivers are dried up and the water becomes small in the river, then the people use to catch fishes with a sort of net like basket after they caught them have them dried up, and carry them to their market, charge very dear for them, so that no body would buy them for temporary use except for sacrifice to idols.

My dear friends before whom this account may come, I cannot be ashamed to describe to you the meat common in use in my country, I mean of flesh of beef, snakes, bush rats, ground pigs and many other insects that creep in the ground.

Dogs and horse are very common, if dog got mad they would kill it and eat, and we use to walk in our farm looking for holes where rats and other insects hide, if we find we dig it up in searching for rats and insects and catch them and eat some of them in the farm and the rest will carry to the market for sale. Money use in my country are cowries five of them would purchase enough food for a person in the time of harvest.

2nd
Men's trade in my country are the following, viz, farmer cloth making blacksmith taylor carpenter magicians phisicians [sic] slave trader & travellers.

The farmer continually work in their farm all seasons of the year and the produce they sold in the market every year and get their profit from it. The cloth maker continually making their cloths and brought them to the market every day and get their gain by it. The blacksmith made their shop in the street some about seven or eight of them in one shop, making hoes cutlasses and knives and many other things by making these things got plenty of gains.

The tailors were set in their houses and if any man have any work to give he is to go after them, they made trousers caps and gowns like those of Mandingoo. The trousers in my country is not long than knee, and clothes all are made in form of bed sheets, some in a day and some for cover in the night, that is the work which the tailors use for get their living.

The carpenter they don't have much to do as the others did, their work is bowls, coffins, and door. No more because the houses in my country have no windows the wall built of clay and the roofs are bush woods or sticks no nails required in those house, no shingle want in those houses in my country. The roofs are covered so leaves is shelter us for many years from shower of rain and heat of the sun.

The magicians they walk from house to house they tell to every person what their Gods enquire of them and so doing they have their daily bread.

The phisicians in my country they pretend to do many things that which is too great, they can heal the sick by their phisical and do man useful to the bodies, but alas I have found they have some sort ever medicine not to ear nor to drink but to worship every morning that the life may prolong or preserve from sickness or diseases, and they have plenty of poison to kill any man quick as razor got into his throat, so men will go and employ the to destroy their enemy, in that way the phisicians will so much so that they get their living.

The slave traders and travellers are one they walk from to through the country to buy people and the things which scarce in one part and carry it to another and sell and make gain, from time to time, they don't care whose child it may be either for the king or the governor they will punish after they purchased him as if commit any crime they chain their foot in the night with iron and in the daily they their both arm or one tied to their necks for fear less they will escape away. They sell them from market of one town to the market of another town until they brought them down to the town that is in the lake side where Spanish and Portuguese use to land their cargoes, and make shop to buy persons and load their vessels with the persons which they purchased."

It is not so necessary for me to still go on in this discourse but however I will tell you that women in my country they were very industrious. I cannot tell you all but I will tell what is my mother is trade she use to make rum out of indian corn. She make palm oil out of palm nut she make blue [?] and sell snuff and she doing complete all domestic service and few of the people in our town they use to put their child in pawn to my mother for money, and my mother bought another girl to help her in doing this work, my mother loved me much because I was her only son my mother told me that she have conceived about twelve times and she born nine children and thus twelve and she miscarried three times and all died save three I was a little boy and I have two big sister. My elder sister born six children one died they left five another one she is young woman she have one son, I loved that child myself my father is a farmer as well as phisician my father have two other wives beside my mother one have two son one is died the other left and the other woman have no child at all. In my country some great men have about fifty wives some twenty some two &c &c you need not wonder how they do to maintain so much women, for some of them have more property than their husband in my country men are not bound to feed and find their wive as white men do and some others, men only to made their houses if them sick he is to see about it, and women use to cook for their husband by turn one today another tomorrow, by this mean one man have some children.

3rd
I am going to tell you about the way of worshipping in my country, but before I begin I will direct you to St. Paul's Epistle to the Roman 1 ch from 24-to-32 verse, in that country we never know whether man have any rights or reason to worship the God of heaven at all, we worship these gods, viz thunder, snakes, stones, mud, wood, iron, brass, palm nuts, shells, dead bodies and some places in the bush we offered sacrifice to a tree.[12] And I never heard Lord save my soul until I came to Sierra Leone, unto the above mentioned gods we prey and make supplication. I am sorry to say however God pour any blessing upon us unto the above mentioned gods ever give the glory, and whenever we met with any misfortune unto them we use to make our requisitions. If too much sickness in the land we will offered unto all kind of gods sacrifice for our deliverance. I never saw a man pray to the Lord of heaven not a day in my country and we never notice the God of heaven as our benefactor his name hardly to be mentioned at all. Every man prays in the morning as follows, Ashoo shoo, war, ju me, mer cueye me. That is to say, devil direct my part, before me you may go, but you must not follow behind me.

Again I say we pray unto our gods to keep us from death and sickness and give us good fortune and gain in selling and out farmer to produce fruits in abundance, we fear nothing but death and sickness, we don't know any thing about Jesus Christ the only son of God who shed his blood for all the world so we live in sin and in shade of death. Our soul may hunger and thirst but there is no food for them, because there is not the word of God (the scriptures) and we never pray in behalf of our never dying souls. I am sorry to say as beast we born as beast we live and as beast we die, in my country. I told you that we worship palm nuts you may not wonder to say how can that be, it is a plain fact every man have them about thirty two in number they put it in calabashes and kept it in their room the produce of their farm they will taste until they offered sacrifice of the same unto the palm nuts.[13]

The palm nuts of them we make palm oil to eat our food daily of the same we make our gods. Look how foolish we are in that country. We worship thunder, for the represent of thunder they made images of woods and few sort of a rock up them unto cabash[14] they offered sacrifice from time to time and whenever roll they cried with a loud voice saying we are thine horses[15] thou art our master we will serve thee, we worship also river and trees in the bushes and many other things which is more foolish thing than these but I will tell you that all our house gods wee generally kept them in a calabash unto them we offer everything what they asked though they cannot see, nor speak nor hear nor answer by a word nor by a sign but we are foolish enough, to believe the magicians for they walk from house to house to try ever mean to ask our gods and tell us what they say, they use to tells of things to come some time it did the same they say.

But allow me to say if there is any nation that forget God their Creator my country will be the head, so we live without God and Christ in my country for whenever I read or hear the wicked shall be turned into hell and all the nations that forgot God I always remembered my country and my eyes goes upon my father and my mother and relatives, Oh! that the Lord would soon cause his gospel to be preached in that land the very place where I was born.

4th
So we live and are until it has pleased the almighty God to pour upon us a very great confusion, and they began to war one city against other they that win the battle will then kill so many in that day the rest they took and bound them all and made them slaves. All their properties they will taken all for themselves ~~killing another one if they were~~ this war is continually and causeless until all persons become barbarous for no man have any feeling for another they keep on selling one another until the warriors become a very large body people. They broken town from place to place killing and selling human being when this warrior comes to one part the people then flee to another part, they continuously pursued their fellow creatures as a lion did its harmless prey from year to year, some time they divided against themselves killing another as if they were not fellow warrior, their hearts is altogether become unfeeling they don't think much in selling their own brother the son of their mother in my country we found that a man sold his own mother, some sold their sons how much more for relative and friends that is a common thing for them to do.

There is no law in my country, as that any more but before time they have law to kill every doer[16] as well as it is in another country, this is another reason we continually selling and Portuguese and Spanish all other slave traders continuously buy us but when I consider what doing to one another I always found but little fault in them thay buying us, for they sailed to that land that wait on shore near the water side or rather in those town which is near to the water side to slaves, with the following articles viz, cutlasses, gun powder, Brazilian tobacco, and every other instruments of war that which is suitable to destroy one another and all so rum and all other strong liquors and every sort of cloths every kind of good things, and we think so much of these goods that cause we to sell one another for it particularly such as taffety and every other red cloths we used to think that the colour is made of human blood so we don't care to pray so much for them.

5th
So this confusion and inrespites proceeds on until, and last of all the war came in to our native place where I was born we use to run from place to place that we may not become their pray, but notwithstanding they troubled us very much inexpressive manner still, and every time when they come against us they will go and surround about one city first and when they broken that city they come another by so doing they have destroyed all our lands and the places were then left desolates and we fled into a large body of army in another part. We have arrived there in three days walk both young and old we will walk all the day long and take our repose in the night water and food we have very little in all our way to that place some persons fail in the way for want of water in food in the way but notwithstanding we still goes on because we wish to escape from those that pursue us, if can we for we run into this large body of army purpose as our refuge. That they may deliver us from our enemy that pursues us and when we reached there they did received us with all gladness we lived there began to rejoice day by day for our deliverance about five days after we reached that place we don't know that the people can in any wise rise against us, see how vain is the help of men they that take part for us to day may rise against us tomorrow.

The people says if they run in that way we will do them no good how is that they going to let, we sit still this they continued until one night we was to go to one village near us there for to buy yams for us to eat we said until tomorrow morning before we go, we slept in that night I was taken my repose in the side of my mother and the middle night the people began to ring bell and calling themselves together thus they reasoned among themselves that they may seize us all tomorrow, we think very little about it because we don't know that they canst [?] serve us as they did, so we slept until the cock crow in the morning, we set out for that village for to buy yams left my mother and I went to my father and fell straight before my father to give him morning service before I should went away that I was know that I should part to see their face no more as I should bid them fare well on earth forever, but all this is a very little matter to me to be compared with the sorrow that use to occupy my mind whenever I considered that I have lost so good kind parents and their is no hope of seen their faces in heaven that endless rest, I am very sorry indeed.

6th
We that going we were about fifteen persons. Me and one of my big sister's sons, one of my father's sister and her son and one girl she is belongs to my mother so we all went out, the people rise against our people and bound great part of them and we began to heard gun firing so much we began to fear until some one tell us that they catched all our fellow country men behind us so we fear to return house by we ourselves for there is no man among us to guide us home we wandering in that place until we found some men of the same place where we going we begged

them to lead us home and they willing immediately they told us to trust [?] on them, but alas they did not lead us home alone but they led us to their own house and separated us into a different places but me and my mother they put us in one room no more to say but next morning as the cock crow they led us to same place from whence led us yesterday me and my nephew only tow, the rest were all left behind. The about ten o clock they sold we two to one man that man is a slave trader they deliver us to that man, he took every out of that town, the same day for fear perhaps our parents will come for us. Shall I tell you what I have in that day, O yes but I say it is beyond expression. In that day the man took us we were coming toward the sea.

The Continuation of the narrative
James Will[17]

I lift up my eyes towards heaven and considered that I cannot my father and my mother no more than the sorrow that justified my breast is more than I can describe but how painful it is to part universe to part to meet no more it is a very saurful [sic] thing to part in that manner to forever to meet no more here on earth so they carried us until night is come and we slept in one town in that night and next day early in the morning the man delivered us to his brother to bring us down toward the sea that white people may buy in order that he may make great gain, when we walk until night we slept so we did until we come to the water side one white man bought me and my nephew together, and the man bought so many slaves they put us into chain the chain is hanged about our necks and we all bath young and old left naked as we born They chained us all according to the length of the chains some forty some thirty and some twenty and five so it is very bad thing to men chained together if one wish to go out busy himself the rest all we must go either through rain or the burning sun, so we live and still punishing my our master, they whipped us for every little fault and cutted all our backs, we lived in chains about two months our master died and they another town there have more punishment, than that place from we came we were punished with hunger and thirst and the chain is still upon our neck and there many of us died but God so good to spared me and my nephew still, in that town we about four months and many of us have died and gone to eternity, and there they took again to another town we and the chain again about our necks the same day we reached to that town for we live canoe[18] all of the nights. The same very day again they removed us to another place[19] there we lived and many died and some very sickly so many were before but we began to left but few. And there they took chain from our necks and they tied us all with cords, but we felt little happy, for chain that which is so heavy & chain past taken from our necks and that gentleman which we met in that town have so many so many hundreds of slaves and he still buying more and more and more fast as they bringing them. And that time we lived there about four months again, and after that they brought us down to the water side we were in sandy ground of the sea shore[20] When we saw the roaring of the sea we were very much afraid we hardly bear the sight of it, but is not be compared with the fear which we feared when first we were brought before white men we supposed they are men eaters, we never satisfied until some of our country men encouraged us and said it is not so, we believed their saying because they been to Portuguese country with said master, and about four days after that, one morning we just awoke from sleep they began to make us sit by ten tens, and soon they began to take us in the most largest vessel in the harbor, for there were about five vessels in the harbor me and my nephew sat down together and we were in one number to be taken to the vessel with our fellows, and my nephew got up and said unto me that he is going to drink water and I told him to come quick that we may not become separate from one another and whether to live let us live together and whether to die let us die together and he went and soon got up, they re-counted us, and suppose that they miss in counting us, so they put another boy in his stead or in room and they took us to the vessel and my nephew left on the shore with other multitudes of slaves and the vessel filled with slaves and she sailed away on the very night so we part from each other until this day so I found that, we have suffered grief and pain and last of all we have past to more here on the face of the earth.

So I bid my land adieu and we were on board about four days after we embarked it appears as the people in our board saw the man of war brig coming after them and so they were very troubled been restless all night and very early in the morning they began to fight against each other at once, because they having got ready all the night and we who were the cause of this war between these two vessels we were locked down below the deck and it is not much longer before the man of war brig prevail against us and they killed much of ship crews and the English prized us and we were sailed to the Colony of Sierra Leone and was arrived in the month of October in the year 1830 and next day we were landed on shore and we were very glad for what we have once again permitted again to tread on the face of the earth and especially when we saw some of our own country people come, and told us about the kind dealing of white men we felt grateful unto our God the white people have compassion on us and delivered us from men dealers and make us free from slave, but remember what I have foresaid on twenty page I said we fled to our country men for refuge, they did us no good. but read down the twentieth page there you will find what they have done to us, it is because they are tyrant and barbarous creature. The more is because they have no fear of God before their eyes, why, us because they have the devil for their father and his works they do.

8th
We met Governor Findlay in the colony and there is no more school in the colony for the King's boys so they bound us out as an apprentices unto our country men, and other nations, but they are the inhabitants of Sierra Leone, both boys and girls were bound out some for seven years and some for five and they set the big men and women at liberty.[21] It was on the 19 October 1830 when they gave us out but me and other girl were given to Mr. Thomas Will in Freetown and he gave me to one of his country men there live until this man died and I went back to

Mr. Thomas Will.[22] One morning me and other boy went to our hawker shop and we come near to the gallows tree we saw so many people standing around the gallows tree for a man was going to be hanged and as they led him upon the steps of the gallows tree so the man began to crying and I asked the other boy what the man saying he told me. Said he, James, how can I tell that but I suppose the man was praying, I asked him what he was praying, he told me says the man is murderer for if he down pray God will cast him down into fire. When he die I was very much afraid when I heard about that fire in the world to come that is first day that I ever heard hell since I was born and my heart was very trouble until I became altogether restless and one night I heard my master's wife as she praying and she said Lord Jesus save me from my sin, and I was thought she said Lord save my sin, and I quickly caught that word from her mouth and I began to repeat it for myself every time whenever my heart surrounds with fears of hell I use to say Lord save my sin, though I don't hear English language but my heart is always telling me says is the way to pray so I continually do it until one day I asked a girl name Nancy what the word Lord meant she told me another thing She told me says is the ground on which our house is built and I was astonished, so I began to reason with myself I said it cannot be that a person can pray to the ground or to the earth, but we can pray to the its maker. I use to pray in our tongue and said as follows – onyly barme, onyly barme –.[23] That is to say creator of the earth save me so I use to pray from time to time until in one night in a vision I dreamed a good dream it appear in my dream as if I have taken up in heaven among a very large body people and all clothed in white and the people filled with love they embraced me we ate some sort of ground nut in white basons [sic] and after that we began to singing the place look as a very fine morning for the heat sun was there so we walk along unto one broad gate one woman went in the gate with tears on her cheek and I so I awoke from my repose with a voice of a certain woman the have converted news our house the praise God and I was awoke with her voice and in the morning I told my dream to my mistress and she told me saying it is the lord about to begin his glorious work in my soul and I was very glad, and then I ceased from watching and praying, and then I was come more harding [?] in my sins because the dream hast deceived me, and I was ceased of think of death and hell which waits my immortal soul, so I become as the foolish souls that dream of heaven and make their empty boast, So I continue in my sins an inequity and it hast pleased the Lord in his wise counsel and I visited with a disease and fierce affliction and I was owns it as the reasoned of my sins and advance of my iniquity thought I use I every time to pray but it is not as when I was first convinced of my sins in the year of 1831, that is a year when I was first convinced in the way which I have been convicted and excited if I was been continue for a while I would have been convicted, had I not been deceived by my grandless decain [?]; but see soon as I began to be careless and unconcern so I began to forget my God to whom I use to pray from time to time for I use to pray every where in the bush whenever I sent for wood, and when I lived in house I use to pray in my head and soon as I ceased from the method and constitution, the spirit prayer was then depart and the spirit of conviction is gone, and the Lord was so good and kind that he hast not leave me to myself but he still warming me by his holy spirit during all these times in the year of 1835.

In the year of 1835 there was in the Colony a good revival of God's holy works, and I was invited to Marroon chapel in Percival street on Wednesday evening on the fifth of August 1835 for to hear Rev. Benjamin Crosby and us soon as I went in the chapel we met another man preaching that is Mr. James Wise one of the Wesleyan[24] Local preacher he commenced to keep the service before I went in the chapel and I was caught up very quick with conviction and I feel the weight of my sins on my back as it were and the Lord hast opened my eyes to see that I am in the high way to that endless destruction from that day I began to pray and asking pardon from the Lord Jesus Christ and on the 19th of August 1835 while I was alone praying and wrestling with the Lord in the twinkling of an eye the Lord hast entered in my heart and wrought in his glorious work an hast gave me his holy spirit in my breast through the meritorious suffering of Jesus Christ and next morning I was able to tell sinner around what dear saviour I have found, and the devil began to come against me and told me I am but an apprentice under a man I have began to serve the Lord too soon but I was keep on to watch and pray and not much long before I was able to revisit the devil and was fled from me able to tell to my fellow Christian either in my class meeting or love Feast that it is my disposition to the Lord here below and find my way to heaven by his own assistance, and I have no more shame to recommend the Lord Jesus Christ to every restless souls. The Jesus Christ without hesitation that he is the fountain of happiness to every troublesome soul that will cry to him from right and end and the first time I can stand before my fellows to exhort them my appointment was at Wilberforce, my text was the 5th verse of the general Epistle of James I have exhorted my fellow creatures and the lord have poured on us at great blessing and we have a very glorious meeting it was on Sunday evening the tenth of June 1838.

Since the lord have gave me his holy spirit the Lord still helping me so I never have any disposition of going back into the world until this present movement though I often tried and tempted but his holy spirit always comfort me and I always enable me to say let hell oppose and devil rage but the will of my God must be done and his will, I must do or shall do. While here on earth I dwell and the lord generally help me in all I do and I have always found him to be an all sufficient God to my soul's satisfaction on every point and his word is forever sure.

So the Lord helped me and the time that I was bound for is finished on the 19 October 1837 and I was discharged and my master has employed me for my office for I use to keep his shop since the 5 May 1834 and there in the same office until today when I was discharged my master bought a lot for me and there I have built my house in forth street.

But though I was once lost my father and my mother but now I have found that the Lord have done for me than my father or mother ever do for God have keep from harm and all danger by day and by night the Lord preserve my worthless when many have pass from time that boundless eternity therefore I will still praise him for what he have done for me and I will still trust what is to come both for time and for eternity.

I have my appointment tomorrow Sunday in the evening in two places one at Murray town and the other at Wilberforce one at 5 o'clock and the other at 8 o'clock I cannot able to attend the both but I attend the one at Wilberforce by the help of God if am spared to the day and I tell Rev Mr. Badger that he may send another person to it for me so the place may neglected by me, and I began to learn to read since I came This country because I love the word of God and soon I was learn to write and far as read far as I can write.

End
Freetown
Sierra Leone
Saturday the ninth march of 1839

CASE NINE

Joseph Boston May

Author: Joseph Boston May
Region of birth: Iware, south-eastern Oyo
Date of birth: *c.* 1817
Year of enslavement: *c.* 1825
Place of writing: Sierra Leone
Date of Account: October 1838
Year of death/last known year of activity: Died 8 March 1891
Published: No[1]

Source: 'The Life and Experience of Joseph Boston May',
MMS, Sierra Leone Correspondence, Fiche Box 25,
Box No. 280, 'Sierra Leone Odds Papers',
Fiche No. 1879, #3

Introduction

Joseph Boston May was a Yoruba Liberated African and Wesleyan Methodist minister in Sierra Leone. May was probably born in 1817 in the town of Iwarreh [Iware], near the Ogun River in south-eastern Oyo. He was originally named Ifacayeh (Ifákayé, 'Ifá covers the world') by his father, a *babaláwo* (a Yoruba diviner) in honour of Ifá, the Yoruba deity of divination.

With the disintegration of the Oyo Empire after *c.* 1817, Ifacayeh's father Loncola moved the family to the town of Ikotto in search of greater security. But both Ikotto and Iwarreh, along with the neighbouring towns of Okiti, Ajerun and Ajabe, were captured in the late months of 1825 by warriors of Ojo Amepo, an independent Muslim raider who had once been a military chief to Afonja, the secessionist ruler of Ilorin. Ojo's raiders took

Ifacayeh, his mother, brother and sisters. Ifacayeh's father avoided capture and subsequently came to the raiders' camp to ransom his family. However, according to May's account, his father's resources were insufficient to redeem the entire family. Ifacayeh was left with his captors and taken to another town before his father could return.

Ifacayeh was held in domestic slavery. His new enslaver kept him for nearly a year until his material circumstances declined, and he was forced to sell the child. His second enslaver held him for three months before taking the boy to a town five days away and selling him to a merchant involved in the long-distance slave trade to the coast. In late September or early October 1826, Ifacayeh and a group of other enslaved people were marched to the Lagos lagoon and carried by canoe to Badagry. Here he was sold to Portuguese slave traders and, after three months confined to a barracoon, was placed on the Brazilian brig *Dois Amigos* in January 1827.[2] The vessel and its cargo of 317 enslaved men, women and children were destined for Salvador de Bahia, before the crew of HMS *Esk* intercepted the vessel and diverted the slave ship to Freetown. There, Sierra Leone's Mixed Commission Court liberated Ifacayeh along with 307 other survivors.[3]

May's account is dated October 1838. This is the first of a number of testimonies collected by the Wesleyan Methodists in Sierra Leone and The Gambia between October 1838 and June 1839. After writing this account, May spent eighteen months in London, sponsored to study at the Borough Road Training College of the British and Foreign Mission School Society. He returned to Sierra Leone in 1841. For most of the 1840s he was principal teacher at New Town West School, Sierra Leone. In 1847, he resigned this position to begin mission work in The Gambia.

Text

Introduction

With patience have I tried to write this. It was my long desire to write something like this long ago, or as a memorandum like, of my conversion and how God hath bountifully dealt with me since I learn to know myself, but I could not able because I am not qualify to write for myself what I desire; but however the Lord still spared my life and I improve more little and little till Mr. Dove Wesleyan missionary with his wife & other came from England at this time the 19 November 1837 and brought some little books with him, and as I went to the mission house to be instructed as we general do he read one of his little books to us and give two or three away he then told us that it will be very good if we can make or write something like this of our conversion or our Experience. Then I was exceeding with rejoice because it was my wishes.

Now as I was about to begin it I was greatly discouraged in many instances till I almost give it up; because sometimes when I think of begin it opportunity will not allow me, and when it occurs again in my mind to begin I do not know how to direct my English more especially this is what keeps me back it discourages me till I almost entirely give it up and say it is of no use but however being it is my long desire even until now I then take a little more encouragement and endeavoring to make it so just as it is now not with pure and perfect English so that you need not stop or doubt of the great errors you shall find there.

Joseph B. May

The Life
and
Experience of Joseph Boston May

I Joseph B May of the Colony of Sierra Leone was born in Aku Country, a heathen nation, a country full of idolatry and I was taking captive with my mother, a brother, and a sister[4], and when it came to the ear of my father he immediately came from where he was with money; redeem my mother, brother, and sister, the money was finished, immediately my father went, to get money in the next Town to redeem me, but Alas! alas! before he came back again I was sold to another man and carried to a very far country, where I doubt not my father and mother will seek for me day[5], and night, with mourning, and groaning; but still I will not be found of them, there I was sold from one place to the other untill I was gone very far with groans, and tears, from my parents, and native country, but thanks be to God who has brought me to better country, to looking forward to a better, better country above, the heavenly Canaan. So I was carried on until I was brought to the place where I saw a large body of fresh water, which we cross over with canoe in a few hours, and came to that country where the Portuguese are: I stop there about a month, and then sold to the Portuguese of the same place; for some articles &c. At first I was affrighting, my heart was in great perturbation, lest I should be sold to the same Portuguese, at last I was sold to them, I wept some; with tears and groans; I was many days and nights; because I get into the hands of a nation whom I know not. Moreover I have no hope of seeing my parents and relations no more for ever but I know not that all of us shall have to see each others' face, in the morning of the resurrection. And more I have heard that the Portuguese buy people, and carried them to eat in their own country; I partly believe it, because if any person or persons do not look fair, nice, and beautiful, they will not buy, they bought many of us, men, women, and children, we were about one hundred and forty or more, we stop there about two months or three, in their hands with chains round about our necks and then we were carried and put in vessel on the sea, I was in a most deplorable state, bitter weeping and moaning, lose all my friends, parents, and relations; and now I know not where I am going; and what shall become of poor me Joseph; but the omniscient Jehovah 'who

> moves in mysterious ways
> His wonders to perform
> Who plants his footsteps on the sea
> And rides upon the storm'

Knoweth where he carried me to a land which flowed with Gospel Light. We have wandered about, and travelled in the great ocean, by the hurricane, till at last my Lord, and Redeemer, hath brought me here and landed me safe in this colony aforesaid in the year 1826, when I supposed to be about nine or ten years age, then I exceedingly rejoice, and thankful to the Lord that he has put my feet upon the shore again. I was in the Liberated yard for about three weeks, and then brought up to Regent's school, a village in the mountains by the order of the Governor; to be instructed, and I was instructing till Mr. Edmund Boston one of the Church Missionaries, took me to live with him there I received more instruction, he was a very kind man to me and loved me very much, he give me a little bible on the 11th of September 1828, which I got with me until this very day, only it is now very old I love it well. I lived with the same man until his death in the year 1830. I then came down to Freetown in 1834 live sometimes with several of the Europeans, some who will not let me go to church or chapel at all but swearing and cursing, damning me soul and the church to go to hell but give me any sort of work to do on the Lord's Day which I never will do which altogether on this account I left them and lived with another who wish not that I should go to any chapel at all, but the large Church Saint George, he say there I can hear a white man preach, I must always go there alone, on Sunday of every two weeks, but to any other place I must not go; he say that it is black men who preaches in the chapel, and they know nothing at all. So I must not go to hear them any more, but thanks, and praise, be to the Lord who has open the eyes, ears, and hearts of the blacks; some a worshipper of idolatry, trying to do like white men; preacher of the Gospel of Christ; and has open my eyes, and heart the _____ to shout his praise. On Friday evening, one of my fellowservant J.C. went to one of the Wesleyan Methodist Chapel, in finery but when he returned home he was in deep conviction after this; over; he told me that his heart troubled him very much and he felt very bad, he continue to go to chapel every time until one evening ~~on Tuesday the month of April~~ 1835. He invited me, to go with him to chapel. I was afraid to go because I was ordered to go no chapel or church at all but St. George[6]: but it was my wish to go as long I were with him, both of us went to Ebenezer Chapel, one of the Wesleyan Methodists, where I hear that warm and levity or heart searching preacher Reverend Benjamin Crosby which is the first since I ever hear a Methodist preacher, struck my heart with conviction.

FIGURE 2 Joseph Boston May (back row, second from right). Courtesy of The John Rylands Research Institute and Library, The University of Manchester.[7]

CASE TEN

Joseph Wright

Author: Joseph Wright
Region of birth: Oba, Egba Alake
Date of birth: *c.* 1815–17[1]
Year of enslavement: *c.* 1827
Place of writing: Freetown, Sierra Leone
Date of account: June 1839
Year of death/last known year of activity: Died at Lagos, 7 June 1855
Published: John Beecham, *Ashantee and the Gold Coast* (London: 1841)[2]

Source: MMS, Sierra Leone Correspondence, Fiche Box 25, Box No. 280, Fiche No. 1868 and 1869, #13

Introduction

The narrative of Joseph Wright is the only account in this volume to have been previously published in a collection of slave narratives, namely Philip Curtin's *African Remembered*. The eminent historian of Sierra Leone, the late Christopher Fyfe, first brought Wright's narrative to the attention of Philip Curtin, and the inclusion of Wright's account in *Africa Remembered* has made his testimony one of the best-known among scholars of the slave trade over the past half century. Wright's account is included herein for multiple reasons. First, this introduction presents new information relating to Wright's life and in particular the slave voyage he experienced. Second, this volume contextualises Wright's account among many compiled by the MMS during this period.[3] Third, while Curtin stated that the version in *Africa Remembered* 'contains some corrections of punctuation, grammar, and spelling but otherwise adheres closely to the original' it was in reality in a much abridged and edited format that smoothed his prose. Finally, the research for this volume uncovered a second narrative titled 'Statement of Joseph Right Concerning Himself' (Case 12 below) and it is important to read both side by side to determine if these texts are by and about the same individual.

Joseph Wright, whose birth name is not known, was born of the Egba Alake, though he later titled his narrative more broadly as 'a native of Ackoo'. The Methodist missionary Thomas Dove observed that the Egba Joseph Wright 'has all the marks and scars in his face indicative of the Akoo tribe to which he belongs'.[4] Wright was enslaved during the destruction of the forested Egba settlements. He was likely from Oba, one of three Egba towns captured in a single day by the Ife–Ijebu forces in late 1826 or early 1827. *Africa Remembered* did not identify with certainty the slave vessel that brought Joseph Wright to Freetown. Curtin concluded that the ship was likely 'to have been the *Velas*, a Brazilian vessel sighted twelve miles from Lagos at 12:30 P.M. on 16 March 1827, by Bullen's flagship, H.M.S. *Maidstone*' though he also noted that there was no evidence in the historical record that there were any enslaved on board this vessel.[5] Indeed, the *Velas* is unlikely since this vessel was not brought before the Mixed Commission Court (likely because no enslaved people were on board) and the Registers of Liberated Africans have no record of any Africans disembarked from this vessel. Rather, it is more likely that Wright was on the *Henriqueta*, a Bahian slave vessel that reached Lagos on 2 September 1827 and proceeded to take on board 569 enslaved people. The vessel was captured 'on the 6th of September a few hours after leaving port by His Majesty's Ship Sybille'. Twelve Africans died on the twenty-three day voyage to Freetown.[6] The vessel's capture fits Wright's description: the capture took place the day after the slave ship departed Lagos, at coordinates roughly 70 miles to the south. The voyage of twenty-three days to Sierra Leone also fits Wright's recollection that 'we landed to Sierra Leone in about a month after we sailed'.

In Sierra Leone, Wright resided at the Liberated African village at York. Little is known of this period or of the training he received in order to become a literate member of the Wesleyan church, though the Methodists maintained the King Tom Institution in Freetown for postprimary education, and Wright undoubtedly went there.[7] In 1842–44 Wright visited Britain with the sponsorship of Methodists backers who wished him to continue his education. Upon his return to Sierra Leone, he learned that Samuel Crowther had delivered the first-ever sermon in the Yoruba language in January 1844 and joined a number of Yoruba Methodist converts in the colony to follow Crowther's lead.[8]

Of Wright's later life, Curtin simply noted that he 'died in the later 1850's still less than fifty years of age' and presumably in Sierra Leone.⁹ In fact, Wright died in June 1855, and the notice of his death in the *Wesleyan Missionary Notices* presents a more complete conclusion to the narrative of one of Sierra Leone's best-known Liberated Africans

> A native of the Aku country, Mr. Wright was kidnapped in his youth, sold to slave-dealers, and stowed board a ship, with hundreds of others. The vessel was seized on the passage by an English cruiser, and the miserable slaves set free on the happy soil of Sierra-Leone. There the young Aku was taught, was converted, began to preach the Gospel, and gave such proof of a call to the ministry, that he was sent to England to be trained at our Theological Institution. He profited much by his residence at Richmond, and returned to his own country an able labourer. There he has faithfully discharged his Missionary duties for more than ten years. He learned that his relatives were found at Abbeokuta, and this year he resolved on making a journey for the purpose of visiting them. This he was permitted to accomplish; but, while with his mother, he was taken ill. He reached the celebrated slave-port of Lagos, on his way back to Sierra Leone; and there, feeling near death, wrote a beautiful, wise, and touching letter to his son, whom he had sent to England to be trained at Westminster Training Institution. There also he rendered up his spirit into his Master's hands, on the 7th of June.¹⁰

Joseph Wright was thus one of the fortunate few Liberated Africans who was able to travel in reverse the passage of Atlantic slavery in order to reunite with family.

Joseph Boston May eulogized his departed compatriot in a letter sent from the village of York where Joseph Wright had first been settled in Sierra Leone. May's reminiscences confirm certain particulars of Wright's life history: that he was 'a native of Obbah [Oba]' and was sold into slavery when he 'was then about ten or twelve years of age'.¹¹ In Sierra Leone he had married and had six children. May recounted that Wright had 'heard that his parents were still alive' and was 'urged to see them before their death' though he does not state how this information travelled from Abeokuta to Sierra Leone.

Wright likely contracted dysentery at Abeokuta and returned to Lagos.¹² Having returned to the region of his birth – now transformed by war, refugee flight, new settlements – he reached the Atlantic coast once again and died at the port where he had been sold to Brazilian slave traders three decades before. His funeral at the Wesleyan mission yard at Lagos was attended by 'a large number of Sierra-Leone emigrants, among whom he laboured in former years'.¹³

Text

The Life of Joseph Wright
A Native of Ackoo

I was born heathen in a heathen Land, and was trained up in my youth to the fashion and customs of that heathenish Country, but the Lord, who would not have me to live to be old in that unhappy Country, hast brought among us war and confusion as the wages of our sins.

I was born of respectable parents, but they are not very rich, my father is a member of Council, and he have two wives, besides, those of his father which he left to him at his death, according to the law of our country.[14] My mother is the first wife my father have, and she has bear us five children unto my father. We were all boy except one girl – and we all were with our parents until this last tumultuous war which is the cause of our separations, the manner of that war reminds me of the saying of the wise man. Though hand join in hand sin shall not go unpunished, the war have been heard of long ago, but our fathers know not how to repent of the impending Wrath of God, therefor the evil hath fulfilled upon us. At the time we heard of that war in a far distant land, we confidently thinking they will not come to us. Alas, in space of about seven years after they came to us unexpectedly.[15] To our surprising they come and besieged us round about. These people that raised up this war they are not another nation. We are all one nation speaking one language. Nation rise against nation, and kingdom against kingdom, and therefore the cannot stand.

The war shut us from all business. They fighting us with all their strength and we fighting against them with all our might, but not with hope of escape. In this miserable state we live for about seven months, destitute of all food. We have nothing to eat, in order to have strength to fight enemies. In this hard case of ours, we had no real God to go to for help, but we constantly sacrificed to our gods. There is a god which we call publick god. It is god of man, and not of woman. No woman ever allow to go or pass by the mountain where they place that god.[16] The name of that god was Carowah.[17] To this we all looking for help, and to another by name of Sarbertaroo. This is woman god, the females often killing pigeons, fowl, and sometimes bullock as a sacrifice for their god.[18]

And these was to overcome the war which had besieged our city. besides thousands of private gods the people kept in their houses, all these was in vain. At last the famine has overcome us, so that the chasing man of war could not forbear. One night in about seven months after the war had besieged us, all the mighty men of war, has consulted together to go to another Country in order to buy us some food to preserve we children of the land. And so they did, and in this band were my father and mother. They go to get us some food too, for they pity us when they see we perishing with hunger. At the time they ready to left me and all my brethren, they knew not that they would never see us again in the flesh, or else they would never left us, or they would have given us final kiss as dear children, but they knew not what would take place after they left us. Short time after they were gone with all the mighty men of war, for fearing the enemies would break upon them in the way. Maybe the enemies knew this that all the chasing men of war hath gone for food, in foreign country. So they getting ready to take the city before the people which gone for food should come. The town become very poor for want of people to fight, because at the time when my country knew the men of war were going for food, the most part of the people determined to go, knowing they would be safe if the enemies should break upon them in the way.

The city in danger of taking every day, because there remained but women and young men and boys in the town. In a night, before the city was taken, people were trying to make their escape, and many had escaped. When I heard of this, I took my brethren with me, and we come to the gate of the city,' to make our escape if possible. The gate was quite crowded, so that the strong trod upon the feeble. Doubtless there were many dead from being trodden upon. Had I and my brethren attempted to go over the wall, we would have been trodden upon and would have died. The wall we build round the City was so high and strong, and had beside a large and very deep ditch dug round behind the wall; there was no way to pass except through the gate, and we were obliged to come back to our father's house, there to remain to see what would take place in the morning.

Oh sorrowful, sorrowful morning! When the morning came, I and my brethren took a walk about in the town to see what the people were doing. We found the city in sorrowful silence, for many had fled and many of the aged men had put an end to their lives. Among these, was one in our house, my father's near and very dear relation. He was full of morality. He had put an end to his life too. His name is Ahkarlah, but since he became the Chief Priest of Carowah, the public god of man, his name was changed to Abborreh for so they call the chief priest of the city.[19] His manner of dressing was remarkable. The day when he was going to officiate, he would put on all white, white garment, white cap, he would put on all white. He would be attended by all the other ministers, and all those whose office was to attend the ministers of the said god; and when they were about to come out from the closet of the priest, warning would be given to the women in the yards to hide. And also warning would be given to the market women, to hide themselves, or bow down their heads beneath their knees, or cover their faces with their handkerchiefs; for they are not allowed to see the priest in his ministerial dress-or if they do, they die for it for they always remained very long, when they carried a bull to sacrifice.[20] And when they coming in the night one would stand before, hailing, giving warning perhaps maybe some women yet remain in the streets.

And when this aged relation of our father, to whom we should have looked for some guidance, had put an end to his life, of course there remained no hope for ourselves. I brought my brethren back home. The enemies had fully taken the city. When I saw none of them pass by my father's house to take us for slaves, I then took my brethren with me. We came out in the street, and when we walked about 50 fathoms from our house, we saw the city on fire, and before us the enemies coming in the street. We met with them, and they caught us separately. Separated me from all my brethren, except one of my father's children born to him by his second wife. I and this were caught together by one man. By the time we left the house of our father, I saw my father's mother pass the other gate. She, I had no hope of seeing again in the flesh, because she was an old woman. Doubtless they would kill her. Many were killed. They killed our Captain, "jurgoonor" (for so they called the Captain) by the river side, and they killed Barlah in his gate. He was second to the king. He was a very high man in the city. Nothing could be decided without his presence.

The city was taken about nine o'clock in the morning. There were two citys beside our own that this enemies hath besieged on the same day. Our city was taken in the morning and the other two were taken in the afternoon about two o'clock. The enemies satisfied themselves with little children, little girls, young men, and young women; and so they did not care about the aged and old people. They killed them without mercy. Father knew not the son, and the son knew not the father. Pity had departed from the face of mothers. Abundant heaps of dead bodies were in the streets, and there were none to bury them. Suckling babies were crying at the point of death, and there were none to pick them up. Mothers looked upon them with contempt-a lamentable day!

These three Cities were consumed in one day, and many of the inhabitants were taken as slaves by the enemies, among whom was one of our chief men of war they punished severely. His name is Offersopuh. In this manner they punished him. They first his private. After that, they put rope on his neck. Then they dragged him about a quarter of a mile. Thus they put an end to his life. They took revenge on him because he was valiant in fighting them. Very many of the chief men of war they punished more severely than I can mention, especially Kings. When they caught any of the king they punished them severely and unmercifully, and when they met with any of the Chief men they treated them with contempt, and after that they killed them, and thus they continued, picking those people who had escaped to the mountains and in the bushes.

I was brought the same day the city was taken to Imodo, that is, the place where they made their residence when they besieged us, or rather in the camp. When I came to that place, the man who took me in the city took me and made a present to the chief man of war who commanded the band which he belonged to; for the custom was when any of their company went with bands of war, if he catch slaves, half of the slaves he would give to his Captain. I was with them in the camp about ten days, during which time they used to send me for fire wood. In one of the Cities they took the same day they took our own, there I saw some people burned in the city.

They dug out many dead bodies from their graves. They dug them out in order to take off the grave clothes to sell for money; for the manner of dressing the dead in that part of the world quite differs from that of this country. In this manner they dress the dead. If the dead been a man of fortune, he would be dressed by the Council. They would take all his valuable clothes and dress him carefully, with all costly apparel. The dress will make him about four feet high from the ground. Perhaps will be about twenty large pieces of costly cloth, besides those that they lined the wall where the dead man lie. And then they will make a large coffin about five feet high and about four feet wide and properly dressed with all fine and costly cloths. After that, they would send for king's drum (or band). About twelve or fourteen men will take up the coffin upon their shoulders, and one would stand before giving out country hymns and followed by thousands of people singing after them, they would go round the city with this beautiful coffin. And when they had gone round they would come back to the Place where the dead person laid. After all these amusements, the relations of the dead would give warning to the Councils when the body should be buried, and in the night when the body was to be buried the Council drum would beat.

The market would be broken about eight o'clock in the evening and they will come to the place where the body laid, and abundant of apparel would be prepared to line the bottom of the tomb, and plenty of money would be laid bottom of the grave. And then they will laid the body of the dead upon these things, and then cover him over with dust, this is the way they bury the dead.

We do not bury the dead out of the house as they do in this country. We bury a person in his own room but if the person be a slave, we bury him in the piazza. The house where the dead person is buried is not to be forsaken, but to be taken possession of by another person. So a dead body may be remain many years and not spoil. This is the cause why the enemy dug out the dead bodies order to take the money and fine clothes with which the dead bodies were dressed. But this cannot be done unless the city is taken by the enemies.

While I was with these enemies in the camp I saw many wonderful instances, all which I cannot now mention. I saw a child of about eighteen months old cast out of the camp because the child was so young that nobody would buy him. That poor orphan was there crying at the point of death for about two days, and none [took] pity to pick him up. Another time I took a walk about in the camp, I saw my own brother. I was not allowed to speak to him, although they knew him to be my own brother. Few days after this, the person who I then belonged to sent me home to his wife for sale, and I was with his wife one day and a half. She sent for a trade man to examine me. They stripped me naked. The man examined me all over.

They went aside from me to make a bargain. In few hours after that, the man came again. My mistress told me to go with the man and fetch some rum. just as I went out of her sight, the man stripped me of my clothes and sent it to my mistress. Then I knew that they only deceived me by saying go with the man to fetch me some rum.

Then I went along with this man who had bought me from my mistress. The man tried to feed me and make me clean as possible for the next market day: for one day out of six is general market day. One morning at the cock crow the man started me, for next day would be market day. We walked mournfully, and when we came to the village near the place where the market is to be held the day after, we then sleep. It was then a late hour. Early in the morning we came to the market. Many hundreds of slaves, we were put in rows, so that we all could be seen at one view by the buyers; and in about five hours another trade man came and bought me. He put me in a canoe at once and we sailed all that night. Next morning, we came to another slaves market by name Krodoo and there we remain whole day, for the man wanted to buy more slaves. At the time of evening, the canoe was quite loaded with slaves and we sailed for his home directly. We arrived about twelve o'clock in the night. The town where we had just arrived, by name of Ikko, is the place where the Portuguese traded. Early in the morning we were brought to a white Portuguese for sale. After strict examination, the white man put me and some others aside. After that, they then made a bargain, how much he would take for each one of us. After they were well agreed, the white man sent us to the slave fold. When we entered into the slave fold, the slaves shouted for joy for having seen another of their countrymen in the fold. These are the articles the Portuguese paid for slaves: tobacco, rum, clothes, powder, gun, cutlasses, brass, iron rods, and jackey which is our country money.

The inhabitants of Ikko are very cruel people. They would even sell the children of their own bosom. May God almighty make bare his holy arm in sending the gospel to this benighted land.

I was there in the fold for about two months, with a rope on my neck. All the young boys had ropes on their necks in a row, and all the men with chains in a long row, for about fifty person in a row, so that no one could escape without the others. At one time, the town took fire, and about fifty slaves were consumed because the entry was crowded-so that these slaves were burnt.

During the time I was in that cruel place, their king was very sick. Then the business of his attendants was to ask the diviner, whatsoever he commanded to be done for the recovery of the king's health immediately attended to. During the time of the king's sickness, the slaves often met with goat or sheep sacrifices and money put on the top of the sacrificed beasts, to appease the god of their land. This money the slaves always took as good luck, for the money generally amounted to 2000 half pennies, £4-3-4. This large sum of jakay they used to put upon the top of the sacrificed beasts, and one jakay is worth as much as an English half penny. Alas, the worthless prophets with all their Ododowor and Obbahtahlah (for so they call their god) were not able to do any good for the king in regard to his recovery .... This king of Ikko ... never recovered from his disease; for he died. Three days after his death we came away over the river to prepare for shipping; for their custom was, when the king died, to sacrifice about one thousand slaves for the celebration of the king's death; for we supposed at that time, if we still remained in that cruel town, and if the king's slaves should not be enough for the celebration of the king's death, doubtless they would ask our master for some slaves to make up the number. We all believed this was what induced our master to bring us over the river in haste for shipping. The place that they brought us to, it is Igaye, and we were all naked both men and women; so that we hardly had any rest in the night for we were very cold. Next day, early in the morning, we were all brought down close to salt water for to be put in canoes. We all were heavy and sorrowful in heart, because we were going to leave our land for another which we never knew; and not only so, but when we saw the waves of the salt water on which we were just to enter, it discouraged us the more, for we had heard that the Portuguese were going to eat us when we got to their country. This put more to despair, and when they began to put us in canoes to bring us to the Brig, one of the canoes drowned and half of the slaves died. After they had done with loading the brig, they stowed all the men under the deck; the boys and women were left on the deck. The Brig sailed in the evening. Next day we saw an English man-of-war coming. When the Portuguese saw this, it put them to disquietness and confusion. They then told us that these were the people which wilt eat us, if we suffered them to prize us; and they also enticed us, if they should ask us how long since we sailed, we must say it was more than a month; and they also gave us long oars and set us to pull. About ten men were set on one oar, and we tried to pull as far as we are able, but it is of no avail. Next day the English vessel overtook us and they took charge of the slaves. We were very poor for water. We were only allowed one glass of water a day and we were allowed only breakfast, no dinner. Many of the slaves had died for want of water, and many men died for crowdedness.

One day as I sat by the fireside where they were cooking, boiling water was thrown on my head, and my head became all peeled and sore, and this pained me very much. All the slaves thought I would have died, but the Lord nourished me in that painful time and I am not dead. Glory be to his name for his Tender care over a poor wretch like me.

We landed to Sierra Leone in about a month after we sailed from Igaye.[21] It was great joy among the slave that day, for we supposed we should never see land anymore.

After we were landed at Freetown, they sent us boys to Mr. B Pratt, manager of York, in order that we may be instructed. There, we were placed in school. We begin at once to learn to read English book, which book I have cause to praise God for while I have life and breath. Through the reading of these books I came to know that High and Glorious name of Jesus Christ the Saviour. I have to acknowledge that although I read these books which teach me to know Jesus Christ the Saviour, I did not believe in him as I ought to have believed. Although I did not embrace or believe from my heart when first I read the word of God, I had great love to it. I liked to hear reading, and I liked to hear the minister preach to me Jesus. In five or six years after I came to this country, I began to learn to pray morning and evening, although I did it not from the heart; for I did not know the nature of prayer at the time. In the year 1834. I began to attend Methodist Chapel. I praise God and I have to praise him if I be faithful to the end that I have joined Methodist Society, for they are not careless about my soul. They do not only tell me that the heaven is happy place, but they do teach me the ways to it. May God Bless this Sect or body. May the work of God prosper in their Land. From the day I met in class, I begin to seek the peace of God. That was from I 5 June 1834. Bless be God! On 25th of December 1834, I obtained peace of God. From that blessed day I went among my friends, telling them that the Lord is Good, inviting them to come and taste for themselves.

CASE ELEVEN

Joseph Right

Author: Unknown
Region of birth: Yoruba
Date of birth: Unknown
Year of enslavement: Unknown
Place of writing: St. Mary's Island, The Gambia
Date of account: 1839
Year of death/last known year of activity: Unknown
Published: No

Source: MMS, Sierra Leone Correspondence,
Fiche Box 25, Box No. 280, Fiche No. 1868
and 1869, #12

Introduction

Alongside the well-known account of Joseph Wright (number X above), the Methodist archive contains a second document with the unclear title of 'Statement of ~~John~~ Joseph Right Concerning Himself' though the actual text begins by identifying the narrator as Joseph Wright. Both texts are dated to 1839 and appear alongside one another within the archival collection. The Methodist archive catalogue lists the two sources as written by the same individual. However, in this lesser-known text, the perspective shifts from third to first person, and it is less clear who actually wrote the document. Other Liberated Africans – including Samuel Crowther – have more than one known version of their testimony. The question, then, is whether this is a different version/draft of Joseph Wright's account, placed within the archive immediately before its better-known counterpart.

A closer examination of the text suggests that this is not the case (a conclusion I reached only after the publication of my 2017 *Slavery & Abolition* article which suggested both accounts were by the same individual). This account was actually recorded at St. Mary's Island rather than Sierra Leone. This does not preclude the possibility that the text was written by the same individual: missionaries often moved back and forth between The Gambia and Sierra Leone mission fields. Moreover, Joseph Wright's more famous account does not actually specify its place of composition, though Philip Curtin and other historians have taken it to be Freetown. The ambiguous title of 'Statement of ~~John~~ Joseph Right Concerning Himself' can also possibly be explained if this particular version of the narrative was composed by someone else.

The greatest hint that these are two different narratives by two different individuals comes from the texts themselves. Both accounts identify their narrator as 'Accou', a term in colonial Sierra Leone for Yoruba speakers. Both identify the Europeans on the coast as Portuguese, and both speak of their personal turn towards the Methodist church in 1833–4. But apart from these commonalities, the recorded experiences of enslavement are markedly different. The short account begins by stating that 'Joseph Wright states that he was not seized in cause of a War, as they did with others although being of the same Accoo tribes'. From there the text recounts how the narrator's father refused to sell a passing merchant a horse, and the disgruntled man then returned with a large group of men to kidnap the child. But this account is certainly irreconcilable with (the other) Joseph Wright's detailed account of the wars that ravaged the Egba settlements in the 1820s and led to the enslavement of himself and many others.

Text

Statement of Joseph Right Concerning Himself

Joseph Wright states that he was not seized in cause of a War, as they did with others although being of the same Accoo tribes. Stating that as far as the best of his knowledge could extend that the cause of his being brought away from his Country was that a Certain Merchant came one day to his Father and asked him to purchase a horse from him. his father then told him that he would not part with the horse. the above Merchant then without reply went away and Hired Large Number of people who came and seized all the property of the said Father and being on the same day that the so named son Joseph Wright was take to a slavery where he were then taken to another Country and was chained for one month, the Mother of the named Joseph Wright was said to have been away from home when this accident happened the father of the said son went to a certain town where he knew that the people would call at. That was in order to Wait them there, the father then got many of his people back by paying for their Redemption, in this same town I meet with my father's brother who asked the people what did they ___ took me away for, they said that they would not let me go unless two slaves be placed on my stead. My father's Brother then told them that he would be there tomorrow morning at 6 o'clock if possible he might get to slaves to Relieve me from their hands, and they well knew that my father's Brother would call in the morning as he had promised them, they then took me to another country and when my father's Brother came in the morning alas he did not find me there, these people then having stolen a King's servants wife, the king had a quarrel with them on this point and they requested by this this King to get the woman back they then went took me there to change me in order they might get the woman back but alas their hope was disappointed for when they took me there they could not get the moan, they then sold me to a Portuguese man with several others of my companion. We were all fix with a rope on our necks for 2 months time, the Portuguese having taken us on board his vessel we set sail the next morning and is at sea for 3 days. They then saw the Man of War coming on towards us, it found that some of us were taken very sick and when they saw this man of war coming on they then take and cast some of our companion over Board and several of us who were sicken they threw them alive over board, frightening us that this Man of War will kill every one of us and threw us overboard and Thanks be to God that I was not __ overboard as some of my companions were, the Man of War then take us down to Sierra and I staid at Sierra about 5 or six years at Kent in school and thanks be to God that I am by the goodness of providence spared me until now and am joined with those who love & serve God – in 1833 being the same year whereof I commenced to know something of God and trust that the same God who so delivered me from the hand of those Enemy who should have perish me forever had I not been by the goodness of God escaped out of their hands and was brought down to Sierra Leone. My last words and earnest prayers on this report is that God may Bless British Europeans throughout all Kingdoms & Dominions Amen & Amen.

CASE TWELVE

James Gerber

Author: John Christian Müller
Region of birth: Unknown, likely Yoruba
Date of birth: Unknown
Year of enslavement: (Re-enslaved) 1848
Place of writing: Abeokuta
Date of account: 1 January 1849
Year of death/last known year of activity: Unknown
Published: 'The Sufferings and Deliverance of James Gerber, a Twice-Liberated African', *Church Missionary Gleaner*, 1850–1, Vol. 1, 20–3.

Source: John Christian Müller, journal extracts for the quarter from September 1848 to 1 January 1849, CMS Yoruba Mission, CA2/O72/8

Introduction

This is a narrative of the re-enslavement of James Gerber. Gerber was a Liberated African who lived fifteen years at Sierra Leone before returning to Badagry in 1843 to become a trader. In 1848, while on a trading excursion inland to Ijaye, he was enslaved for the second time in his life. The account was written by John Christian Müller, a CMS missionary based at Abeokuta, following Gerber's redemption. An amended version of the narrative appeared in the 1850–1 edition of the *Church Missionary Gleaner*. The published version of the ordeal mentions that Gerber left his position with the CMS at Badagry to trade with Abeokuta and Ijaye but omits the fact that this trade included guns and gunpowder.

Text

Monday January 1st 1849 being new year's day

This evening James Gerber returned from slavery at Lagos to the joy of us all. He was 15 years at Sierra Leone, lived as a communicant of our church at Hastings.[1] Arrived at Badagry with wife and one child in the year 1843. Gerber was employed as laborer of the society at Badagry till he took up a trade for himself, dealing with Abbeokuta and Ijayi in some species of European articles as for instance guns and powder. It was towards the close of the month of August last year that Gerber proceeded to Ijayi for the purpose of selling off his goods. He took up his abode under his brother's roof. On a certain day many people entered the yard telling: that Ikumi the chief wished to see them. But neither Gerber nor his brother trusted this people. Then they tied the hands of Gerber's brother and carried him together with his slave into Ikumi's yard. Gerber returned into his room resolved to defend his person as well as he could. None ventured to draw nigh unto him. The people assured Gerber, that nothing should happen to him and that Ikumi having thoughts of peace wishes only to see him. After such repeated assurances Gerber at last yielded and went with the people who were however not satisfied till they were in possession of his weapons. Having arrived at Ikumi's yard, he commanded Gerber, his brother and his brother's slave to prostrate. Whilst they were doing this, the tyrant took up his sword and slew Gerber's brother not knowing however who it was for the bloody man made no choice before, whom he would kill. Thus had the hand of providence directed Ikumi's sword not upon the innocent slave or the innocent Gerber, but upon a slave-dealer. These two persons were then immediately taken away from the presence of Ikumi and thus it came to pass, that Gerber fell into the hands of the chief of Yjayi as a slave. He was soon after this event transported to Ibatang with many other Egbas and sold there. Having been so maltreated, that both his head and body were covered with sores, no man desired to purchase Gerber at Ibatang. His master, who bought him ~~from~~ of Ikumi thought that he (Gerber) could play the acts of a witch and therefore he can not be sold. Enraged this tyrant tied Gerber's hands upon his back and fastened his head to two sticks notwithstanding all the entreaties of his wives and his own brother, who said that the man had committed no fault. Let him die! I am able to pay for this slave, was the language of this master. So little is human life esteemed in the eyes of a slavedealer. Poor Gerber fainted, his strength being almost gone. They loosed his bonds. An Jebu man pitying his wretched condition bought him for 6 heads of cowries.[2] He was then carried from Ibadan into the Jebu country, where Gerber was to undergo again severe trials. At length in October last, he arrived at Lagos and was sold to the Portuguese on the same day. Gerber was of course instantly laid into chains. Several attempts were made to ship him together with other slaves, but they failed, because of the man of war cruising about. In the meantime the friends of Gerber sought his redemption. But this worthy attempt of theirs seemed then to be quite hopeless, for a vessel had been announced to arrive soon at Benin, and that the slaves should be held in readiness to be shipped in a moment. Accordingly these poor slaves were instantly in the night dispatched from Lagos and arrived at Benin 4 days after their departure. On their way thither Gerber called upon his companions in the like affliction to pray to God, that he may deliver us into the hands of the British. They all did thus pray with the fervency of their hearts. The living God heard the prayers and sighs of these poor creatures, for they were scarcely hid 4 weeks into the bushes on their arrival at Benin, when the news reached that the vessel above mentioned had been capsized in the sea and all lives lost safe one. The slaves were thus obliged to return to Lagos again. And Gerber could be redeemed by his friends, arrived at Abbeokuta last week and is now living among us breathing the air of liberty.

CASE THIRTEEN

Thomas King

Author: Thomas King
Region of birth: Emere, Egba
Date of birth: Unknown
Year of enslavement: *c.* 1825
Place of writing: Igbein
Date of Account: 7 April 1850
Year of death/last known year of activity: Died at Igbein, 23 October 1862[1]
Published: 'How Thomas King Became a Slave', *Church Missionary Gleaner*, New Series, No. 12, March 1851, 138–41.

> Source: Journal Extracts of Thomas King for Quarter ending 25 June 1850, CMS Yoruba Mission, CA2/O61/36

Introduction

Thomas King was a CMS pastor and Egba Liberated African who participated in the early Yoruba Mission. King was enslaved as a child after a battle which destroyed his village. His account provides much of the chronological detail for the spread of violence into southern Yorubaland, following the collapse of the Oyo Empire. King asserted that his hometown, Ẹmẹrẹ, was destroyed in 1825 and that another Egba town, Kesi, was destroyed about two years earlier.

Taken into slavery, King was sold to a European slave trader and subsequently was liberated by a ship of the British fleet and settled in Sierra Leone. King's account states that he was enslaved 'about the year 1825 in the beginning of November' and that 'before a fortnight after my capture, I was sold to one of the Havannah slave traders at Lagos' where he remained for '[a]bout three weeks'. If these dates are accurate then King was likely on board the Havana-bound slave ship *Iberia*, which departed Lagos on 27 December 1825.[2]

Legally emancipated by Freetown's Mixed Commission Courts in January 1826, King was subsequently educated in CMS schools and graduated from Fourah Bay Institution in 1849. A year later he returned to Abeokuta via Badagry, where he was improbably reunited with his mother, whom Samuel Crowther had redeemed from slavery. He worked in Abeokuta as a catechist, being made a deacon in 1854, and ordained in 1857. He died there on 23 October 1862 after working at the Igbein station. He worked with Samuel Crowther on translating the scriptures into Yoruba.[3] King's account is written in his journals while travelling inland from Badagry to Abeokuta in early 1850 as part of the inchoate Yoruba mission.

Text

Sat. 30 Proceeded on gradually this morning as it was dawning but our walk today was a gentle one. We met with great number of people to day before we had reached Awoyade coming to meet us, among whom was Mr. Phillipp the schoolmaster, many schoolchildren, & church members. About one o'clock we entered the town. Our arrival caused great joy indeed among the people. Were the friends of Africa to witness the scene to day and hear the many blessings the people implored upon their heads by the return of those whom they had given up for lost, they would see how much their services are much regarded. The people are deeply sensible of the good that the British Government had done by their generosity in restoring their children freely to them from slavery. Mr. Crowther's house, where we first came, was entirely crowded. The road from Igbein, Mr. Crowther's station, to Ake leads through a market. We could hardly have chance to walk, for too many people, till we entered the yard. Among those who came to meet us in the way was my aged mother; but she was too old to recognize her son among the crowd. When I was pointed to her, so much was she overcome by feelings that she sat down in great amazement weeping, while all the by standers were rejoicing with her and blessing the people of England on my behalf.

April 7th Lord's Day Psalm 13th, 5th verse. My heart shall rejoice in thy salvation. This indeed was the language of my heart today, when kneeling together with my aged mother at the communion table as partakers of those holy pledges of our savior's dying love. The text well suits the language of her heart as well as mine, as it will be seen by the following narrative respecting my parents and relatives. On the morning of that unhappy day that I was separated from my parents about the year 1825 in the beginning of November. I left home about eight o'clock for farm about three miles distance from home, in order to get some corn. My mother and elder sister, about a fortnight previous, went to Ishaga, a town about fourteen or fifteen miles distance from hence for trade. About three years before this, my elder brother, having left home, had joined the war party; but as the fact was not known to us to be such, we concluded that he was either killed or sold. My niece and I, my sister's daughter, were the little ones that were left at home. I stayed with my father, but my niece was left to the care of her father. No sooner had I got to the farm, and just cut sufficient corn for my load, than the repeated reports of muskets at the town gate acquainted me of my dangerous situation. All my endeavour to escape had utterly proved a failure, as I was surrounded by a number of men, who were very eager, as to whose lot my capture should fall. At last, as a kid among many chasing wolfs, I was caught by one of them. It was a day of inexpressible sorrow to me. About the space of an hour, they had taken three gates, one only being left which the people in the town endeavoured to secure, as it was the only road for escape. As soon as the intelligence reached my mother, for our sakes she hazarded her life by returning to the town. But to her great disappointment her son was gone.

We left the encampment about three the next morning for Ikporo, the place of their rendezvous but formerly the town of ~~Shodekkah~~ Şodeke[4] the late chief. As it was dawning, we came to Kesi, the town of Andre Wilhelm[5] and Goodwill, destroyed about two years since. About nine o'clock we arrived at Kemba, the town of Mr. Marsh destroyed two days before they came to ours.[6] At Ikporo I stayed five days; I was sold one evening to a mahomedan trader who carried me the same evening to Ikereku, the town of Mr. Philip, which was not yet destroyed by war. We went to Oko the next day when I was sold to an Ijebbu trader. To be short, before a fortnight after my capture, I was sold to one of the Havannah slave traders at Lagos. On the way all along as I was coming, I had been cherishing the hope of making my escape at any time an opportunity should offer itself. As it was a current report that whoever is sold to the whiteman became an inhabitant of another world, as the Europeans were then reckoned to be, all hopes of escape now vanished from my mind. About three weeks after I reached Lagos the sad intelligence that our town was reduced to ashes reached us. A few days later, with heavy hearts and sad countenances, we took leave of our shores without the slightest hope of visiting it any more.

At the destruction of our town, my mother and niece were both taken together and carried to Oko, where a woman bought both of them together for twelve heads of cowries, a sum not exceeding 3 pound. She brought them to Ijebbu, but sold them separately. After my mother had stopped four years in Ijebbu, she was then sold to Lagos by her master. My father in the mean while escaped and came to Oko, but it was after my mother was sold to Ijebbu. At last he came to Abeokuta, but was at last unfortunately killed in the battle which they fought with Oluyole the late chief of Ibadan about fourteen years ago.

After a few years stay at Lagos the master of my mother being himself a slave, escaped and she was sold to another man at the same place. At this time she heard of my brother being at Lagos, but no opportunity afforded of seeing each other. The wife of my mother's master being an Egba woman on a visit to this place brought my mother with her in the hope of finding some one to redeem her. But as my brother was then in slavery, nothing could be done toward her redemption and she went back with her mistress to Lagos. A short time after my brother escaped, and came to Abeokuta. At the time of the insurrection which took place at Lagos previous to the time that Akitoye was expelled from the throne of Kossokoh, hundreds of slaves from Lagos made their escape. My mother at the time came with them. But as none of them could get to Abeokuta without being conducted by someone to the town, all such conductors reckoned those who were thus brought to the town through their means as their captives, and demanded from them as much as they pleased. To the man who conducted my mother in the manner above described was paid the redemption money by Mr. Crowther. Thus my mother had been in hard servitude under six or seven different owners, and would probably have died under the same, had it not been for the arrival of the missionaries here a few years ago, when her redemption as well as my brother's was effected by their means.

Could the friends of Africa witness the heart melting sight of the parents that have those children restored again to their bosoms whom they ~~gave~~ have given up for lost, after the expiration of twenty-five years, they would know how their services are acknowledged by the people here. Before two years had expired after my arrival in Sierra Leone, I was informed that my sister was brought to Porto Novo, whose master took her for his wife, and she had been blessed with about four children. Should the chief of that place be favoured with a Missionary, I would humbly hope that their deliverance from spiritual bondage might likely be effected by ~~the~~ his means ~~of such Agent, should their bodily liberty be proved beyond my power to effect, though I earnestly wish it also~~. My brother died about seven months before my arrival here. So the language of my mother is somewhat like ~~or similar to~~ that of Cornelius to the Apostle, 'it is well ~~that thou have sent you come~~ It is well done that though hast come.' The sight of both the Sabbath school and Church was very gratifying. The eagerness and fixed attention with which the people apply to learn is a matter of ample gratification. Since the separation of my niece from my mother nothing was heard of her.

I remain Dear & Revd. Sirs
your obedient servant
T. King

CASE FOURTEEN

James Barber

Author: Edward George Irving
Region of birth: Ijemo, Egba
Date of birth: Unknown
Year of enslavement: 1826
Place of writing: Abeokuta
Date of Account: December 1854 or January 1855
Year of death/last known year of activity: Unknown
Published: *Church Missionary Intelligencer*, Vol. VII, 1856, 65–120

Source: Edward George Irving, Journal of a Visit to the Ijebu Country in the Months of December 1854 and January 1855, CA2/O52/18

Introduction

Edward George Irving recorded the testimony of Liberated African James Barber at some point in December 1854 or January 1855. Dr Irving was a medical missionary and political advisor to the Yoruba mission. His 'Journal of a Visit to the Ijebu County', which contains the testimony of James Barber, chronicles their journey through Ibadan, Ijebu, Ode and Abeokuta. James Barber was an Egba Liberated African who reached Sierra Leone in 1827. By the time Irving wrote his journal Barber was a 'Native Catechist' at Ibadan and accompanied Irving on his travels. Barber's testimony was published in the *Church Missionary Intelligencer*, Vol. VII, 1856, 65–120.

Irving records little detail of Barber's journey and emancipation at Freetown. What Irving does learn from Barber is a uniquely precise account of a particular period of the Yoruba wars. Barber's hometown of Ijemo was captured by an allied force of Ijebu, Ife and refugee soldiers from Oyo.

Barber was enslaved and incorporated into the allied forces. He participated in sieges on several Egba towns before being sold to the coast. Irving records how Barber 'was with the army which besieged Ikreku. The town, he states, was destroyed in 1826, as it was the year previously to his being liberated at Sierra Leone, which he knows to have been 1827'. Barber therefore places the fall of Ikereku Idan, one of the Egba villages, in 1826. Barber's testimony is central to reconstructing the chronology of the Yoruba wars in the nineteenth century. From Barber's account, Robin Law has suggested that the fall of Ikreku in 1826 occurred four or five years after the fall of Owu (in late 1821 or early 1822) and preceded the allied army's occupation of Ibadan *c.* 1827–8.[1]

Text

From Mr. Barber, native catechist at Ibadan, who accompanied us, we derived much information. A native of Ijemo, he was taken captive at the destruction of that place, and followed his new master into the Ijebu country. He was with the army which besieged Ikreku. The town, he states, was destroyed in 1826, as it was the year previously to his being liberated at Sierra Leone, which he knows to have been 1827. It has been already said that Owu was the first town destroyed. After this fell Ikija, whose ruins we have described. From thence the conquering army of Ifes, Ijebus, Yorubas, proceeded against other towns of the Egbas. Kesin and Emere soon fell. They then settled in the Egba towns of Erunwon and Ijemo, and a part pitched on the road to Itoko. Here they found cause to quarrel with Ijemo, and destroyed it. Itoko next fell. Returning to through the ruins of Ijemo they passed through Oba and Itoku to Ijeun – towns also of the Egbas – where they settled. The Ijebus, wishing, on account of the slave-trade, to have the army nearer them, invited them to come to their country. A quarrel at the same time fell out between the two chief leaders of the army, Laboshide and Maye. Hence a division took place in the army. Laboshide, heading his party, went with the Ijebus, and the king gave them the town of Ipara – of which I shall speak by and bye – to pitch in, the people of Ipara removing to a neighbouring town, Ishara. Maye went and settled at Iporó. From these separate places the two divisions of the army went out daily, kidnapping and destroying the smaller Egba towns, the Ijebu slave-traders always offering a ready market for their captives. The Egba towns of Igbore, Imó, Igbein, &c., joined their strength together in an attempt to destroy the camp at Ipara. Marching all night, they arrived before daylight – a favourite time to attack in Africa. Entering the town, they began to kill; but the enemy, rallying, defeated them with much slaughter; and, as a consequence, Igbore, Imó, Igbein, &c., fell in turn. About a twelvemonth after this, or less, a quarrel was sought with Ikreku, and easily affected, as follows. A party of Maye's army at Iporo went, *more solito*, to buy provisions at Ikreku. After purchasing certain articles they refused to pay, and beat the women who attempted to prevent their leaving without doing so. Her husband's relations set upon Maye's men in turn, and at last the chiefs drove them from the town. This was quite sufficient. Messengers were sent to Laboshide, at Ipara, for aid. He besieged Ikreku from the south, Maye from the north, and both were defeated. A reconciliation now took place between the two chiefs. Maye left Iporo, where he was in too close neighbourhood to Ikreku after his defeat, and joined Laboside at Ipara. From this quarter – south – they besieged Ikreku the second time; and although the town was assisted by the Egba towns of Itoku, Oba, and Erunwon – but their aid proved vain – Ikreku, after a few months' siege fell; and, as a matter of course, Itoku, Oba, and Erunwon, shared its fate, the three latter being stormed and taken in a single day. It was after this army removed to Ibadan, destroying all the Bagura towns mentioned in an early part of this journal, and the others which were left, till no one remained.

CASE FIFTEEN

Peter Wilson

Author: Eliza Wilson (his widow)
Region of birth: Owu, Yoruba
Date of birth: *c.* 1811
Year of enslavement: *c.* 1824
Place of writing: Kissy, Sierra Leone
Date of account: 1860
Year of death/last known year of activity: Died in Kissy, Sierra Leone, 1860
Published: Published locally in Freetown

Source: CMS Sierra Leone Mission CA1/O6/53

Introduction

Peter Wilson's narrative, composed posthumously by his wife Eliza, begins by stating that Peter was 'a native of the Aku Tribe, born in the Town of Owu; and was early sold into slavery to Portuguese slave dealers'. The Owu War (*c.* 1816/7–1821/2) was a catalytic event in the expansion of warfare in Yoruba territories following the collapse of the Oyo Empire. Wilson may have been enslaved during this conflict, though his narrative does not provide any details of how he came to be enslaved.

Wilson's narrative is unique because the details are not simply drawn from personal memories. Rather, Wilson researched colonial documents and 'endeavoured to gain and collect the facts of the events … even the minutest particulars respecting his liberation from the bondage of slavery'. Wilson was uniquely well positioned to do so, working for many years as a domestic servant to Michael Linning Melville, a Scottish barrister and judge who had been lieutenant-governor of Sierra Leone and then sat on Freetown's Mixed Commission Court. These details were recorded in a posthumous account written by Peter's wife Eliza in 1860, based on what her late husband had uncovered. Published locally in the Liberated African village of Kissy, Wilson's life history recounts in tremendous detail that he was 'rescued from the holds of a Portuguese Brig called the "Anizo" which was captured while on her destination for the Brazils, by HMS *Maidstone*; Commodore Charles Buller, on the 26th of September 1824; and after a lengthened passage of 43 days, he, together with his fellow captives were safely landed and emancipated in the Colony, on the 8th November'.

Wilson identified the slave ship (actually the *Avizo*) on which he was on board, the circumstances of their interception at sea, and the exact date of their arrival, despite forty-six years in the colony. The *Avizo* was a Bahian slave vessel whose crew purchased 467 enslaved people at Badagry. Wilson's identification of HMS *Maidstone* under Charles Bullen (rather than Buller) corresponds with the register of the Sierra Leone Slave Trade Commission.[1]

The memoir states that Peter's birth name was 'Lai-guan-dai, signifying, his being deprived of his father during infancy'. Unfortunately, it is difficult to find a registered Liberated African whose recorded name is phonetically similar to 'Lai-guan-dai', though it may be a twelve-year-old boy on the Avizo whose name was recorded by British officials as 'Laign'.[2] The name may be a corruption of the Yoruba name '(E)legunde' or 'the masquerader has come'.[3]

Text

A
BRIEF MEMOIR
OF THE LATE
PETER WILSON
MEMBER OF
KISSY ROAD CHURCH

BY

HIS WIFE
ELIZA

1860

MEMOIR
OF THE LATE
PETER WILSON

PETER WILSON, the subject of this memoir departed this life on Tuesday the 8th day of November 1859; at his residence in Fisher Street, Freetown, in the Colony of Sierra Leone aged 46 years. He was a native of the Aku Tribe, born in the Town of Owu; and was early sold into slavery to Portuguese slave dealers. His country name *Lai-guan-dai*, signifying, his being deprived of his father during infancy, may in some measure have led to his so easily falling a prey into the hands of the slave hunters. By the good Providence of God, he was however rescued from the holds of a Portuguese Brig called the 'Anizo' which was captured while on her destination for the Brazils, by H.M.S. Maidstone; Commodore Charles Buller, on the 26th of September 1824; and after a lengthened passage of 43 days, he, together with his fellow captives were safely landed and emancipated in the Colony, on the 8th November; 'most remarkable in its becoming the very month and day of his death.' From a peculiar assiduity natural to Mr. Wilson he had endeavoured to gain and collect the facts of the events above related even the minutest particulars respecting his liberation from the bondage of slavery. He had carefully kept memorandum of them, together with a sketch of the slaver (a Brigantine) in which he was captured, and the number of slaves in her at the time of her seizure; which were 465; and that out of this number 43 died on the passage; and 424 landed in the Colony, comprising 222 men 102 women, 66 boys and 34 girls. He was then about 13 years of age at the period of his arrival; and after having completed the accustomed years of Apprenticeship, under the care of a Liberated African of his Tribe or nation; he subsequently entered the Service of M.L. Melville Esquire, then Registrar of the Mixed Commission Court of this Colony; in this place he remained for several years as a domestic-servant; and his general deportment obtained for him, most excellent and high commendations, both from the gentleman and his lady, above every flattering eulogimns his friends could here bestow on his past memory. – It affords his friends great cause of satisfaction while endeavouring to fulfil the obligations of a family, in doing justice, without any exaggeration to the merits of their deceased relation; by presenting a few out of many testimonials of the character of deceased. His good behaviour eventually procured for deceased a subordinate situation in the Office of his master; who afterward gave him the following recommendation dated *Sierra Leone 6 June 1848. This is to certify that Peter Willson Messenger in the Registry of the M. Commission, which situation he has filled with satisfaction to his superiors for Eleven years, is a most obliging person – he is in fact for beyond the generality of his country people in all these qualities as well as superior to them in intelligence.* I have known him for 16 years and place the utmost confidence in his veracity and integrity' M.L. Melville.[4] Whoever regarding the studious habit of deceased, and the state of intellectual culture at this period, this piece of encomium could not be considered of too strong a colour.

About the year 1833 Mr. Wilson entered into Matrimonial engagements with his first wife on 17th March at the village of Kissy; by which marriage he had a son whom he christened after his own name Peter. He was baptized and admitted a full member of the Church Missionary Connexion in that village in the year 1839 on the 24th February. Of his consistency in his religious profession, we would refer our friends to a publication entitled 'Letters from Sierra Leone,' written by a Lady;

which work gives a faithful but concise account and character of deceased; whom this lady thus describes *another pleasing feature in his early career what we find noticed by persons of high respectability is, that he was not indifferent to religion* and further adds *his spare time always given to reading the Bible; his regular attendance at church, and constant sobriety and steadiness, evince pious principles not always to be found amid even the most influential members of the Liberated African community.* Mr. Wilson served also in the Sierra Leone Militia corps, where he rose to the rank of Sergeant. – His first wife having died about the twelveth year of their marriage, deceased took a second wife in 1845; with whom he was married on the 2nd June, in the same village.

Sometime after he was employed at the Cape Light House; and not long he removed with his family to Freetown. – His health being found after the lapse of a few years, to be affected by the peculiar nature of the employment; he obtained a temporary leave of absence for the recruiting his health – about the year 1854: and during this interval he turned his attention in a small line of Trading speculation, as soon as he was advised to resign his post; With the view of extending the business of his Trade, Mr. Wilson undertook a voyage to Lagos in January 1859; to re-visit again those scenes of his childhood days; from whence he was barbarously torn away from his father-land and relations by the cruel hands of the Slave Masters. He remained about 7 months down the Coast, and returned in August; and not long after his health seemed gradually to fail: which soon confined him in-doors, and latterly to his bed. Our friend Wilson evinced in his last ours of dissolution the same tranquil and consistent spirit which always characterised the man, as he daily became more and more conscious of his approaching end. His hope was built on that Rock from whence he obtained bot Help and Consolation. – During the time he was confined to bed; when suffering from pain, he was overheard to make use of this Prayer 'I thank thee O Lord and Heavenly Father that thou hast not taken me away by a sudden death, but hast laid me down upon the bed of affliction; Have mercy upon my soul: this is the time now, that Thou hast made thy Sure Promise; Do Lord look upon me &c.'

On another occasion he thus prayed 'Almighty God assist me true for I am now going unto the throne of my Father; O Lord save my soul, Oh Blessed Saviour, save my soul and Pardon all my sins!'

As his physical strength and frame was gradually yielding to the hand of Time his view of an eternity seemed in no way obscured; his mind was entirely divested of all those anxious concerns which is so often displayed at the death-bed scenes of persons of his calling and business; as he had been a tender father; kind and affectionate husband and master, an honest and upright citizen he had no scruples to embitter his last moments; friends, wife, children and servants grieved at his sudden fate; yet not a murmur escaped his lips; he displayed in the last hours of his illness that degree of resignation to the will of Providence, which only the Hope of a crucified Saviour can impart to a dying sinner; *who has faith in God; and who looketh for a habitation not made with hands, eternal in the Heavens.*

We record the following dialogue which took place between deceased and a gentleman, a religious professor, who formed one of the numerous visitors who daily called to console their christian brother's illness – among other subjects.

This friend put the following questions to the suffering patient Ques. Mr W – do you think you will be spared from the sickness? Ans. no, I believe that I shall die. Ques. and if you die, where do you think your soul shall go? Ans. To Heaven. – Ques. Do you feel that the Spirit of God dwells in you? Ans. Yes. – Ques. Do you also believe that the Lord Jesus Christ died for you? Ans. Yes. Do you feel in the Spirit, that all your sins in the body, thoughts, words and deeds are all forgiven? Ans. Yes. – Ques. upon what do you presume that all your sins are pardoned? Ans/ Because Christ died for sinners, and he has made his *sure promise* that whoever shall come to him with all his heart and mind and worship him truly, shall obtain eternal life; and besides I have always felt the spirit of God in my mind when I was in health; but since I have been afflicted I feel it more and more, and it is that which comforts me, and assures me that I shall soon quit this sinful world &c. – and many more encouraging words which he from time to time expressed to comfort the hearts of his family. When asked if he would desire prayer to be offered (by the former visitor referred to) deceased expressed a most ready and willing consent. In reply to another friend as touching his approaching end; he declared himself to be *on the way to God, and therefore had no doubt of fear*. Shortly before his death he one day asked his wife 'Do you think that you are a christian? if so it will be good;' and quoted a passage in Matt. 1–3.

He then added, 'the Lord to whose kingdom I am going requireth me; and after my death, do you continue to follow him and change not; and if you so continue, the Lord will bless you.' It must be truly said of Mr. W. – that having served his God with faithfulness and simplicity of heart, he now gathered his feet and slept in Jesus. He was for many years one of the Class Leaders of Kissy Road Church.

Of his example of meekness, humility and amiability of disposition every one acquainted with late Wilson will be ready to say in the language of the Psalmist *'Mark the perfect man and behold the upright; for the end of that man is peace.'*

Mr. Wilson has left his widow Eliza, and his only son Peter by his former wife to deplore his sudden loss which will be long felt by all his friends family and acquaintances.

CASE SIXTEEN

Susannah Bola

Author: Unknown (possibly Valentine Faulkner)
Region of birth: Igbore
Date of birth: *c.* 1815
Year of enslavement: *c.* 1824
Place of writing: Ebute Metta
Date of account: *c.* 1873
Year of death/last known year of activity: Unknown
Published: No/unknown

Source: 'Mrs. Bola of Igbore' in CMS Z/30
'Biographical Accounts of Nigerian Converts to
Christianity Early-Mid 19th Century', 25–9

Introduction

The next two narratives by Susannah Bola and William Doherty are second-hand accounts recorded in Nigeria in the latter decades of the nineteenth century. The source, catalogued in the CMS Archives as 'Biographical accounts of Nigerian converts', appears within an archival series described simply as 'Miscellaneous papers and artefacts for which the provenance is unknown'. The archival catalogue dates the manuscript to *c.* 1873 and attributes it to an unidentified 'CMS missionary, or catechist, who was resident in Ebbu Metta in the mid-19th century'. There are several possible candidates for author based at Ebute Metta around this time. The most likely author is probably Valentine Faulkner who was based at Ebute Metta on the mainland adjacent to Lagos Island in the 1870s.[1] However, the account by Joseph Bola refers to 'Mr Faulkner' in the third person suggesting that he was perhaps not the amanuensis.

Susannah Bola's account is one of few in the CMS archives relating to the experiences of women. The account of Susannah Bola is also one of the very few testimonies by Liberated African women. Both this text and that of William Doherty are heavily mediated, with authorial interventions stressing the 'degradation and horrors' of the slave route. The narrative records that Susannah's birth name was Karunwi and that she was taken on a Portuguese vessel at about the age of ten.

There are some chronological issues within the text describing, as it does, events more than a half century prior. The narrative states that Karunwi 'must have been born about 1820' and was enslaved around age ten during 'the war in which Igbore [her hometown] was destroyed'. We know that Igbore fell in 1824 – not *c*. 1830 as the account suggests – so she was likely born no later than 1815. She then spent six months at Lagos in a barracoon until '[a]t last a Portuguese slave dealer bought her'. While we do not know the vessel, her departure date from the coast *c*. 1824-5 comports with the account of Sigismund Koelle's Igbore informant, Gbiludso or Thomas Cole, who was 'taken by the Dsebus' and had been in Sierra Leone an estimated twenty-five years by the time Koelle conducted his interviews in 1848–9. Cole stated there were a 'great many' of his country people, though he did not state if he meant the Egba in general or those from Igbore specifically.[2]

The account states that Susannah 'was placed in the King's Yard until she was removed to the Bathurst King's yard, this institution was afterwards removed to Charlotte'. At Charlotte, she 'had the privilege of being taught by Mrs. Crowther (now Bishop Crowther's wife)'. The Crowthers married in 1827 and were based at Bathurst in the early 1830s. Susan Crowther, who taught Susannah, assisted the resident missionaries and ran classes for female Liberated Africans in spinning cotton.[3] Susan was herself 'a rescued slave, having been captured by His Majesty's ship *Bann*, Captain Charles Phillips, on 31 October 1822, and was landed at Sierra Leone in the same year as Crowther'.[4] Susannah's husband, Joseph Bola, was also born at Igbore some two decades before his wife and had served as *Balogun* (warlord) of the town before becoming an early mission convert.[5]

Susannah Bola's history is also one of several in this volume in which a victim of enslavement in Africa experienced an improbable reunion with kin. Her testimony concludes with a recollection of how '[f]rom Lagos she went to Abeokuta where she met father Anrubu and other relatives. This she thinks was about eight years before Mr. Townsend's visit'. Henry Townsend, the first CMS missionary sent on a 'mission of research' to Yoruba territories, reached Abeokuta in 1843. The first known reverse migration of Liberated Africans from Sierra Leone to the Bight of Benin occurred in 1839, and the dating within Susannah's account, however imprecise, indicates she was among the first Saro returnees from Freetown to Yorubaland.[6]

Text

Mrs. Bola like her husband is a native of Igbore; her country name was Karunwi, she must have been born about 1820. During the war in which Igbore was destroyed Mrs. Bola was taken prisoner, by an Ijebu man who took her to Lagos; she was then about 10 years of age. She remained six months in the slave barracoon; who can picture the degradation and horrors of those six months!! At last a Portuguese slave dealer bought her & took her on board his slave ship. This poor child was not to be lost, although she had to pass through much suffering; after they had been at sea a few days, they were sighted by a man of war, who soon opened fire; the captain was killed & the vessels boarded by the English. It is easier to imagine than to tell how the poor creatures would tremble before the new comers, one hope, might animate them, that new comers might be better, & could not be more cruel than the old one. As a little heathen girl Mrs. Bola would know nothing of that love which, through much tribulation was bringing her to a 'good land' where she would be taught to worship – not dumb idols, but the God of love, who willeth that not even one little one should perish. The captain who had charge of the slaver, took her to Freetown, where the poor creatures were landed. Karunwi was placed in the King's Yard until she was removed to the Bathurst King's yard, this institution was afterwards removed to Charlotte.[7] Here she had the privilege of being taught by Mrs. Crowther (now Bishop Crowther's wife) when baptised she received the name of Susannah. She remained there one year & was put out to work for Iyapo, with whom she stayed until she married John Over a constable; he was not a good man; she left him on account of his taking another girl to live with him. When she separated from him, her relatives in Sierra Leone supplied her with money to pay her passage to Lagos, they also put her under the care of a man named Moses who was going to Ishehin.[8] From Lagos she went to Abeokuta where she met father Anrubu and other relatives. This she thinks was about eight years before Mr. Townsend's visit.

CASE SEVENTEEN

William Doherty

Author: Unknown (possibly Valentine Faulkner)
Region of birth: Egbado
Date of birth: *c.* 1817
Year of enslavement: *c.* 1832
Place of writing: Ebute Metta
Date of account: *c.* 1873
Year of death/last known year of activity: Unknown
Published: No/unknown

Source: 'Biographical Accounts of Nigerian Converts to Christianity Early-Mid 19th Century', CMS Z/30

Introduction

William Doherty was an Egbado Liberated African who, like Susannah Bola above, had his account recorded by a member of the CMS as part of a compendium of biographical accounts of Yoruba converts. This account also displays a strong element of intervention by the amanuensis, depicting the region as 'a nation metted out & trodden down'. But Doherty's account contains descriptions of enslavement and British naval intervention not found in other accounts. In particular, he recalls that the naval crew that intercepted his vessel included 'two black men Şolekan & Ona' who 'told them to rejoice for they were free'. These two men were probably Liberated Africans recruited into the Royal Navy, likely with little volition on their part.[1] This is the only account in this volume which mentions African crew members acting as translators to reassure those on board intercepted vessels of the intentions of the British crew.

We do not know when Doherty experienced enslavement and the middle passage. His account places his enslavement soon after when 'the Ijebu people went to war against Abeokuta'. This may be a reference to the 1832 conflict between Abeokuta and the people of Ijebu Remo. Doherty also refers to the Queen of England and Freetown's Queen's Yard (earlier King's Yard) indicating Doherty arrived in Sierra Leone after Queen Victoria's ascent in 1837. Doherty described how a British naval 'Oko elêfin (ship with smoke)' pursued his slave ship. The Royal Navy first introduced paddle steamers into the West African Squadron in the 1843.[2] Doherty's account describes a period of compulsory labour on public works in Freetown, a common practice forced upon recently landed adult, male Liberated Africans. Doherty's account also states that he and other Africans on board the vessel were sent 'to Waterloo, where they were to settle down under the supervision of Mr. Doherty'. This is possibly a reference to Richard Doherty, Governor of Sierra Leone, from 13 June 1837 to 16 December 1840. Doherty also speaks of his conversion and the 'Rev. W. Young'. William Young was based at Waterloo during 1837–9, 1840–4 and again in 1847, periods interspersed with appointments in other villages of the Sierra Leone peninsula.

William Doherty later became a native catechist and returned to Lagos by steamship in 1854. The CMS sent him from Abeokuta to establish a mission presence at the town of Isagga. In 1862, Dahomean forces captured William and seventeen Egbado Christian converts at Isagga, and he was held in slavery to one of the chiefs of Dahomey.[3] For several years the CMS sought his release and in 1866 sent an envoy including his son, S. W. Doherty, which was ultimately responsible in seeing William freed from slavery for the second time in his life.[4]

Text

William Doherty

He speaks English so I can give the principal events of his life in his own words. He says his country name was Agigboṣo (* Ajibosho) & he worshipped Oṣaroko God of the farms, an iron idol. He was born in Idele an Egbardo town. When a boy, about fifteen years old, the Ijebu people went to war against Abeokuta & destroyed Idele on their way. Agigboṣo escaped to Immoshe, a tributary people of the Egbas; Immoshe was destroyed by Egbados & Agigboṣo was taken prisoner. The soldiers seeing he was a strong healthy boy, sold him privately without letting the Balogun know & divided the money among themselves. His master took him to Otta, while there his master was king to him. After a time some soldiers on march stated in Ogilusi's house & troubled him, so he gather all his property & servants that he could, & went to Ọtọ, on the island of Ido. While there his master beat him until he nearly died: his friend Pajo went to Lagos & told Abioro his (Ajigboṣ's) relative that his master would kill him. One night Abioro came to Ọtọ, when Pajo put Agigboṣo into a canoe; Abioro told Agigboṣo that his slave had been made a slave in Abeokuta & he would send him to her. They landed at the King's wharf in Lagos; Abioro put him in a little place in his house, where he could not stand up, on pretence of hiding him from his master; but did not give him any food. Abioro went to look if he were there, when he said to him, 'Abioro you are my relative; you take me out of my master's hand & you don't give me any food, let me go: if they catch me no matter.' Abeoro replied 'never mind, I come back to day & carry you to Abeokuta.' The same night he returned, Agigboṣo had a sword & two knives which he fastened round his waist, when this was done Abeoro said 'come follow me,' so they went out together. I have noticed a peculiar fashion the natives have i.e. unless engaged in palaver, or earnest converse they seldom walk together, but one behind the other, Indian file; thus Agigboṣo followed Abioro to the gate of the slave barracoon. Abioro walked in, but Agigboṣo drew back & turning round found himself surrounded by a crowd of people who seized him. He drew his sword but his arms were held, he fought & struggled hard & in wrestling the sword was wrapped round & round his arm, & his hand severely cut, before they could deprive him of it. He was then by main force dragged inside & heavily shackled with irons; next they beat him in a most violent manner, & then using a flat wood, a kind of castinado, they beat the palms of his hands, regardless of the wound until there was scarcely any skin left. Next he was thrust into an inner prison, while they fetched a white slave dealer to see if he would buy him. After much examination, as to whether all his limbs were sound, he consented. After the slave dealer was gone, they again beat him most barbarously; he was then joined on to a gang; (each gang consisted of twenty-five) at night they were pushed into a room the keeper saying 'go in' & freely using his whip to make them go closer; & so closely were they packed that one could not move a limb without the whole moving. But why go on describing the revolting horrors of a slave barracoon: how truly may the words of the Prophet be addressed to their keepers 'With forced & with cruelty have ye ruled them.' No white man was allowed to have charge of a barracoon for slaves. Every morning the poor creatures were driven to the lagoon & upon their return were obliged to rub themselves over with oil so that their skins might look bright & healthy; their food was not only bad, but insufficient. When the slave dealer bought Agigboṣo he hoped soon to be taken from that den of cruelty; but was disappointed on finding that he would have to remain, until his master, had made his compliment of slaves. He thinks this was about three months (during which time he & some others had been calling upon the God of Heaven to make the white man take them away to his country for surely said they, the whiteman's country must be better than this place, where we are so cruelly treated). They were taken to the wharf, their chains taken off, which was a great relief & told to get into a canoe. So thoroughly abject was their appearance that the people & women who were looking on, lifted up their voices & wept aloud, to see such suffering. The slaves in that canoe were a living testimony against the argument of the Infidels who maintain that the African does not possess the same susceptibilities & reasoning faculties as the European. Upon seeing & hearing the signs of sympathy for their woes, like the exiles in Babylon, they chanted a parabolic refrain, the meaning of which was 'Those of you who reach Abeokuta tell Sodeke we are lost to his & our country & sold as slaves to the White man. Tell our friends to mourn us as dead.' When animals are ill-used they either become stupid or violent; but these poor children of Africa had been browbeaten & trodden under foot, yet on the least touch of kindness, their hearts respond with patriotism & tender affection; rather must their friends sorrow for them as dead, than as dragging on in misery.

Surely Africa has been 'a nation meted out, & trodden down.' The canoe was taken to the beach where they were landed & again shackled with chains. Having been so long shut up in a close room, they suffered much, especially thirst, from being exposed to the scorching sun. At night they slept upon the sands & suffered still more from the cold & heavy dews; some of these died & when the morning dawned the dead & living were found chained together. To elude the English vessel, they were hid in the bush through the next day, early in the morning, they gave them hot Eko or Agidi without akara (country bread) to eat, & that had to suffice until next morning. At night they were driven along the sands by palm torch lights as far as Benin, & at day-break they were put in a shed & given warm Eko without soup. The overseer took a glass & after searching sometime to see that no English ships were about, struck off their chairs & ordered them to get in some surf boats. When they arrived at the side of the slave ship the Capt (a man of giant proportions) took hold of their hands & flung them on deck as he would a bale of goods. All being on board, they were put down in the hold which was so full they had to fit in close together. Each morning they were called up & fed on dry gari & salt beef, with one measure of water, five men fed at once one bucket of gari. After they had eaten they were allowed to stay up & catch the breeze for one or two hours, as it sent the Officers off the vessel; then they were sent back into the hold, & the poor creatures would fight & struggle for places near the port hole. If the masters heard it, they would go down & flog them all round. The children were not so hardly treated as the adults. When they had been at sea nine days they sighted a man of war. Immediately the sailors saw they ship they went to the slaves & told them to pray hard to good as the thief-man was coming & if they were taken prisoners they would be treated very badly & put on an island, without work or food. Some of the slaves, who had been in Lagos a long time & had heard another account of the English ships pinched them & whispered, no! no! pray for them to take us, they are good people, who will set us free.

They were soon called out of the hold & put to work, all the sails were spread & the ship ran very quickly leaving the (Oko elêfin (ship with smoke)) steamer behind them. In a few hours they were greatly amazed to see the steamer in front of them. The sailors & men immediately lowered the boats & jumped in, leaving the Capt. & slaves in the ship. The capt stood by the ship, the steamer then steamed round the slave ship three times; a boat was lowered & the Capt & two black men boarded her. The Capt of the steamer walked to the Captain of the slave ship & taking the flat side of his sword beat him with it, in token of victory. Then the hatchway was opened, rum, honey & water was placed in abundance before them, of which they were told to drink freely; the two black men Ṣolekan & Ona told them to rejoice for they were free. Cooked gari & soft beef was then placed before them & they ate as much as they pleased. Şolekan told them to return thanks to the God of Heaven & Earth for they were free to do as they liked. They were beginning to realize they were no longer slaves when they came in sight of Free Town. In the distance the houses appeared to them to be too small for human dwellings & fear again for a short space took possession of their hearts, until Şolekan & Ona reassured them by again telling them 'god is your friend & with you, you are all free, & will soon meet many of your own country men, dwelling in peace & plenty.' When the anchor was cast, they were told they could not go on shore naked; they must wait until the boat with clothing came; at last each man a pair of trousers & shirt given him, the women a gown, the children were also suitably clothed. Those they were told was their first present from the Queen of England. When they were dressed & in the boat, the Housa man in charge of the boat told them they must all join in singing what he told them.

'Ibogbo oiyimbo ti Olorun fe.'

The meaning of which is

'God bless all the White men'

The landing was crowded with those who had been previously brought there, a motley group; mothers with aching hearts, Rachels seeking their lost children, some found them, others had to go away empty, for them the night of weeping had not ended. Sisters & brothers, relatives & friends, one common sympathy had drawn them together.[5] The tyrant had severed them from home & friends; but with all his degrading cruelty he had not been able to quench 'the spark Divine.' Now that they were free, one hope, one desire, animated each heart, to meet again the loved ones, who had been enslaved like themselves. Mr Doherty says none but those who have witnessed such a scene can imagine it.

As soon as these glad yet sad meetings were over, the newly arrived were led to the Queen's yard, where they were well fed & met many friends & acquaintances. After they had time to rest & relate to each other the sad tale of their woes, those who had arrived previously, would reassure the newcomers; then their hearts would be at rest & they realized they were once again free. England has done much, indeed it is a glorious privilege to set the captive free, wherever he may be found. But the work is not complete she still needs to train & send out her sons more freely than she has yet done. Teachers are still needed, to make known the truth which shall set them free indeed. The strong men were divided into bands of twenty-five, a constable was placed over each band, who led them out to repair roads & do other necessary work.

They were left quite free & could do as they liked about going to church, but were gently led to adopt the habits of Christians. Each Saturday afternoon they were given a piece of soap & told to wash themselves etc. & not to work on the morrow, it being the day the great & Good God had set apart for men to rest & thank Him for all his kindness to them. Thus they were taught the first lesson in Christianity ...

When Agigboṣo had been in the Queen's Yard about three months, they were told to fall in a line round the yard and divided into little companies of five men. To each company was given one iron cooking pot, one soup pot, & one kettle. Each man had given him one shirt, one pair of trousers & three pence & were then told 'The Queen of England this day sets you free to work for your own living, be careful not to steal or fight.' A policeman then led them to Waterloo, where they were to settle down under the superintendence of Mr. Doherty who sent a policeman with them to point out a place where they were to clear the ground & build themselves houses; until the houses were completed, each man received three pence per day for subsistence. When finished each man was shown his own room & left to provide for himself. Next they were encouraged to take a wife, from among the women who had been brought like themselves from their country.

PART TWO

Enslavement in Africa

CASE EIGHTEEN

Awa

Author: Unknown
Region of birth: Ibadan
Date of birth: Unknown
Year of enslavement: c. 1864
Place of writing: Lagos
Date of account: 12 November 1865
Year of death/last known year of activity: Unknown
Published: Parliamentary Papers. Vol. 50, class B, no. I, Glover to Russell, 6 December 1865, encl.

> Source: Deposition of Awa, a slave woman of Mr. Henry Robbin at Abbeokuta, 12 November 1865. Appears in triplicate in CMS Yoruba Mission, CA2/O11/32, CA2/O80/39. The deposition was also forwarded to the Foreign Office (FO 84/1250), 'Deposition of Awa, a Slave-Woman of Mr. Henry Robbin, at Abbeokuta' (Enclosure No. 1 in Slave Trade No. 25, 12 November 1865); the Colonial Office (CO 147/9) and published in the Parliamentary Papers (PP. vol. 50, class B, no. I, Glover to Russell, 6 December 1865, encl.)

Introduction

The next two testimonies were recorded in Lagos in 1865, four years after Britain's annexation of the coastal kingdom. These two accounts are second-hand recordings of the experiences of Awa and Daniel Dopemu, who both claimed to have been held in slavery by Henry Robbin of Abeokuta and had fled to Lagos to seek protection from British authorities. Henry Robbin was a Sierra Leonean returnee to the Bight of Benin and prominent African member of the Church Missionary Society congregation at Abeokuta.

Robbin was a trader and cotton producer, who had previously visited Manchester to study techniques for the introduction of cotton production to the Bight of Benin.[1] He was also a son-in-law of Samuel Crowther and had spearheaded Abeokuta's cotton production with Samuel's son, Josiah.[2]

Several scholars have made use of Awa's account.[3] The account of Daniel Dopemu is less known, though Dopemu assisted Awa in bringing her case before the police in Lagos. By 1865, the 'fugitive slave question' was a pressing matter for both colonial officials in the recently annexed colony as well as for missionaries and Christian converts.[4] Awa and Daniel Dopemu were part of a larger wave of enslaved women and men who reached Lagos seeking refuge with British colonial officials and missionaries. We cannot disentangle the accusation of slaveholding against Henry Robbin from the increasingly adversarial stance of Governor Glover and British officialdom at Lagos towards the Egba in general and Saro returnees in particular.

Awa's account appears in triplicate in the CMS archives. Her account also appears in the Colonial Office correspondence for the Lagos colony (CO 147) and the Foreign Office correspondence for the suppression of the slave trade (FO 84). The testimony in all of these sources (listed in full below) is identical. It is unclear which is the original, though it may very well be the Colonial Office version as the deposition was taken before the justice of the peace. By contrast, the FO 84 version was type-set and printed locally. While this source is not exclusive or perhaps original to the CMS archive, it is one of the few accounts of female experiences within British missionary sources and relates directly to the activities of the mission.

As a deposition, it follows different conventions than other testimonies in this volume and, as a colonial court document, raises different interpretive challenges. Africanist historians including Richard Roberts, Kristin Mann and Trevor Getz have noted the utility (as well as limitations) of court records in looking at individual life histories, particularly the testimony of the enslaved and formerly enslaved.[5] The earliest colonial courts recognized slavery and openly heard cases relating to the enslaver-enslaved relationship as well as to slave trading. In Lagos, such cases could involve members of CMS congregations and inland mission stations, raising sensitive if not embarrassing questions about the relationship between slaveholding, church membership, British subjecthood and protection within and outside of British formal possessions.

While other narrators in this volume wrote or dictated their accounts, Awa's account was taken in an unfamiliar setting in which her interests were secondary. But Awa's testimony shows some of the discursive strategies employed to voice her grievances against a high-profile African merchant and convert.[6] John Hawley Glover, Secretary of the nascent Lagos colony, informed Foreign Secretary John Russell that he found the testimony convincing. Despite describing Robbin as 'a British born Sierra Leone subject, generally considered the most influential and respected of the Sierra Leone emigrants residing at Abbeokuta', Glover took Awa's statement as proof 'that the Church Missionary Society's agents in Abbeokuta cannot but be aware of the system of slave dealing and concubinage which exists among their congregations'.[7]

Text

Deposition of Awa, a slave woman of Mr. Henry Robbin at Abbeokuta.

I am Mr. Henry Robbin's slave at Abbeokuta. I was brought from Ibadan to Abbeokuta and sold to Mr. Robbin. I met several other slaves with him. I remained with him about a year, during which time I was one of his mistresses. When he returned from Sierra Leone the last time, myself and three men (his slaves) came to meet him in Lagos, and accompanied him to Abbeokuta. On our arrival at Abbeokuta, four of my companions (Mr. Robbin's other female slaves) were missing: and I have not been able to get any information respecting them. Thirteen days after our arrival at Abbeokuta, Mr. Robbin ordered me to go to Okeodan[8] (with several others who were going thither) to assist in bringing from thence to Abbeokuta some rolls of tobacco. When we arrived there, I was sold, on the ninth day, by one Osanyipeju (a relative of one of Mr. Robbin's principal mistresses at Abbeokuta, who had previously gone to Okeodan to sell two of Mr. Robbin's female slaves) to two women for two rolls of tobacco, which was paid in my presence. I was then sold by these women to a man at Porto Novo with whom I remained for two moons. This man brought me to Lagos thirteen days ago. I saw one Dopemu three days ago, who I knew to be one of Mr. Robbin's slaves. Dopemu informed me that he was to have been sold by Mr. Robbin to Okeodan; but that he had managed to escape to Lagos. Dopemu took me to Mr. Willoughby the Superintendent of Police. I am certain that Osanyipeju had not sold me without Mr. Robbin's authority; as he had on previous occasions, been selling slaves for and at the express request of Mr. Robbin. The four women who were missing when we arrived at Abbeokuta from Lagos were familiarly acquainted with me: their names are Ebo (a native of Ibadan) Ajisomo (native of Efon), Lakanye (native of Ijayi) and Akitunde (son of Lakanye). Since I was sold at Porto Novo, two women and a child, viz. Roki, Eyinle & her child (slaves of Mr. Robbin) have been sold; they met me at Porto Novo.

Mr. Robbin's principal mistress was a woman of the late Alake; for trading this woman he had to pay heavily; this occurred just before the Alake's death. He had ten women up to the time I was sold (myself included). He has three children. At Illugun where his women are kept, he has three men and a boy; and at his farm, he has three men, whom I know; his other men slaves are kept in Ake; but the number I do not know. I have attended Sunday School for about a year at Abbeokuta; and have been constantly employed to carry to, and count cowries for Mr. Townsend from Mr. Robbin's principal mistress. Mr. Townsend has often addressed ~~himself to~~ myself and other companions from Mr. Robbin's yard, both in school, and while counting cowries in his compound, and must be fully aware, as is all of Abbeokuta, that I and my companions were Mr. Robbin's concubines.

In the beginning of December 1864, myself and eight others (two of us being his concubines, the other seven being young ones in course of preparation) were sent to the Aro gate to bring up cowries; for staying too long, we were all placed in cell under the wooden floor of his room (without air or light); but on Mr. Faulkner remonstrating with Mr. Robbin, we were released the next day. On another occasion, for being saucy, I was shackled to a post for six days, with another concubine, who has since been sold, by name of Elatutoon; during that time, we were only fed twice; viz. on the third day, a country woman (Nuphe) by stealth brought us Agidi and palaver sauce with water. This was on Saturday; on the next day, while Mr. Robbin was at church, one of his concubines brought us some beans, cooked in oil, and water; but on hearing this, every one was kept away from us, until we were released. On the second day, a little girl succeeded in giving us water.

Agoonoko, wife of Ali one of Mr. Robbin's slaves, wears shackles on her legs and goes about, shackles was put on her by Mr. Robbin for supposed adultery. Flogging is another punishment in Mr. Robbin's harem; the instrument being a whiteman's horse whip administered either by Mr. Robbin or Debare, brother to Mr. Robbin's chief concubine.

Three of Mr. Robbin's concubines attend the day school at Abbeokuta church; but since one has had a child by Mr. Robbin, she had not attended.

Awa
X

Awa   her
*   X*
*   mark*

CASE NINETEEN

Daniel Dopemu

Author: W. Benjamin Way (Chief Magistrate, Lagos)
Region of birth: Unknown
Date of birth: Unknown
Year of enslavement: Unknown
Place of writing: Lagos
Date of account: 31 October 1865
Year of death/last known year of activity: Unknown
Published: 'Sale of a Slave at Abeokuta by a British Subject', *The African Times* (London), 23 December 1865, 60.

Source: 'Deposition of Daniel Dopemu, A Christian Convert at Abbeokuta', CA2/O9/19[1]

Introduction

Daniel Dopemu, alongside Awa whose account is discussed in Case 18, provided testimony before the chief magistrate at Lagos that Henry Robbin had held him in slavery at Abeokuta. Dopemu's account is contained within a document series otherwise comprising the petitions of Europeans and Sierra Leonean returnees to the colonial government at Lagos. The printed account appears alongside a petition from Henry Robbin and other prominent merchants and converts. The document was 'directed to Henry Venn' (the CMS lay secretary) and 'enclosed in a wrapper inscribed "with the compliments of the Acting Colonial Secretary of Lagos"'. The wording reflects some of the tensions between colonial officials at the recently annexed Lagos colony, missionaries in the interior, and slaveholders among their congregations.

Text

Deposition of Daniel Dopemu

I am a slave to Mr. Henry Robbin at Abeokuta. I was bought by him four years ago for fourteen and four head cowrie.

I was employed to bring the Reverend Mr. Moore to Lagos in a canoe belonging to my master, in returning the canoe & cargo were seized and confiscated in consequence of a bag of shot, that was found concealed in a bag of cowries. I got Mr. Moore's friends to buy the canoe at the public auction and returned in her to Abeokuta.

My master asked me whether it was I who put the shot in the bag of cowries. I told him no, he then said fortunately it is not you for if it was you who did it, I would have killed you.

Five days afterwards my master called me and said I would return you to your former master as I heard you have got a disease and I would lose my money.

The Christians at Abeokuta on hearing it came and begged him not to sell or return me to my former master, they asked the amount for which I was bought, he told them he bought me for thirty one bags of cowries. As they all knew that he had only paid fourteen bags for me they all returned without saying anything more.

Mr. Robbin then put me in chains in which I remained for five days in his house and after that he handed me over to one Lumeye a slave dealer who shaved my head and kept me in chains at his house for seven days and was preparing to take me as he said to Okeodan. Lumeye said to one himself that as the people had begged Mr. Robbin and failed, I should be quiet and not run away as he would not sell me at Okeodan as he was requested by Mr. Robbin but that he would sell me to the son of the late king of Porto Novo who would treat me kindly.

After Mr Robbin had handed me over to Lumeye I am told he went to the Reverend Mr. Townsend and informed him that my former master had claimed me from him and had taken me away.

After I remained in chains at Lumeye's home for seven days I was glad to find on the night of the seventh day that the chains fell off from me during a very strong wind that was then blowing. I then wrapped the chains in my cloth and escaped. I left the chain in an Oro bush at Illugun, I came through Oko-obba to Mokoloki, and from thence to Otta in a canoe, and to Lagos overland from Otta. This is the tenth day I escaped from Abeokuta.

I was told by Captain Davies a few days ago that Mr. Robbin has written to himself and Mr. Beckley to say that my former master had claimed me from him and taken me to Porto Novo and they should happen to see me they should not believe any word I may say against him and that he believes I was taken to Dahomey.

(Signed) Daniel Dopemu
X his mark

On the 31st day of October 1865
The foregoing deposition was sworn
To by Daniel Dopemu at Lagos
Before me
(Signed) W. Benjamin Way
Chief Magistrate

CASE TWENTY

Jack Macumba

Author: Jack Macumba
Region of birth: Kajoor
Date of birth: *c.* 1790
Year of enslavement: *c.* 1801–3
Place of writing: St. Mary's Island, The Gambia
Date of account: 6 June 1839
Year of death/last known year of activity: Unknown
Published: No/unknown

Source: MMS, Sierra Leone Correspondence, Fiche Box 25, Box No. 280, 'Sierra Leone Odds Papers,' Fiche No. 1880, #12

Introduction

Jack Macumba was a local preacher with the MMS's Gambia mission. Macumba was born in the kingdom of Kajoor in northern Senegal. He was kidnapped and enslaved while on a journey with his father from Ganjool near present-day Saint Louis. Macumba was enslaved on Gorée island during the period of the Napoleonic Wars (*c.* 1803–15), during which time Gorée had an enslaved majority.[1]

Macumba left Gorée on an English ship bound for The Gambia upon the official cession of Gorée to the French (25 January 1817). Macumba reached St Mary's in early 1817, noting in his account that he left Gorée 'the same day' the French formally reoccupied the island. The restoration of Gorée to the French saw many British merchants transfer to the recently founded Bathurst. Many brought with them their enslaved domestics whose labour was utilized to hastily construct government buildings and traders' houses. Macumba began attending MMS church sermons in the early 1820s.

Other sources in the MMS archive indicate that Macumba remained enslaved in the years after Britain's 1833 Act for the Abolition of Slavery came into effect in August 1834. Macumba was one of six enslaved people named in a petition to Lieutenant-Governor George Rendall and forwarded by the missionary William Fox to Secretary of State Lord Glenelg. Fox complained that despite the 1833 Abolition Act, '[s]lavery exists in this infant colony, a fact this too notorious to be denied, altho' it may be of a different species to West Indian slavery, and perhaps of a somewhat milder type, tis nevertheless slavery to all intents and purposes, and as such I presume is inconsistent & unconstitutional'.[2]

In October 1835, Macumba appeared before the Colonial Secretary of The Gambia alongside his enslaver, Antoine Pierre formerly of Gorée, who 'set his hand and seal as a solemn act of manumission of the said "Jack Macumba" alias "Byebonny" from and after this Twenty eight day of October'. The record of Macumba's manumission contains a peculiar detail: the payment of 165 dollars by Charles Grant. Grant was an early colonial settler at Bathurst and a pioneer of the export of mahogany logs felled along the Upper Gambia.[3] His name features in several accounts in this volume from The Gambia. The peculiar spectacle of the 'redemption' of an enslaved person in a British colony post-abolition was in part in response to the recommendation of the lieutenant-governor.[4] Fox reported Rendall's suggestion that 'while they continued on this Island or any of its dependencies they were not slaves' but if they were to 'purchase their freedom and they might then visit any of the French Settlements without risk of being taken into slavery'.[5] Upon gaining his freedom, he became a local preacher with the MMS Gambia mission. At this time, he was approximately forty-five years of age. A certificate of Macumba's manumission is included in the MMS archive.

Text

Statement of Jack Macumba

I Jack was born in my native country called Kajoor and was journying with My Father to Gangoul[6] and when we returning home we call to a Town named Marour and lodged their. then I was sick. now this Town is a very large town and My father left me in the house wher we was and go in the town to see some friends then about two Oclock in the day their came some men from Ndakourroo[7] to plunder then they came to the place where I was and met me laying down in sickness then they catch me and many others persons more then thirty. and journying with us to came to Ndakourroo the man that catch me told me that if they make piece with the man of Marour then he will send me back to my native country. Then we walked three day's before we reach to Ndakourroo then when we reach their this man sold me to a man named Farra Pierre then this man take me to Goree The time I come to Goree a man named Corramel Farrasair[8] was the Governor of Goree and this Mr. Lloyd's Brother[9] was the captain theirof because the English been belong to Goree that time. Then I was in Goree till the French's came to make war they arrive in their in the night and was fighting till the day light before they took Island from the English. then a man came from Senegall was the King this man named Mamayour then he reign their about two month's + half then their came four English men of war again each three mast and four Brigs beside the men of war they arrive in Goree at twelf Oclock in the day then they land four boats on shore full with Officers then the Frenchs took these officers and put them in prison and about nine Oclock in the night their came another large boat from the men of war and met a Merican Brig laying at anchour then they cut the chain and took her to the men of war then they write their letters and send them by this Brig because the English and the Merican's have peace that time and the Mericans have peace with the French's too therefor they send their letters by her and tell the Frenchs that if they dont deliver the Island to them they will set the Island on fire. then all the Frenchs fled in their men of war the same night. then me and a man named Pierre Bonnay[10] he was the commandant of the Island that time he hear the English language well then I was with he and the Officers which was in Prison to light lantern's + to fire gun's to call the English's to come now these English was in Goree again then I was in Goree till the English give the Island to the French again then the same day I get in one of the English vessels to come to St Mary's to Estalish it then I was a ship carpenter that time. and they got to pay me 3/9 per day half belong to my master and the other to me then I work in St Mary's six months and got nothing in that work. then I go in the bush to cut and to square timbers for my master. then I came to Goree again and build a schooner for my master and when the schooner was finish I got to go trade in her and when ever we came back to Goree then can let me go shore but to stop in the vessel. then I was in much trouble till my master load the vessel with some stones then I and my master came to St Mary's and when we landed all the stones I go to the captain of St Mary's named Veapilton and tell him that I am a ship carpenter and wanted to stop here and work and tell him that I got to give my master half the money and the rest for myself and when he here this he was displeased for it and he asked me if I dont want to work for myself alone. but although I was in trouble but I been want to pay my master for my freedom before I got free if I been tell the captain say yes he will make me free without paying any money. then I stope here to work and I went with my master to Joe Wilson to writes it in books one for me to keep and the other for my master to part the money that I shall work. in the same day both me and my master left here he go to burnt lone linae and I go to Kyeye to work for Mr Deann and at my return here I met him here then Mr. Deann paid me and I give him the first time 25 dollars. and when I give him this money he was so please because he not been believe that I shall give him any thing in my wages. Now in all these times I was in the darkness be because I was in the religion of the Mahometens. till when Mr. Morgin[11] came here before I hear some thing about Christ till one day I heard him Preach and Cupidon was to interpret him in Jollof then I here the sayings and was so please but I was not yes in the good old way but I was in the habit to go in. for some times when I go to my bed I cant sleep because of thinking for my sins because I here Mr. Morgin said if any man got a wife and not marrieze her he is commit adultry this is what I think of so much because I been keep a woman without married her then I was in the habit to married her. and Mr Morgin got to teach me to read till Mr. Hawton[12] came from England and Mr Morgin left me with him to learn me to read then I always go in the night because I got no time to go in the day till one night I go and Mr Hawton told me that I dont loan enough and he told me to go till next time this I was greave and go home and not went again till Mr. Dawson came[13] then I begin to go again till Mr. Dawson manage me then I got into the good old way and begin to seek forgiveness from God. untill Mr Marshall came here.[14] then I was alway's Pray to God that he may pardon my sins and on Sunday night at eleven oclock as I lay on my bed some thing came to my mind as a dream but not exactly because I was not quite asleep and told me that I was a child of God and that God was my Father and immediately I got up and went out to make water and when I came again I fall on my kneels and prayed and felt much happiness in my heart then as I praying I lifted up my hand as if I could took hold of God. but some thing told me in my mind that you must put your hand down for God is in every were then I put my hand down and praying all night and not went to bed again because I cant sleep again then I heard some thing like a voice saying unto me thy sins be forgiven thee then I feel much joy in my heart. then I opened my mouth as if some thing thaugh me to say may God almightly help one to live in is glory here and hereafter. Then I went to be baptized because I was baptize in the French's religion. and when I told Mr. Moister he say that it is very good and he baptize me then one day again about two oclock in the night I dream as if many mighty men were assembled and I was brought before them to speak the words of truth and all these me wanted to deny what I said then of these men as if he was there headman stood in the midst of them and asked me why all these men assembled against the to day what you said then my answer to him was that because God is a true God and when I have said this he told me to hold fast on these words and go on in them then awaked out of sleep and give praises to God and kneel down and prayed and I was though without no doubting that my pray's were heard. that might I was not afraid of death. because I heard something said unto me that if any of my fellow men die in there sins it is their own fault then Mr. Fox came out.[15] all the missionarys which came from England I been said that their cant be no better missionary's then they to me but the time seen Mr. Fox God has join me and him and not only me but all the Poor people as me because he helped them vey much. if it was our own power we shall never part with him but we want him to go and see his Family and Friends because as we wanted to see him so his Family but we hope that he will embrace his Friends in good health of life and body. and return back to us again untill now I am Feeling the goodness of God in my mind untill this vey same day. because I hoped a hope in God that I know it cannot Fail and now I am thanking God. and hope that Mr. Fox may reach his native country in safty.

Here I have ended my Statement
Jack Macumba Local Preacher
St Mary's River Gambia June 6th 1839

CASE TWENTY-ONE

John Cupidon

Author: John Cupidon
Region of birth: Wolof
Date of birth: Unknown
Year of enslavement: *c.* 1814
Place of writing: MacCarthy's Island, The Gambia
Date of account: 9 April 1839
Year of death/last known year of activity: Died 1853
Published: No/unknown

Source: MMS, Sierra Leone Correspondence, Fiche Box 25, Box No. 280, 'Sierra Leone Odds Papers', Fiche No. 1880, #5

Introduction

John Cupidon was one of the first West Africans employed by the MMS Gambia mission. He began his career with the mission around 1822 as a translator and catechist, and in 1831 he was appointed assistant missionary to the Reverend William Moister.[1] In addition to penning his autobiography, much of his correspondences to the mission house are included in the MMS archive.

The narrative of John Cupidon includes one of the most detailed accounts of enslavement in the MMS archive. Cupidon reports that he was born in the country of 'Burhabol' or 'Burhold'. He and many members of his village travelled to what is likely the kingdom of Siin, where they were attacked and violently enslaved in a day-long battle with a local king and his army. After his enslavement, Cupidon was transported to Gorée and sold. He first arrived with his enslaver at Bathurst around 1816, as he notes visiting the island 'when it was in building'. Cupidon added that he had 'live[d] with this gentleman about two years before Saint Mary's in The Gambia was stablished', suggesting he reached Gorée around 1814.

Many of Bathurst's first government buildings and traders' houses were hastily constructed by enslaved domestics transported from Gorée and Saint-Louis by English traders.[2] His enslaver then took him to France and London for several months, and then back to The Gambia, where he worked for the Scottish merchant Charles Grant. Grant taught Cupidon to read and write, as well as having him trained as a carpenter. Cupidon purchased his freedom around 1822 with wages he had earned as a shopkeeper.[3] He was baptized and began working with the Methodist Missionary Society, translating sermons into the Wolof language. The Methodist John Morgan, who baptized Cupidon, later explained, 'The French at Goree had given him the name Cupidon, and the Missionary baptized him John Cupidon.'[4]

The details of Cupidon's enslavement in the account below are contradicted by the published account of the missionary William Moister, who wrote, 'John Cupidon was born at Goree. His parents were slaves, consequently their son was not free-born.'[5] Several historians have reiterated Moister's assertion that Cupidon was born on Gorée to enslaved Tukulor parents.[6] However, Robert Maxwell MacBrair, a Wesleyan missionary who reached The Gambia in 1836 – prior to either Fox or Moister – wrote in 1839 that Cupidon 'was of respectable parentage, but had been taken captive and reduced to the condition of a domestic slave'.[7] While many scholars have accepted the assertions of Fox and Moister that Cupidon was born into slavery on Gorée, Cupidon's own account and the earlier publication of MacBrair suggest Cupidon was born free in Africa.

Cupidon's account is the only one in this volume written on MacCarthy's Island, known both before and after British rule as Janjangbureh. The Rev. John Morgan accompanied the original West India Regiment expedition in 1823 and selected a plot on the island for the Methodist mission. In 1832, John Cupidon and Rev. Moister established a mission school at MacCarthy's.[8] Cupidon and his wife became the head schoolmasters at MacCarthy's Island, and by 1836, the school had nearly fifty students.[9] In 1838, Cupidon and the Reverend William Fox travelled to Bondu, Senegal, where Cupidon translated sermons into the Fula language.[10]

During his time at MacCarthy's Island, Cupidon's house was destroyed by a mob gathered by French merchant John Messervy after Messervy failed to obtain Cupidon's plot of land. Cupidon returned to St Mary's Island in the early 1840s and served at Bathurst and Barra. In 1846, he entered into a dispute with another missionary, Matthew Godman, over the issue of marrying church followers to unbelievers. Within this disagreement, Godman beat Cupidon's wife, leading Cupidon to offer his resignation. The resignation was originally refused, but after an additional dispute, Cupidon was dismissed in 1848. He died in 1853.[11]

Text

I was born at Parter a town belong to the country of Burhabol where I was about twelve years of age. my father followed a prince who was going to unite for a crown at seean. he being a relation to the prince. left his home and went with him. hoping to enjoy the benefit of his reign. or to be chief of some towns in his reigning over the kingdom. The prince and his mother and their people and my father with him they left Goyjar, a town in the east end of Burhol at sun set and reached seeann at cuck crow[12] in the morning and lodged in one of its town till day light when day Break. the prince and my father left the prince us mother and her people in their lodging for the capital to see the King. in a day or two they left the capital for his own town. and his mother too to her appointe town. I was with my father to this great man as place. for some time before my father as house hold came after him from Burhold. When they enter the country, they send word to him and he went to meet them. and soon after this he begin to build his own town about day as walk from the prince as town but I believe we live only one rain in this place on the dry season a whole town break of from Burhold came after my father on the same evening they came they found him went to the capital. but the came back the same night and found our town was full of strangers the same Evening they arrived the news was reported to the King that a body of people is came from a nother kingdom to his ground and are lodging in such a place running my father as town day light early in the morning. the King himself with a part of his army stood before our gate and fill the plain with his horses and fool men. who we left in the capital a short time at midnight is now calling my father from our gate. he went and the King said to him I came for the strangers that came to you this last Evening. he said to him they are no strangers they are my people who were left behind and now came after me. If you ask me to give you them you ask me my wives and children when he said this he went in the yard he tell his people and the strangers what is about to take place. and tell them that the King is came to take them as slaves. Then they began be ready to fight. When the King saw the movement in the yard he knew that he cannot get them without using force. he then no sooner form a ring round this large thorn hedged yard then the fight began just when the sun rised a little and continued till it fall from midday the thorn hedg and the corn burns caught fire. this found many died and many wounded and still many dieing in the yard. Some of my sisters and my self was in one hut and the balls was going through the hut at all the time of the fight. till one of my sister was hurt in her small finger by a ball. My poor father too was also wounded in both of his thighs. the houses caught fire the women and children all come out the enemies floked in and took us all away to the capital with the King. but my father was left in ruine with his nephew among the dead. his mother my father as sister was setting by them. All this was done without the prince my father as frind as hearing any thing about it. till all was over. But when he heard it, he rode to the place with some of his men. but found only dead men and the wounded who were ready to die of theirs wounds doubtless he ordered his people to bury my father as deaths and took him to his town with him there he died and was buried by him. When they took us all slaves to the capital. the next morning the king gave order to select all my father as wives and children and let them all go home. but keep those who caused the mischief this was morning the man who caught me brought me to the sea side of Goree and sold me there to a dark color Mulatto woman.[13] When the man who sold me was gone she asked my where I came or where I belong to. When I tell her my country and parents she said ah child your father was my husband as good friend she further more says. When my husband was King over Seean. you father was a chief of – naming some places in the Kingdom. about a day or two she want to send me by land with a man to the nearest side to goree to get me across to the island. But when we was about to leave she heard that there are people lieing in waite to take me as soon as I come out. This liere in waite was a man who came from the same town I belong to and was send by the chief to the sea side to buy some things for him. he heard of me from the next town he lodged, he got few men to assist him to take me but when the woman came to hear that she not send me by land again the same Evening a small batit belong to her daughter as Husband in Goree arrived she directly send me on board to sleep there that night The next evening we set sails and landed in Goree the early the following morning after day or two I was taken to an English gentleman as house, who married the old woman as daughter to be his servant. I live with this gentleman about two years before saint Marys in The Gambia was stablished. When it was in building he went up there for a short time. and went back to goree but he left goree again a short time after our arrival for Senegal and about three weeks we left Senegal in a French vessel for France and from France we landed at Portsmouth and ride to London. There I stop a few months and was send out again to The Gambia. to waite for him till he came out. in a short time after our reaching The Gambia he also arrived But not long before he left the coast for England for good. Before he left he told me that he going to left me with one good gentleman. nam of mr Charles Grant who I hope will take care you. by the asst of this gentleman I got my liberty for one hundred and twenty Spanish Dollars. This was about the time the first missionary. the Revd John Morgan comeout to The Gambia and was lodging in Mr. C. Grants house.[14] Al that time I knew nothing at all about religion until providence brought me to live with this man of God in one house. and mr Grant was so kind as to see me always to attend service in Sunday or in other time in the week. and being this bless with a nother us good a master as the former and also with a kind and graceful minister I soon became different to what I was before. a little while after this I was Baptized and admitted in society on trial and some time serve as an interpreter in sunday evening or in Wednesday evening till I was fully engaged for that purpose. but at length I given the salary to the cause. One Sunday evening in June 1824 I heard mr Morgain preached in a native house just neare where the mission is now built. under this sermon my conscience was awakened. trouble ceased my mind. But thanks be to god like Jacob I wrestled with the angel and prevail. I found pardon a liberty with God. the next morning I went and sett the minister of it. some time after this I became the class leader and a local preacher About October in 1831

I was taken assistant missionary this was in the time of the Barr point war.[15] I being one the Bathurst Millitia much time was not allowed to enter fully into my employment untill the nine of March 1832. I embarked with the Revd. William Moister to commence the mission on MacCarthys Island where I been labouring till the Revd Thomas Dove was sent up and after him the Revd William Fox. our excellent minister who has been labouring two years amoung and who we now sorry to part with. Thank God their labour has net been in vain in the Lord.

MacCarthy's Island
April 9. 1839
J. Cupidon

CASE TWENTY-TWO

Mary Ann Gay

Author: Mary Ann Gay
Region of birth: Gorée, Senegal
Date of birth: Unknown
Year of enslavement: Born into slavery
Place of writing: St. Mary's Island, The Gambia
Date of Account: 24 May 1839
Year of death/last known year of activity: Unknown
Published: No/unknown

Source: MMS, Sierra Leone Correspondence, Fiche Box 25, Box No. 280, 'Sierra Leone Odds Papers', Fiche No. 1880, #11

Introduction

Mary Ann Gay's testimony is unique as the only account in this volume and uncovered in the MMS archive for West Africa which presents a woman's testimony in the first person. Mary Ann was born into slavery on Gorée, unlike the other narrators in this section who were born free on the African mainland before being enslaved and taken to Gorée before reaching Britain's Gambia colony. Women were a majority of the enslaved labour force in the households of both Gorée and Saint-Louis.[1] Enslaved women, including Mary's mother, played an important role as producers of both goods and people, reproducing the enslaved population.[2]

Mary's account, like that of Jack Macumba in Case 20 and John Gum in Case 23, mentions the role of a Captain Lloyd. Captain Edward Lloyd, along with his brother Lieutenant-Colonel Richard Lloyd, had been stationed at Senegal. Richard was British commander of Gorée from 1804 to 1808 which Edward was captain in the Royal African Corps stationed at

Gorée. At Gorée they formed partnerships with the island's wealthy *signarés*. Both men moved to The Gambia from Gorée, bringing with them mixed-race women and children as well as enslaved domestics. The Lloyds subsequently became one of the wealthiest colonists and landowners in Bathurst.[3] The eminent historian of The Gambia, Frances Mahoney, describes the Lloyds as 'autocratic patriarchs in a complex extended family system, who could bring pressure to bear upon the colonial government'.[4] In her account, Mary describes how she 'lived in Captain Lloyd's house because he was married to my masters Daughter and was there to mind him and his wife and children's till he took his son and Daughter and put them in my hand to take them to the school'.

Like Jack Macumba's statement, Mary Ann Gay's account speaks to the ambiguity of slave status within The Gambia and especially among those enslaved to French subjects from Gorée. Like John Cupidon, Mary was enslaved to a woman on Gorée reflecting the role of women in the colonial economy of a French port city.[5]

Text

Statement of Mary Ann Gay

I Mary Ann was born in the Island of Goree to a bond mother belongeth to a lady named Mary Tress. theirfore I was is slavery till I was married and got eight children. and their father took one of them which was a man child named Gabriel Piere to Senegall to teach him to read and write. till the time he can read and write well then his father brought him to Goree again and ask his master to give him his son and he pay his freedom then the master say except they give her ten slaves or the value of then she cant let him have freedom then his father go and try till God helpeth him and he got eight slaves then it only left two more to make it ten and he brough these slaves to goree. the sames day his father arrived to Goree with these slaves the son died and after this all my children died till if left one. the one that left come to St Mary's for some work and was sick here very bad and Captain Chown sent for me to come and take care of my son. then I got unto a vessel and came to St Mary's and was here with my son till my son died and was buryed by the Revd. Richard Marshall. and I left alone. the time I came from goree I lived in Captain Lloyd's house because he was married to my masters Daughter and was there to mind him and his wife and children's till he took his son and Daughter and put them in my hand to take them to the school so I continued to take them till one day the minister called Mr. Marshall ask me what for I can come to chapel then I tell him that when I was in Goree I go to chapel every time and he asked me if I got some children and I told him that I been got eight children and they all died and tis you who burried the last one lately and he ask me if I dont think that I soon die myself also and I told him said yes and he told me to come every time I see the flag up in the evening and in the morning and so I begin to come every time without missing then I heard him Preach and I feel that I was a wicked woman in my heart. and so I begin to pray to God that he would save me from the wrath to come till I feel in my heart that God had save me and forgive me all my sins and at last Mr. Marshall was sick and I come in the mission house to mind him in his sickness till God has taken him from this world of tears to a better world and I left in the mission house with Mrs. Marshall and her son and got to sleep their till Mrs. Marshall left for England and I was left alon. untill seven months time before the Revd. Wm. Moister came from England then John Cupidon take me to him and tell him all my character and tell him that I am their mother in the Gospel and so Mr. Moister loved me much and take me as a mother and so am I and whenever he sick I come to mind him and his wife then when I see how the people of God love me and make me to hear the word of God I said that I dont want to go back to Goree and when my master heard it he send for me to come and I wount go. now all the things I have in Goree my master take them all and take from me the value of eight slaves instead of me but I left all with them because the God whome I seeking every time his great deal better then all these things. after this they sent to me to pay them for my freedom but I refuse till when the time the Revd. Wm. Fox came from England my master heard that these missionarys love me so much she send me a letter to tell the missionarys to pay for my freedom but I wount and wount let no body know any thing about it untill now when Mr. Fox come to St Mary's and see me and hear every thing about me he love me so much as Mr. Marshall and Moister and took me as his own mother now my heart and mind was increase in the church of God more and more so I love the house of God more and never mist to come in his house then Mr. Lloyd called me and tell me that I am a foolish woman now because I go to church too much and tell him said yes because I want my sins to be pardoned and so I continued in the way of God and to tell all my fellow neighbors to come and serve God for he is the God of all gods. and when some of the people which I live with in one yard begin to come with in the house of God Mr. Lloyd call me again and tell he that I want to turn all his people's heart to come to church and I tell him that I dont carry any body with me only who want to go himself. and when Mr. Lloyd heard it he take the key's of the gates to lock them himself while I went out to church. so some time when I know that today shall be meeting I go to the mission house and sleep their untill one morning at five oclock I awaked into sleep I went to Mr. Lloyd to ask him the key of the gate because I want to go to the prayer meeting he wount let me have it because he know that I want to go to the chapel. and therefore I went to my house and kneel down on my knees and pay to God with all my heart and weep before him now when the day was light I came and tell Mr. Fox all about it he told me said never mind tanta soon all done away then one day I sleep in the mission house and at midnight I was sick and was very ill and in the morning Mr. Fox tell me to stop in the mission house but I tell him that I can go to our house then I go and lay in my house and Mr. Fox lend to the Docter to come and see and when the Docter came Mr. Lloyd sent the Doctor back and tell him that she dont live in my house this time she is in the mission house and the Docter go back and when Mr. Fox and his wife come to see me they ask me if the Docter been here I tell him that I dont him and he send Piere Sallah[6] to go and ask the Docter why he not come then the Docter till all what Mr. Lloyd tell him so I say down with my sickness and Mr. Fox and Mrs. Fox was so good and to help Poor people he got to look after me he and his wife and do all I want for me till in his Eternal Mercy raised me from the bed of sickness. one time again Mr. Lloyd got some plabour with one of his men. the man been got his wife in Mr. Lloyd's house till his wife conceived and bare a child and about one week the child Died and some one go and tell the man that Mr. Lloyd make till his child Died and the man was wax and go to the governor and required it to the governor. then Mr. Lloyd said that tis me that go and tell the man that Mr. Lloyd been flog your wife and kick her in the back side that make you child die and say that to me who tell the man to go to the governor and report him but all this I never think it in my heart nor do it but God knows all our heart this was the cation Mr. Lloyd strive me in his house then I came to the mission house and weep before Mr. Fox and Mr. Fox heard my cry and tell me to come to the mission house and live their and I tell him say yes then Mr. Fox send all the school Boy's to go and fetch my things from Mr. Lloyd's house and now I am in the mission House. thanking God and Mr. Fox also because the greate things which he done for me here all me Trouble's and Trials ended.

Mary Ann Gay's
Statement
Saint Mary's River Gambia
24 May 1839

CASE TWENTY-THREE

John Gum

Author: John Gum
Region of birth: Wolof
Date of birth: Unknown
Year of enslavement: c. 1812
Place of writing: St. Mary's Island, The Gambia
Date of Account: 28 May 1839
Year of death/last known year of activity: Last mentioned in Methodist archive in 1859[1]
Published: No/unknown

Source: MMS, Sierra Leone Correspondence, Fiche Box 25, Box No. 280, 'Sierra Leone Odds Papers', Fiche No. 1880, #10

Introduction

John Gum was a formerly enslaved African and local preacher with the MMS's Gambia mission. Gum's account does not name his country of birth. He writes instead that he 'was caught by a King named Macodoo Maia in the time of famine' and sold to an enslaver at Gorée.[2] Based on his account, he probably reached Gorée around 1812. Gum first visited The Gambia in 1816 on a voyage led by Captain Alexander Grant.[3]

Gum likely began attending the Methodist church around 1828, as he reports first attending the sermons of the Rev. Samuel Dawson. He was baptized a few months later. In 1834, the Rev. William Fox noted that Gum would make a good addition to the small group of native preachers working for the MMS.[4] The mission could not hire him immediately, however, because Gum was still enslaved. The next year, Gum and a few other enslaved West Africans at Saint Mary's Island sent a scathing criticism of the institution of slavery in the British Gambia to Lieutenant-Governor George Rendall.[5] It is likely that the MMS provided some financial assistance so that Gum could purchase his freedom soon after. Once he was manumitted, the MMS hired John Gum as a local preacher.

Text

Statement of John Gum

I John Gum was a free born in our Country and was caught by a King named Macodoo Maia in the time of famine he catch me and sold me in the Island of Goree by a man named Malick Cumba which was a head man for the mason's then I was in goree about four years then Captain Grant brought my master and I to go and Establish James Fort.[6] and paying me as a labourer for four Dollars a month and my master got to take my wages and from thence we came to Saint Mary's to Establish it and in the rainey season we go back to goree and after the rains we come back again to St Mary's and about four years Captain Lloyd send me to goree to work for him then I tell him that I cant go then he send some conistable to take me to the vessel. so I go on board and go to Goree and work for him about eight months for three shillings and nine pence a day but I dont receive no money from him in the work I work for him he got the money till now and after this I came to St. Mary's again and took my journey to run away to my country and was caught again by some Mindingoes and brought me to St. Mary's again at the same time Captain Findle[7] was a King governor in St. Mary's. then they want me to go to goree. then I run and go to this King and tell him and he told me that you cant go. go and set down nobody cant take you to goree if you dont want to go. the same time Samuel Dawson was here. till one day on wenesday evening I come to the Chapel and heard him preach in the twenty first case of Saint John at the fifteen verse and John Cupidon was to interpret it in the Joloof language then I heard what they say then the words entred in my heart after the meeting I go home and was thinking it all night and not went to sleep I was in a great hurry that the day where light quick till I go and ask the minister what shall I do to be saved because I know in my self that I was a great wicked sinner. and when the day was light I came to him and ask him master and he tell me say said on John then I ask him said what must I do to be saved because I heard the words which you said last night and they entered in my heart and I know that if I die now where I am I shall lost for ever because I am a sinner and he told me that whenever I see the flag up I come to chapel and every friday when the meeting is concluded you stay and I will tell you what must you do to be saved then I tell him that I want to be baptize and he tell me that before I baptize you you must meet in class till three months before I can baptize you because I must look at you first wether you are a good man or not. so I continued to come in the member till three months without missing then he baptize me then some times if I got time I come to the school to learn to read because that time I dont know any thing about reading then I continued in this way till I feel in my heart that all my sins were forgiven then a Missionary come from England named Richard Marshall[8] was a very good man and I come to see him then Mr. Dawson tell me that this man is a good man he will take good care of you to lead you and teach you to read as I am. then Mr. Dawson return to England and left me with Mr. Marshall and I live with him and he got to teach me to read very well till he died the time he was sick I never went away from him till the same day he his taken up to heaven then I weep for him very much. then after seven months time the Revd. William Moister came from England and meet me in the member and love me very much. he always come to Mr. Lloyd's house and see me and to teach me their because I got no time to go to school because I was engaged in slavery. after this I got a wife named Mary Joab and he baptize her he was her godfather and Mary Ann Gay was her godmother and he married us. and she lived with me about eight months and she died then I was without a wife till about one year and eight months before I married to one of Mr. Lloyd's girl named Siloy Sair which got to look after Mr. Lloyd's children. now what I gave this girl before I married her is about thirty dollars. and the same time I went to married her I give her thirty Dollars again. it was the time of the Revd. William Fox[9] this man was so good to me he help me much and love me so much too. he married me with my wife then Mrs. Fox love my wife so much too then I live with girl till she got Belly about seven months time till one day she dressing Mr. Lloyd's Daughters and the little one go and got to dirty herself in the dust then my wife was wax and flog the child because if the child dirty herself her mother got to flog my wife thenfore my wife flog her then her mother was wax and tell Mr. Lloyd about it then Mr. Lloyd came and was very grieve and flog my wife till he has kick her on the back side then my wife fall down and was not able to get up till some people take her up and carry her in her house and she was lie down now all this I was not present their but been working in the chapel that Mr. Fox build and at nine oclock I came home to get some breakfast then I met her lay down then I ask her what is the matter with you and she hide this from me not want me to know it but tell me that she dont feel well her back side pain her then I tell her to try to get up and walk about because it is not fit for you you to lay down always and after a few day's she brought in bed and the child was hurt and the child died. then one old woman in the yard with me she came and took the child and wash him and bring him to me and tell me to look where the child hurt then we find that he was hurt on the back side and his breast. the old woman told me that it is the kick that Mr. Lloyd kick your wife when she god Belly that is the reason your son died then I went to Charles Grant tell him all about it then Mr. Grant called for his jury's in the same night and the Docter to required it then the Docter took the child and look at him and told them that the child his hurt you better call his mother and ask her if she ever fell down when she got Belly then the ask her and she said she never fell down except the time Mr. Lloyd kick her on the back side and she fall down that was the only time I fell down. Then when they know that Mr. Lloyd got the fault they all assembled themself to help him and want to do me bad. then they help him till they hid all this Fault then begin to trouble me then Mr. Fox helped me till they not do me nothing again then after this Mr. Lloyd took my wife and carry her one the other side of the Island to mind his Field and to work at the Farm he got their. all this he do he do it to punish me but God was on my side to take my part. I was in the mission house working and saw they carring my wife away then I came to met them to stop my wife. Then Mr. Lloyd's son called Edward Lloyd took hold of her and pluck her out of my hand and took hold of my shirt collor and tore it. Then I let him because I not want to fight Then I went to the governor George Rendell[10] to tell him but I dont find him because he was distant to some other country then I went to the secretary and tell him all about it but he told me that he got no business with the marrieg people. Then my wife to go this farm and was their about one month and five day's then I was to perish with hungry but an old woman named Mary Ann Gay got to give me some thing to eat. Then when the governor came Mr. Fox tell me to go and let the the governor know about it Then I go and tell him and he told me to go and fetch her Then I go and when I go I tell her to come and go home but she told me that she was afraid to come for when she come with out her master know it they shall flog her.

The same day they take my wife to this Farm I came out of Mr. Lloyd's house and take my box away and want to take my wife's they wount not let me have it. but I take mine and carry it to Jack Macumba's house. Then my wife was in this Field till one month and five day's before she come back and pass in the house where I was and give my compliments and go to her master's house to sleep and in the morning she came and see me again and go to see Mr. and Mrs. Fox then Mr. Fox told her that you see your husband is went away our of your master's for your sake theirfore you must go after him dont be afraid of nothing I will help you and god shall help you also then she came and set down to Jack Macumba's house where I was and in the evening her master sent a girl to call her and she told the girl that she cant go then the girl go and they send another girl to call her again and she tell the girl that she cant come I live with my husband and theirfore when these girls go home Mr. Lloyd's son named Edward and another gentleman named John Hughes[11] came and met me reading and my wife was sitting behind me and they went behind me and took hold of her to take her by forst but she wount go then John Hughes answered and said that if the woman been belong to him he shall make her go by forst then I get up and took hold of my wife then Edward Lloyd told me that he know what Mr. Fox want to do he want to make every slave free but he cant then the master of the House get up and told them to go out of his yard then they go out and in the morning I go and tell Mr. Fox about it then he told me to go to the governor and tell him then I went to tell the governor but I met Edward their was complaining and I tell the governor all my business and he tell me to go with my wife wherever I want and set down their with her no body cant Trouble you again then I came and set down with her in a very good way but there is many enemies between me and her. I lived with her till she bare me a son called William Fox. now the place where I was I not been pleased with the master of the house because it was belong to Mr. Lloyd then I came out of this place and tell Mr. Wilkinson about it and he told me to go to the chapel yard at Soldier Town and make my house their then I went and make my house their and their I live untill now then Mr. Wilkinson died. Then the Revd. Thos. Wall came from england and and meet me their and was a very good man to me. Then my wife hare another son called Thos. Wall and not many day's he died and the Elder one named Wm. Fox was sick and about six days he died also Then about one week my wife run away to her master's house because some onee tell her that if she dont get her freedom she cant never go to Goree and see her mother and Family. but if you run away and go to your master if your husband not get no body to work for him he soon pay for your freedom then she runaway for the sake of what they tell her and go live with her master Then I went to fetch her and her master tell me that before she come I must pay her freedom First then she must come back. and pay for my freedom also Then I come and tell it to Mr. Fox and tell him that I not care for myself because I am a man but she is a woman but Please lent me some money to pay her freedom and if you got some work I work you will render it to what I work then Mr. Fox tell me that he very sorry for me but go and ask them how much they will charge for her freedom and I will pay it for you out of mind own pocket then I went and ask her master. then her master called her and tell her about it and she said that she is very glad if I pay her freedom then she shall got lieve to go where ever she likes. then her master told me to give her two hundred Dollars before she give me her freedom's paper then I come and tell Mr. Fox then Mr. Fox tell me that he not able to give two hundred Dollars but he can give them one hundred if they like because she is not a man she cant work as a man but if they want he can give them one hundred but if not I cant give more then it so we left her in her master's house untill now.

Where I am now I am ashame to go out in the town for the great trouble which my wife do to me. I have do her good but she like to hear what my enemies tell her till she do it and make me to walk amongst my enemies with this great trouble.

But thanks be to God for his mercy endured forever for we know that all things work together for good to them that I love God.

This is the way I continued and thanking Mr. Fox for he is very kind as to fight for such a Poor fellows as we. but God in his great mercy shall render it to him at the last day. May God bless him and all the missionarys who send him here to Preach the gospel to our ears and to help such a Poor Fellowe's as we are.

    here I have end
   My Statement
    John Gum Local Preacher
    St. Mary's River Gambia
     May 28th, 1839

PART THREE
East Africa

CASE TWENTY-FOUR

George David

Author: George David
Region of birth: Ngindo
Date of birth: *c.* 1843–4
Year of enslavement: *c.* 1855–6
Place of writing: Frere Town
Date of account: 29 November 1876
Year of death/last known year of activity: Died at Frere Town, 28 September 1884
Published: No/unknown

Source: Biography of George David, 29 November 1876, CA5/O6/7

Introduction

George David was a 'Bombay African' and catechist with the CMS in East Africa. George was born *c.* 1843–4 among the Ngindo people of present-day coastal Tanzania. George – who identified his birth name as Kitenga Sholo, Wa Alingoeka – does not specify a place of birth, though he stated that he was born to the west of Kilwa Kisiwani on the Swahili Coast. After his enslavement, George was taken to Kilwa and then Zanzibar *c.* 1855–6. Kilwa was a key port city, and much of its slave trade was directed to Zanzibar, as both Kilwa and Zanzibar were under Omani control. The port of Kilwa was one of the centres of the East African slave trade. After the Sultan of Oman settled on Zanzibar around 1840, the slave trade from Kilwa expanded to meet the increasing need for workers on the clove and palm plantations of Zanzibar and Pemba.[1] The activities of Arab traders in the Red Sea also created a vast slave mart at Zanzibar, where the enslaved were brought from present-day Uganda, Kenya, Tanzania and Malawi.[2]

At Zanzibar, George was 'bought by an Arab from Muscat' and later 'taken to a place called Shargi' (likely Sharjah on the Persian Gulf in the present-day United Arab Emirates). Coastal cities such as Sharjah relied largely on revenues from pearl diving, which in turn was dependent on enslaved shipboard pearl divers. The growing demand for slave labour in pearl diving during the second half of the nineteenth century meant that the African population of the coast grew to one quarter of the total population by the turn of the twentieth century.[3]

George David was captured by a vessel of the Indian Navy, which made a small number of captures between the Red Sea and Persian Gulf in the 1850s.[4] He arrived at Bombay in early 1858. Along with the Bombay Africans William Jones and Ishmael Semler (both mentioned in this account), George David attended the Indo-British and Robert Money schools in Bombay and trained for a time at Sharanpur. The three men were among seven Bombay Africans selected by Isenberg and Price to assist Rev. Johann Rebmann and the CMS mission station at Rabai. Rabai, located seventeen miles to the West of Mombasa, had been founded in 1844 and was the oldest CMS station in East Africa.[5] David, Jones and Semler – who had excelled in their studies at Bombay – were sent to Rabai as catechists. George David married in December 1864, though his wife died within a month. He later remarried to Priscilla Christian, who had grown up at Sharanpur and had been sent to Rabai at the same time as David.

In 1873–4, the CMS decided to expand their mission's presence in East Africa by setting up stations with the assistance of formerly enslaved converts. In August 1876, James Abner Lamb who had recently become the head of the mission transferred George David to Frere Town.[6] David wrote the account below at Frere Town some three months after his arrival there. Eventually, George purchased large amounts of land just outside of the mission estate at Freretown and became part of an emerging mission-trained middle class. The missionary James Abner Lamb anticipated that George David might become the region's first bishop, 'the Crowther of the East Coast'.[7] But George, along with many of the educated Bombay Africans, fell out with John Streeter, appointed Lay Superintendent in 1877, who defined more authoritarian methods and punishments within the mission. In light of Streeter's harsh discipline and a more widespread context of racial condescension towards the Bombay Africans, George co-authored and signed a letter to the British vice-consul in Zanzibar accusing Streeter of exceeding his legal authority, leading to an investigation which recommended Streeter's removal. At the same time, the Bombay Africans wrote a long memorandum to the CMS Parent Committee in London proposing to be stationed in a different location or removed completely from the mission.[8] Ultimately, George submitted his resignation to the mission in 1882. He died at Frere Town on 28 September 1884.[9]

Text

According to your request, I hereby send you a short account of my biography.

The tribe to which I belong is very little known at present; the name of the country is called Ngindo, and the inhabitants are called Wangindo. The country is situated to the west of Kiloa, on the mainland, to the south of Mombasa about 5 degrees from here. As the African parents do not keep reckoning the birth of their children more then two years and a half, so I cannot exactly tell in which year I was born; but I can guess the year, from the time I was taken to be about 14 or 15 years of age. This being in the year 1858, when I look back I consider myself to have been born some where about 1843 or 1844; during the time when the Parent Committee were commencing the mission among the Wanyika. Before I became a slave, one day, my mother told me that a set of men of the same tribe made war with them for some cause or other which I have forgotten now. In this war, my grandfather suffered some loss, either of cattles or men. This loss which my grandfather suffered was unjust one; and so when peace was made my grandfather demanded the loss back. The men who had caused him the loss, agreed to pay him back. But they did not returned him, in the expected time; and so my grand father together with his kinsfolk were displeased, and made up their minds to pay themselves by catching some of their children when good opportunity avails them. This determination remained in their hearts, till I was born, and became a youth of 11 or 12 years of age. When a man belonging to the same parties, of whom my grandfather demands the loss; came with a slave woman to his own village, whether through forgetfulness or whether he had not been informed of it, I do not know; and so he took the woman from the man with the consideration as God having brought her to him for the purpose. The reason for taking her was explained to the owner of the slave, which quite satisfied him, being just according to African ways of dealings. But during the time, my grandfather was making the mischief, my mother and I, were in the township of the man whose slave he had taken. My mother's second husband, whom I call a stepfather, and the owner of the slave, which her father had taken were brothers in law. The man hearing that we were already in his township, he lost no time of returning home with the news to his relation; on his arrival at home, he and his relations agreed to take me instead of their slave; and so he came to our house on the same day, in the evening with three others. They countenance of the men, and the way they were talking with my parents, and the way they sat in the room my parents knew that they were up to some mischief; and so my father told my mother to take me to the bush outside for private business, in order that I may not trouble them in the night.

This was merely a plan for our escaping, which my mother at once obeyed. But as soon as my mother got up from her seat, to take me out, the three men also stood up, as if to pay her respects; but as soon as I got up also, from my seat, I was immediately in the enemies hands. Though three men rested upon my father alone and yet they had to struggle hard to pluck me from his hands. Having got me out from the house, one of the men threw me on his shoulders and started off from the compound, while the other two, were still pushing my father. On the way, about a quarter of a mile from home, I threw myself off from the shoulders of the man, and got myself among the grass, and tried to get home again; but as the others who were left behind had now come, they besieged me on every side, and so no way was left for my escaping, and so I was found again; and they paid me well with slaps. The next morning my parents went over to my grandfather to fetch the woman, which he had taken to redeem me; when my grandfather and mother heard they tidings from my parents, about me, the slave woman was at once given to my parents to convey it over to the man for my redemption; after three days, the woman was brought back to the owner by my parents and I was redeemed.

After a year or two had past, our tribe was constantly visited by Mafwiti (another name for Masai) who for want of cattles, and slaves troubled the people very much. My step father and his brother in law having become friends again, they agreed to go a journey together with family, about two days from home. And the place where they were going was and isolated one through spear and shield of the Mafwiti; their going was merely in search of poor weak sheep which escaped the death of Mafwiti's spear and shield to take them as slaves. Their wishes were accomplished, and we were brought to the desired place. But instead of their remaining here and getting what they came for, my father's brother in law insisted on their going further in search of slaves and properties which he thought the people for the fear of the Mafwiti had hiden in the forest. Through love, and close union with his brother in law, my father was very much blinded of what his friend intended to do to him. Leaving this lonesome desert, we descended down to a river called Muhuehi which very likely takes its beginning from Lake Nyasa, and runs down through uhiao country and ours, and falls to the south of Kilwa. This river, I believe if it should be well explored it will be an easy route for travelling by boat to my country. But as I saw very little of it, and knew very little of it, I cannot speak with great confidence about the facility of the journey in boats. When I stood on the banks of the river with my parents my mother said to me, my son, as soon as we cross this river in a boat we are lost for ever; and her words were true. When we were on the other side of the river, three or four days after our arrival, my father together with his brother in law accompanied the owners of the town who went about hunting wild buffaloes on the other side of the river from where we had come. While they were hunting, my father's brother in law gave orders to the people to tie up my father, either for killing or selling him; but he knew their stratagem, and pretended as having seeing an animal little lower down the hill on which they were, his tip toe walk, and his attentive to the bow and arrows, as he walked down, made them all believe that he was seeing an animal in reality, but as soon, he found himself a good space from them, he started running on the other side of the hill; and standing on the top of the hill, he said to his friend, I know what you are about, but you are too late to catch me now, good bye, I am carrying the news home; my wife and children I know are now become your weakest prey. And so my father went home alone whether he reached our village or no, God Almighty knows. The name of my step father, and his brother in law, I have quite forgotten them. But my grandfather, and my real father and mother, I still remember their names; my grandfather was called Alingwira, my father, Alingoeka, and hence my name was called, Kitenga Sholo, Wa Alingoeka; and my mother, Akilanga Lengwira. Both my grandfather & my father died while I was still with them at home. My father die of small poxs, my grandfather I do not know of what he died off. When the men returned from hunting, they took hold of me first, and then my mother leaving behind my younger brother, he was about 6 or 7 years old, when we parted. His tears for us, and ours for him, was all vain, there was no one here to pity us or say a word of consolation. And so all of us hence, became slaves in one day. I was sold to the Swahili (whom we call Wanasara) who then brought me, together with the others down to Kilwa, unknown region to us. We stayed here about a week, and then left for Zanzibar, in a dhow, this was about the year 1855, or 1856. At Zanzibar we were sold at the market to different masters. I was bought by an Arab from Muscat, who then brought me over to Muscat together with the other slaves of his and friends. At Zanzibar I remained only a month I think. And when we came to Muscat, I was given to a women, of about 24, or 25 years of age; whether I was bought for her, or whether I was made present to her I do not know, but this one thing I know, that she loved me very much indeed; she quite made up her mind, to keep me for herself. But God, who wished to reach me to better friends & better home, opposed her wishes; by striking me with severe sore eyes, which made her afraid of loosing me by death, and so she made up her mind to sell me if I ever should recover again. As soon as I was recovered again, I was put together with the others, who were about to be taken to a place called Shargi, near Bassadore, in Arabia. We were in all 28, slaves on board the buggalow; we landed at Shargi in the night about 9 or 10 O clock. We were immediately taken on shore, for fear of being seeing by the man of war. However, the news of our arrival was soon spread in the town in the morning. About 8 O' clock in the morning, an African man came on horse back, to the house where we had been placed, he took me and another boy aside. We were brought to an old Arab, who looked to be a man of influence over the others, we were nicely treated here by him. We stayed with him about a week, we then saw a ship of two masts approaching the harbour; we were told that she was coming to take us away, we feared very much to go in her, thinking we were going to be eaten. And as soon, as the ship anchored; we were conveyed over to her; together with the rest which we had left in the house where we landed. The name of the ship was called Constance, a small skoona from Bombay.[10] And this skoona brought us to Bombay, where we were put into government schools in the month of March, 1858. In the month of November 1860, we were taken by Mr. Deimler a missionary of the C.M.S. to be trained for East African mission.[11] We stayed with him 10 months under instruction, and then we were sent to Nasik under Mr Isenberg care; where I learnt the trade of a mason and black smith.[12] In 1864, December 19th we got married; and Lady Frere invited us to her house, from whom we received each couples a handsome Bible, to convey it over with us to Africa, in remembrance of her. Few days after our marriage, my wife fell sick so much so, that I was obliged for her sake to remain behind; while William Jones & Ishmael Semler proceeded. On the 26th of January 1865, my wife expired. On the 23rd of May, I also left Bombay, & followed others who had gone before to Mombasa to join Mr. Rebmann. On the 17th of July I reached Kisulutini, and I was glad to see my friends again personally.* After two months past Ishmael lost his wife Grace by name; and he was send back to India to marry again, and to remain there. In 1870, William Jones also lost his wife, he was also send back to India to marry again, and to remain there. And so I was again left alone, in Africa also. Under Mr Rebmann I remained patiently labouring for God, among the Wanyika for 11 years; 23 August 1876, I was removed from Kisulutini by Mr Lamb, and brought over to Frere Town, where I am now labouring with him, in our Master's vineyard.

I remain
Dear Sir,
Your obedient servant
George David

Frere Town
November 29th, 1876

---

*On the 14th of January 1866, I got married again, to one of the spinster which came with us from Bombay, Priscilla Christian by name; with whom I got five children, three daughters & two sons, of which one the Lord took to himself on the 8th of February, 1870.

CASE TWENTY-FIVE

William Henry Jones

Author: William Henry Jones (copied by Charles William Isenberg)
Region of birth: Yao people, Lake Malawi
Date of birth: *c.* 1840
Year of enslavement: *c.* 1850
Place of writing: Sharanpur, Nashik, India
Date of account: 7 August 1861
Year of death/last known year of activity: Died at Rabai, 4 July 1904
Published: 'East African Youths in Bombay', *Church Missionary Gleaner*, Vol. XII, 1862, 6–8.

Source: CMS East Africa Mission, C I3/O38/65D, Autobiographies: William Jones and Ishmael Semler, 1861

Introduction

William Henry Jones was born around 1840 and identified as a member of the 'Wahião' (Yao) from the area near Lake Malawi. Yao territory centred on the region of north-west Mozambique, bounded approximately by the Rivers Lucheringo to the west, Luambala to the south, Lujenda to the east, and Ruvuma to the north. By at least the early seventeenth century, the Yao occupied extensive territory extending from the south-east of Lake Malawi across the Ruvuma.[1] Yet Megan Vaughan describes the Yao as 'a newish ethnicity in the eighteenth century', who were likely formed from elements of the old Maravi kingdom as they pushed into Makua/Lomwe territory in present-day Mozambique.[2] Along with the Makua, they were the foremost slave traders of the region.

Jones was about ten years old when his stepfather sold him to his uncle in order to settle a debt. The uncle took the young boy and tried unsuccessfully to sell him at the slave market of Kilwa. From Kilwa they travelled overland and was eventually purchased by an Omani Arab slave trader at Zanzibar.[3] Jones's new enslaver could not find a buyer for his new captive. They instead returned to the mainland and journeyed through the Zigua country in central Tanzania. Failing again to offload his captive, Jones's enslaver took them both to Zanzibar where after a period of four months he was able to broker a sale. Fred Morton has described Jones's journey as 'the most remarkable experience of a child slave' among testimonies from East Africa and has estimated that he must have walked some fifteen to sixteen hundred kilometres on the mainland.[4]

At Zanzibar, Jones was forced onto a dhow destined for Muscat. The Royal Navy intercepted the dhow and directed it to Bombay. Jones reached Bombay in 1850 and was placed under CMS care at the Indo-British Institution in 1854. He transferred to the CMS African Asylum at Sharanpur, where he wrote the following 'self history' in 1861. The extant version of the account was copied by the missionary Charles William Isenberg. At Sharanpur, Jones oversaw the care of many of the recently emancipated youth sent to the African Asylum in the years after his arrival.[5] Here Jones also got married to an Ethiopian Galla woman liberated from a slave vessel, within whom he had a son, John. Following her death in 1870, he married his second wife, Sally Jones, in 1876 (Figure 3).[6]

In 1864, Jones was one of several Liberated Africans sent to Mombasa to assist the CMS missionary Johannes Rebmann. He worked with the CMS mission in East Africa for the next thirty-four years, principally at Rabai. He undertook several recruitment trips to India between 1878 and 1881 to convince other Africans in Bombay to return to East Africa. But as with George David, Jones came to resent the racism, condescension and hostility of European agents of the mission, in particular the Rev. A. G. Smith at Rabai. Further tensions over salary and a property dispute over a piece of land at Rabai led Jones to resign. 'I fought for Rabai,' Jones wrote to the Parent Committee, 'I fought for the slaves with their masters; I did all I could for mother CMS; and now after many years to be told I have proved myself an unfaithful servant was unbearable, hence I resigned.'[7] In late 1898, he took up a post with the British colonial government with a considerably higher wage. Much like Samuel Crowther and George David, William Jones survived the middle passage and climbed the mission ranks, only to feel the alienation of ascendant racial prejudices of the Victorian era. Jones died at Rabai on 4 July 1904.[8] His two sons, William 'Willie' Jones and James 'Jimmy' Jones, both had significant lives within Kenya's Christian intelligentsia. William became a pioneer in education while James set up a printing press at Freretown, thereby creating the first independent African press in eastern Africa.[9] The press produced much of the religious and educational material for missions throughout eastern Africa in both English and Kiswahili.

Text

Autobiography of William Jones a Native Mhiāo of the Wahiāo negro tribe which inhabit the country north of Waniasa lake.

W. Jones arrived in Bombay in 1853, when he entered the African Asylum, newly formed by some Xian friends, chiefly by the Rev. G. Candy and Mr. Theodore Zorn.[10] The Asylum for the for African boys was then at Mr. Zorn's house at Warley hill, till the death of Mrs. Zorn, who was the real agent and fostering souls of it.[11] Immediately on her death, in 1854, which but for one or two days preceded Mr. Zorn's commercial downfall, the boys asylum was transferred to the Indo British Institution; there W. Jones remained till the beginning or middle of 1856, when the Rev. G. Deimler took him & Ishmael Semler into his house on purpose of giving them special training for future usefulness if possible, in the C.M.S. East African Mission. Mr. Deimler sent these two youths last April to Sharanpur to give them the opportunity learning some trade at the Industrial Institution. W. Jones chose the profession of a blacksmith, & Ishmael Semler that of a carpenter. W. Jones is a stout, somewhat heavy boy, 5'4" high. I give here his remarkable history previous to his arrival in Bombay in his own words, copied from a paper drawn up by himself.

Self History

The Sultan of the country where I lived had a brother. These two brothers lived separately from their father, who lived at a place called Cromacunda, and founded different settlements for his 2 sons, one for himself.[12] As the two brothers lived far from one another, it happened upon a time that the eldest brother went and borrowed from the younger brother something, of which I can make no idea what it was. Accordingly, the time came when the thing lent was to be demanded from the eldest brother, and at that time he had nothing to pay the lender. Day after day he was urged to pay, but had nothing at hand then to pay. It happened once upon a time, the younger brother caught upon the beloved wife of the Sultan, and took her away to his own country. The Sultan, at this time did not know what to do, as to how he will be able to get his wife back again. Accordingly he thought in his mind that by giving me to his brother, as I was a stepson of his through his marriage with my mother, I might be favoured by him and bring his wife back, and keep me in her stead, till he goes to Waniasa to get slaves, through which he may give the slaves and get me back again. My mother was sorry for this though (only) for a moment, because she knew that I was not going among the strangers, but among the nearest relatives. And I sorrowfully wished my mother and brother a welcome (bid them farewell). I thought of seeing them again, though my real father died when I was young. When my stepfather came from Waniāsa he did not directly come to his brother take me back, but came over to Kiloa.[13] (His way, he said, about 1 month's journey, and he said that he was accompanied by 200 to 300 men, slaves.) To Kiloa they go yearly to sell slaves. At my father's brother's

I was treated kindly, and was regarded with every outward respect by everyone who knew me, and I lived with him about 8 or 10 months. As my stepfather did not directly come to take me, his brother thought that it was useless of keeping me till my stepfather comes from Kilwa to his country. Accordingly he took me and brought me to Kilwa to where my stepfather was. Here I met my father with his subjects with him, and my father's brother feared that if he went in the same house where my father was, they would steal me by night, and he would lose me; so he lived far from him. My father knew all this that I was brought over, to be sold; and he tried by every mode in his power, to get me back from his brother, but his brother would not give me up. He informed my father that it was too late for him to get me back again, and that was not the place where they agreed to pay each other's debts. Every day my father used to come with tears; and he tried & borrowed some other things from his friends in order to pay for me, but his brother would not consent to it. About one o'clock one night, my father's brother sold me to an Arab, and told him to remove me as quietly as possible to Zanzibar. From thence I lost my mother and a brother at home, and saw my father no more to the present day. Before I was brought to Kiloa, I fell into many persons hands though my father's brother wherever he used to take me with him for visiting different friends & relatives. In Zanzibar, for about four months my master took me & would to sell me, but no one bought me. From␣Zanzibar, I was taken to be sold at Wazegula with many others. Here many were sold, but I escaped from their hands, and I was not sold because no one wanted to buy me. From Wazequa we went to near Waniamesi – in all these places, for to be sold, but no one bought me; and I was brought back again to Wazequa, and from Wazequa to Zanzibar. Here I stayed about 4 months again, then, sailed for Maskat under Arabs, and finally caught by the English at Mascat at one o'clock in the night, and was safely conveyed to the land next day, where I and about 40 or 50 others lived, till the English ship came and brought us to Bombay. Had my uncle given me again to my father, I should not have had the opportunity of enjoying the privileges which I not enjoy in the Christian land. Yet I am not the worse but the better. Cruelly did the other fellow creatures suffer who came with me from my country; but I was free as a master of those who inflicted the pain on the other, ___ my uncle, who, though he sold me, yet he was kind enough to me little with inferior to my parents (little less kind than if he had been my parents). Every day nearly I think of my country, and I see my country spiritually where I lived, and all the other places I trodded upon; it is open before me more than what Bombay is now.

The above was written by Mr. Jones at my request and has been now copied by myself.

Sharanpur near Nasik

7 Aug., 1861

D. W. Isenberg

FIGURE 3 William Henry Jones c. 1876, with Sally Jones (wife, died 1877) and eldest son, Johnny. Courtesy of The John Rylands Research Institute and Library, The University of Manchester.

CASE TWENTY-SIX

Ishmael Semler

Author: Charles William Isenberg
Region of birth: Yao people, Lake Malawi
Date of birth: c. 1840[1]
Year of enslavement: c. 1843[2]
Place of writing: Sharanpur, Nashik, India
Date of account: 7 August 1861
Year of death/last known year of activity: Died in 1930s
Published: 'East African Youths in Bombay', *Church Missionary Gleaner*, Vol. XII, 1862, 6–8.

Source: CMS East Africa Mission, C I3/O38/65D, Autobiographies: William Jones and Ishmael Semler, 1861

Introduction

Ishmael Semler was, like William Henry Jones, a Yao Liberated African. His account, which he dictated to the missionary Charles William Isenberg, delineates at least eight years in slavery following his enslavement when 'a very little boy'. Semler was held in slavery within a few weeks' journey of his point of capture and, over a period of years, adopted the local language. He was later taken to Mozambique and 'employed in ship work'. This might have entailed scraping dhow hulls; the CMS *Register of Missionaries* described him as having been 'employed in a sailing ship as a boat boy'.[3] Semler was then brought to Inhambane where he was forced to work tapping coconut palms. Being returned to Mozambique, he was placed on board a dhow to Bombay. The Royal Navy intercepted the ship at sea and brought Semler to Bombay in 1850. He was placed at the Indo-British Institution in 1853.[4]

He was one of seven Bombay Africans – alongside William Jones and George David – selected to join the Rabai mission station as catechists. Semler grew disenchanted serving as Rev. Johann Rebmann's assistant and returned to Mombasa in 1873, being appointed catechist at Frere Town. Semler lived a long life, dying in the 1930s.[5]

Text

Ishmael Semler's History

Ishmael Semler is the youth whom the Rev. G. Deimler selected with William Jones from the African Asylum boys and took from the Indo-British Institution into his house, and sent afterwards in April 1861 to Sharanpur. He is of about the same age as W.J., thinner & somewhat more lively & somewhat impetuous. Height 5'2". The following particulars were communicated to me by him, when I examined & cross questioned the boys of the African Asylum.

Ishmael Semler is a Whião. He was taken captive in a war between the Wahião & Wariāsa Sultan's. His father escape; Ishmael was taken captive to Waniāsa and sold. From thence he was sold back to Whião. He stayed about 2 years with the man who bought him. That man died. His people sold him to a Makuba, with whom he stayed 3 years, until he had learned the Kikuba language perfectly. He was then a very little boy & was treated kindly. Thence he was sold with 400 slaves to Matipan, the inhabitants of which place were white, longhaired, and said to be cannibals. There they did not continue long, were taken to Mozambique where he – Ishmael – was employed in ship's work. Then he was taken & sold to a Brahman at the town of Mozambique.[6] The Brahman sold him to a mussulman captain of a merchant vessel, who took him to Cap-Twent; thence to Waniamban.[7] There he remained about 3 years working as a Toddy man (climbing palm trees, & making palm wine [Toddy]) Thence he returned to Mozambique, where he stayed about 1 month, and thence sailed for Bombay. Here he was examined by Government – together with about 20 other Africans. After having been 1 month at the Supreme Court & 3 months more at the Constables, he was taken by Messrs Candy & Zora into the African Asylum. Here he has chosen the trade of a carpenter, and is making good progress in it.

CASES TWENTY-SEVEN TO THIRTY-TWO

James Deimler, Paul Deimler, Lewis Brenn, David Rebmann, Cecil Mabruki, Duiah William

Authors: James Deimler, Paul Deimler, Lewis Brenn, David Rebmann, Cecil Mabruki, Duiah William
Region of birth: Makua (J. Daimler, Brenn, Rebmann); Mozambique (P. Deimler, Mabruki); unknown (D. William)
Date of birth: Unknown
Year of enslavement: Various
Place of writing: Frere Town
Date of account: 1880
Year of death/last known year of activity: Unknown
Published: No

Source: School Exam, 1880, CA 5/011, CMS

Introduction

The final six accounts in this volume are presented collectively as they were composed within a single classroom exam session among CMS schoolchildren at Frere Town in 1880. The exam included scripture, geography, translation, dictation, arithmetic and grammar and prompted the students to write an 'autobiography'. The six children were all liberated by a naval patrol from the same dhow, which had been at sea for only three days.[1] Three of the boys identify the intercepting warship as HMS *Thetis*, whose crew made their first dhow capture in the Red Sea in 1873 – while in transit to the China Station – and who were subsequently reassigned to the slave trade patrolling in East Africa.[2] HMS *Thetis*, under Captain Thomas Le Hunte Ward, was engaged on the East Indies station from 1873 to 1877. It is impossible to identify with certainty the intercepted dhow, which usually lacked ship names and were recorded in British sources simply by point of capture. But the six boys may have been on dhow which the *Thetis* intercepted in the Mozambique Channel on 9 September 1875 with 250 Africans on board, including seventy-five boys estimated to be under the age of ten.[3] The dhow was tried and condemned at the Vice-Admiralty Court at Zanzibar. Those on board were placed in charge of the CMS and taken to the mainland at Frere Town. From 1875 onwards Frere Town was established as the main reception centre for Liberated African resettlement in East Arica.[4]

Many accounts in this volume are by Africans writing many years after their enslavement and after many years of missionary instruction. Their accounts are filtered through both the imperfect remembrances of years and decades (often of a period of youth) combined with the filter of subsequent experience. The following accounts, though shorter and less detailed, were written by youths not long after their experiences of enslavement. While often lacking in geographical and chronological specifics, they have the particular quality of being accounts of childhood enslavement by those who were not yet adults. James Deimler and Lewis Brenn both identify their homeland as Makualand in the Lake Malawi region.[5] The Makua (or Makhuwa) are today the largest ethnolinguistic group in northern Mozambique. In the nineteenth century, Makua captives were deported from south-east Africa to both the Atlantic (Brazil, Cuba, Louisiana) and the Indian Ocean (Mascarene Islands, Madagascar). The surnames Deimler and Rebmann show that East African mission stations continued the practice started in Sierra Leone of renaming Liberated Africans after missionaries.

Text

James Deimler

I came from Makua country and my native place is Mkwaya. My father was fighting with the men of that place, and he was killed. My mother died from sickness. I had three sisters and one big brother. And this brother made counsel with the elders of that town, and sold me to another country named Mkoro. I lived there a few months and we took a journey. In the way we slept near the town, the men of that town came out against us with their guns. Our men were very strong and drove them away to their town, no one was killed. The reason why we fought is because we did not give them anything when we were passing through their town and we went on our journey and came to Mfusi.

I lived there about four days and then came to Barawa, and went into the dhow, many people were there in the dhow. We slept three days in the dhow, and we saw the man of war coming Thetis by name, Arabs put us down in the hold, and they took up the stones looking up and praying; and man of war fired one gun and rect the Arabs sail, they lowered down the boats. One Arab man wanted to jump into the water, and English man cut him with his sword. They took us all to their own ship and they gave us biscuits and water, but we didn't eat them so much because Arabs said, we were going to be eaten, by Europeans.

We saw the English men were treating us very well so we didn't believe about being eaten, we saw they were lying only.

On board the Thetis, there were two Makua boys who were able to speak with us.[6] Arabs were left in Zanzibar, and we came to Frere Town, where we are learning about God and Jesus Christ how he died for us.

Paul Deimler

I came from Mozambique and I had my three big brothers and two sisters and I was very careless boy and I went to the shore to play so the robbers caught me on the shore when I was playing on the shore and I cry very much indeed and they put sand in my mouth and I want to runaway to my father's house and they would not let me go, so they brought to Ubulu and sold me to Banyan, and I became his slave so that Banyan loved me very much indeed. As I grew very careless boy one day I went to play with others boys and my master put chain on my foot and I ranaway to my master's dow and they gave me food and eat it and give thanks unto them. I want to go to Mozambique very much, but they don't worship God. And we came on the shore and we saw the dhow on shore many grown up men, big boys, and small boys, and girls, and we entered and my master which stole gave me place to sleep there and we slept in the dow three days and I saw the man of war named Thetis, and they rush out the gun and the lead cut the mass and the mass fell down and the Arabs took stones and worship and said Lahilalu Mahomed they said three or four times and they put us in for we commanded by the Arabs saying go down go down, and I saw the boat coming near and catch the dow and I went to go in the boat to the English so I want to go in the boat and I fell in the sea and the English caught me up and I was in the ship and they gave me bread and sent it and then we were brought here to be taught to read to write and to sing at first I was not fond of this at all and God send teacher to teach me about him. I thank God that he has brought me here and taught me to this place and to send our teacher I thang very much I forget one thing to tell you that they deceived me, I am going to catch fowls and he said come let us go to catch fowls and the man said I am to bring them but he said to man of the house shut him lest he will run away. I am very glad to see this that I am always my teacher teaches me about Jesus that he died for my sins and that he was nailed on a tree. At first I did no believe in him but now I believe in him and I am his sheep but now I know much of him than at first.

Lewis Brenn

I came from Wanambamda in the Makaw [Makua] country I went up to the Mtili because in our country the men were fighting. Together with my two sisters and one brother and my father and mother and went to another country and we lived in that country about four months and there was famine. And the men of that country caught me and put me in a room for a night on the morning they sold me to the strangers and they sent me to their land I live there one year and they sold me again, and I live one month, to Wananthira I live there two years and I travel with my master to Okurwani. We live at Okurwani one year, and my master told those people to go and sell me, I left my master at Okurwani. I came down with them and they sold me to a king, and that king tied me with a rope round my neck, and told his son to hold the rope and went with me at night-time, and we reached his house after a few days. We went on forward until we came to that king's friend and we live there many days and that man took us at night time through the country on he morning we went in another country and those men wanted to catch us but we ran away in the woods and we cross over mululi and we came to the land called Oniwaroni on another day we came to the Arab's land and those men sold me to the Arabs and those Arabs took me to Ofusi and I live few days we came to Barawa and we went in the dhow after three days we saw the ship the ship which is called Thetis and the Arabs went to fight with them and some of them said do not fight with them and they took us to their ship and brought us to Zanzibar then to Frere Town and the men came and taught use about Jesus Christ and now we love Jesus Christ we pray him to help us to be good children.

David Rebmann

I came from Mkuta land when I was caught there were men and children. They brought me to Mkuta my brothers three and sisters two. I went to play on the sea shore they caught me and put mud in my mouth that I might not cry and they wanted to beat me. My father was a fisherman and my big brother he run away and hid in a wood some were killed when they were fighting some of them died sixteen, they built a tent until they brought me to Arabs those Arabs came to sold clothes and guns and bosees [?] these are the only people Mwabea, Mwadua, Mwalawa and Mwasega [?]. When they finished to sold me and bose and clothes and guns, then they put it on my head, and I pushed down, they took and other men then we began our journey about twenty days in the road then we came to the Arabs of them called Nakafulo took me and he give us mahinde and some kunde. Again we began our journey for many days in a way they gave me big bundle then they said we shall hurt him and they took from me a bundle and pull my ears and I cried. Mtekerika is the chief of their chiefs rest [?] are Namirive Muduli. The men of war said until you will give us yours slaves and they said we shall not give you then they fight forty men were dead afterward we come to the Mbisa then we slept there five days till we came to Arabs and there we lived many days and evening all slaves went to sea shore two by two in a board then all finished and we began our journey and I cried for my family, they told me don't cried after days in a vessel I saw a large a large thing coming from a distance I did not know it what sort of thing it was some Arabs said it is a ship which coming then all begun to said oh ye slaves go inside some of them did not I was standing with the mast [?] then the English came and took me to thethis [Thetis] and they brought me to here. So God love me and he give me his grace his mercy his goodness and before all these things first I want that he may send His Holy Ghost in my heart first I did not know anything but now I know how to read and speak about Jesus Christ.

Cecil Mabruki

I come from Mozambique. My Father and Mother were dead. But my sister was left well her name was called Shiva, she was big I was little I went with my companions we went to making traps for the birds. Then we saw four men coming one of them took the spear and the gun, and the knife in his hand. And the second gun also and the spears and his big knife in his hand they was running after us. And we was running but one of them spoken unto us and said; stand still if ye shall not stand I shall kill you. Then we was afraid to run and we so stand, and they came and tied. Then we came to the river Mwabo [?], and walk little once and came to Okivulani and sold me to the Arab and I sat many days. There he give a little cloth and he was give the name Mabrubi, then I saw three slave women and two boys, were Henry and the other boy Edward and Eli we was place together but not one master. Then we went the place were called Obab Obarawa [?] were the dow it came and we go in about the five o'clock until six o'clock. And we sleep in the dow three days then fife o'clcok we saw the ship. I was thinking it is a trees. When the Arabs saw the ship they said ^words^ us go, down others took stones and worship they think are they heard the ship shall turn back. But they do in vain. One Arab he want to jump to the sea one English man cut off and the sword two pieces, then come to the ship and the men of compassion they was give water and breads. When we want water we was told two boys was Alfred and George and ^we^ was cannot to stand where we come Zanzibar then come to Frere town.

Duiah William

I was running the battle when was running the battle my mother was with womb we come out I my six brothers we go another country it is called Unantavarara they cheat us they said battle is coming then said they are saying wrong we all turn back there said go in they not give us any super [supper] until the morningtime the began to ask each other when land you are coming they where checking me and my mother Usheleje [?] my mother she run by night we remain by ourself he come a short man he set I want this child he buyeth me with two dollar an a cloth an a gun he take me he sent at in his house. I was crying my mother on the road [?]

I got my big brother who was drawing the water I pass my fathers field and I go rite away up and I my fathers O my son is going he ask that man who take me that man I buy him for a two dollar our king has name was mkaferamee [?]. Told my mother the battle is come he sent me to fetch the wood my my mother was catch he fast him with roll in his neck he sent them with anto one man who was called bwanali my mother sit their about one month my father he take me and another man I got their precillar [?] and I sit about two month and I come to the hand of Arab I sit their one month he buyed me another men into five dollar and I said unto me and I go another Arab I and I got coraline(?) their about one month then we go into the boat we saw marikubu big arab when they saw litath(?) coming they sat lakeside(?) la mhomado [sic]. I dont no many days did stay in the sea.

NOTES

Acknowledgements

1 Richard Anderson, 'Uncovering Testimonies of Slavery and the Slave Trade in Missionary Sources: The SHADD Biographies Project and the CMS and MMS Archives for Sierra Leone, Nigeria, and The Gambia', *Slavery & Abolition*, 38:3 (September 2017), 620–44.

Introduction

1 John W. Blassingame (ed.) *Slave Testimony: Two Centuries of Letters, Speeches, Interviews, and Autobiographies* (Baton Rouge: Louisiana State University Press, 1977); Charles T. Davis and Henry Louis Gates, Jr. (eds.) *The Slave's Narrative* (Oxford: Oxford University Press, 1991); John Ernest (ed.) *The Oxford Handbook of the African American Slave Narrative* (Oxford: Oxford University Press, 2014); Aaron Spencer Fogleman and Robert Hanserd (eds.) *Five Hundred African Voices: A Catalog of Published Accounts by Africans Enslaved in the Transatlantic Slave Trade, 1586–1936* (Philadelphia, PA: American Philosophical Society, 2022).

2 On the importance of the distinction between narratives composed by individuals who had once been free in Africa and those who were born into slavery in the Americas, see Paul Lovejoy, '"Freedom Narratives" of Transatlantic Slavery', *Slavery & Abolition*, 32:1 (March 2011), 91–107.

3 Philip D. Curtin (ed.) *Africa Remembered: Narratives by West Africans from the Era of the Slave Trade* (Madison: University of Wisconsin Press, 1967).

4 See, for example, Sandra E. Greene, *West African Narratives of Slavery: Texts from Late Nineteenth- and Early Twentieth-Century Ghana* (Bloomington: Indiana University Press, 2011); Alice Bellagamba, Sandra E. Greene and Martin Klein (eds.) *African Voices on Slavery and the Slave Trade* (Cambridge: University of Cambridge Press, 2013); Pier M. Larson, 'Horrid Journeying: Narratives of Enslavement and the Global African Diaspora', *Journal of World History*, 19:4 (2008), 25–56; Robin Law and Paul E. Lovejoy (eds.) *The Biography of Mahommah Gardo Baquaqua: His Passage from Slavery to Freedom in Africa* (Princeton: Marcus Wiener, 2001); Paul Lovejoy, 'Biography as Source Material: Towards a Biographical Archive of Enslaved Africans' in Robin Law (ed.), *Source Material for Studying the Slave Trade and the*

African Diaspora (Sterling: Centre of Commonwealth Studies, University of Sterling, 1997), 119–40; Sophie White and Trevor Burnard (eds.) *Hearing Enslaved Voices: African and Indian Testimony in British and French America, 1700–1848* (Abingdon: Routledge, 2020). In addition to autobiographical and biographical accounts, scholars of the Black Atlantic are now reconstructing life histories and microhistories from a range of sources. See, for example, Randy J. Sparks, *The Two Princes of Calabar: An Eighteenth-Century Atlantic Odyssey* (Cambridge, MA: Harvard University Press, 2004); James Sweet, *Domingos Álvares, African Healing, and the Intellectual History of the Atlantic World* (Chapel Hill: University of North Carolina Press, 2011); Roquinaldo Ferreira, *Cross-Cultural Exchange in the Atlantic World: Angola and Brazil during the Era of the Slave Trade* (Cambridge: Cambridge University Press, 2012); Lisa A. Lindsay and John Wood Sweet (eds.) *Biography and the Black Atlantic* (Philadelphia: University of Pennsylvania Press, 2014); João José Reis, *Divining Slavery and Freedom: The Story of Domingos Sodré, an African Priest in Nineteenth-Century Brazil* (New York: Cambridge University Press, 2015); Lisa Lindsay, *Atlantic Bonds: A Nineteenth-Century Odyssey from America to Africa* (Chapel Hill: University of North Carolina Press, 2017); João José Reis, Flávio dos Santos Gomes and Marcus J. M. de Carvalho, *The Story of Rufino: Slavery, Freedom, and Islam in the Black Atlantic* (Oxford: Oxford University Press, 2019); Marisa J. Fuentes, *Dispossessed Lives: Enslaved Women, Violence, and the Archive* (Philadelphia: University of Pennsylvania Press, 2018).

5   Historians have also turned to oral traditions and oral histories of enslavement in Africa, even as the topic of slavery and ancestry remains a sensitive subject in many parts of the continent. See Anne C. Bailey, *African Voices of the Atlantic Slave Trade: Beyond the Silence and the Shame* (Boston: Beacon Press, 2005).

6   In particular, Marcia Wright and Edward Alpers have shown how biographies of converts can convey the strategies of enslaved women in nineteenth-century Africa. See Edward A. Alpers, 'The Story of Swema: Female Vulnerability in Nineteenth-Century East Africa' in Claire Robertson and Martin A. Klein (eds.), *Women and Slavery in Africa* (Madison: University of Wisconsin Press, 1983), 185–219; Marcia Wright, *Strategies of Slaves & Women: Life Stories from East/Central Africa* (New York: Lilian Barber Press, 1993); Sandra E. Greene, 'Christian Missionaries on Record: Documenting Slavery and the Slave Trade from the Late Fifteenth to the Early Nineteenth Century' in Alice Bellagamba, Sandra E. Greene and Martin Klein (eds.), *African Voices on Slavery and the Slave Trade: Vol 2: Essays on Sources and Methods* (Cambridge: University of Cambridge Press, 2016), 50–73.

7   The society was known in the nineteenth century as the Wesleyan Methodist Missionary Society (WMMS). On the Methodist Union of 1932, the WMMS, United Methodist Missionary Society (UMMS) and the Primitive Methodist Missionary Society (PMMS) merged to form the MMS. This volume refers to the MMS since its references the archive and contents therein, which are today referred to as the MMS Archive.

8   Sigismund Wilhelm Koelle, *Polyglotta Africana: Or a Comparative Vocabulary of Nearly Three Hundred Words and Phrases in More than One Hundred*

Distinct African Languages (London: Church Missionary House, 1854); P. E. H. Hair, 'The Enslavement of Koelle's Informants', *Journal of African History*, 6:2 (1965), 193–203. See also Christopher Fyfe, 'Four Sierra Leone Recaptives', *Journal of African History*, 2:1 (1961), 77–85.

9   Between 1808 and 1896, a network of courts in the Atlantic and Indian Oceans 'liberated' approximately 200,000 children, women and men. Freetown's courts alone legally emancipated an estimated 99,752 Africans. As many as 72,284 subsequently began new lives in the Sierra Leone peninsula; the rest were forcibly sent elsewhere to fulfil the labour and defence needs of Britain's Atlantic empire. See Richard Anderson, 'Liberated Africans', *Oxford Research Encyclopedia of African History* (March 2021); Anderson and Henry B. Lovejoy (eds.) *Liberated Africans and the Abolition of the Slave Trade, 1807–1896* (Rochester: Rochester University Press, 2020); and Daniel Domingues da Silva, David Eltis, Philip Misevich and Olatunji Ojo, 'The Diaspora of Africans Liberated from Slave Ships in the Nineteenth Century', *Journal of African History*, 55:3 (November 2014), 347–69.

10 See E. Adeniyi Oroge, 'The Fugitive Slave Crisis of 1859: A Factor in the Growth of Anti-British Feelings among the Yoruba', *Odu*, 12 (1975); Oroge, 'The Fugitive Slave Question in Anglo-Egba Relations, 1861–1886', *Journal of the Historical Society of Nigeria*, 8 (1975), 61–80; Toyin Falola, 'Missionaries and Domestic Slavery in Yorubaland in the Nineteenth Century', *Journal of Religious History*, 14:2 (December 1986), 181–92; Kristin Mann, *Slavery and the Birth of an African City: Lagos, 1760–1900* (Bloomington: Indiana University Press, 2007), 160–99.

11 J. D. Y. Peel, *Religious Encounter and the Making of the Yoruba* (Bloomington: Indiana University Press, 2000), 11.

12 Peel, *Religious Encounter*, 9. Fyfe notes that it was the rule from the start that every CMS missionary send home regular journals to the parent committee, a practice that began with the discouraging accounts of Melchior Renner and Peter Hartwig among the Susu in the early nineteenth century. Christopher Fyfe, *A History of Sierra Leone* (London: Oxford University Press, 1962), 94–5, citing *CMS Report 1804*, 317.

13 Journals were kept beforehand and published in the annual reports of the CMS, most famously in the case of W. A. B. Johnson's accounts of Regent. However, the practice of sending regular journal extracts only appeared at this later date. The documents that exist within the archive today are journal 'extracts', likely copied from actual journals, though the exact conditions of production are not known and the original journals are not extant. Peel, *Religious Encounter*, 9. Johnson's papers were edited and published by Robert B. Seeley (ed.) *A Memoir of the Rev. W.A.B. Johnson, Missionary of the Church Missionary Society, in Regent's Town, Sierra Leone, Africa* (New York: Robert Carter & Brothers, 1853).

14 Pratt to Johnson, 8 October 1817, CMS C/A1/E6/73.

15 Robin Law, 'The Chronology of the Yoruba Wars of the Early Nineteenth Century: A Reconsideration', *Journal of the Historical Society of Nigeria*, 2 (1970), 211–22; Law, 'The Owu War in Yoruba History', *Journal of the*

Historical Society of Nigeria, 7:1 (1973), 142–3. Robert Smith was the first to utilize King's narrative. Smith, *Kingdoms of the Yoruba* (London: Methuen, 1969), 150, 205 fn.50.

16 Leo Spitzer, *Lives in Between: Assimilation and Marginality in Austria, Brazil, and West Africa, 1780–1945* (Cambridge: Cambridge University Press, 1989), 40–72.

17 Fred Morton, 'Small Change: Slave Children and the 19th Century East African Slave Trade' in Gwyn Campbell, Suzanne Miers and Joseph C. Miller (eds.), *Children in Slavery through the Ages* (Athens: Ohio University Press, 2009), 55–70.

18 The woodcut of 'How Thomas King Became a Slave' was reused in Jesse Page's biography of Samuel Ajayi Crowther with the caption 'Foulah Capturing Little Adjai'. See Jesse Page, *The Black Bishop: Samuel Adjai Crowther* (London: Hodder and Stoughton, 1908), 25. Other examples of reused images of enslavement include 'James Gerber and His Companions Praying for Deliverance', *Church Missionary Gleaner*, May 1850, 13.

19 The annual roster of CMS mission agents, which often recorded place of birth, provides complementary information on individuals. *Register of Missionaries (clerical, lay, & female), and Native Clergy, from 1804–1904* (Church Missionary Society: Printed for private circulation, 1905).

20 For missionary sources on enslavement in Egypt and the Sudan see George Michael La Rue, 'Seeking Freedom in Multiple Contexts', *Journal of Global Slavery*, 2:1–2 (2017), 11–43.

21 This definition is adapted from James Olney, '"I Was Born": Slave Narratives, Their Status as Autobiography and as Literature', *Callaloo*, 20 (Winter, 1984), 47.

22 I have incorporated well-known accounts by Thomas King, Joseph Boston May and a number of Bombay Africans which have been analysed by Robin Law, Leo Spitzer and Fred Morton respectively. In these instances, the primary sources they utilize are not readily available in print. I have excluded several published narratives which have been discussed by historians including Edward Alpers, Matthew Hopper and Morgan J. Robinson. (See discussion below for the analyses of Law, Spitzer, Morton, Alpers, Hopper, Robinson and others.) In these cases, the published sources are generally accessible online. This is also true of the well-known accounts of Samuel Ajayi Crowther and Ali Eisami Gazirmabe which can be consulted in Curtin's *Africa Remembered* and elsewhere. See Richard Anderson, ''Alī Eisami Gazirmabe' in *The Oxford Research Encyclopedia of African History* (Oxford: Oxford University Press, February 2022) https://oxfordre.com/africanhistory; H.F.C. Smith [Abdullahi], D. M. Last and Gambo Gubio, 'Ali Eisami Gazirmabe of Bornu', and J. F. Ade Ajayi, 'Samuel Ajayi Crowther of Oyo', in Curtin (ed.), *Africa Remembered*, 199–216, 289–316; for the original publication of Eisami's testimony, see S. W. Koelle, *African Native Literature: Or Proverbs, Tales, Fables & Historical Fragments in the Kanuri or Bornu Language* (London: Church Missionary House, 1854), 248–56.

23 See Silke Strickrodt, 'African Girls' Samplers from Mission Schools in Sierra Leone (1820s to 1840s)', *History in Africa: A Journal of Method*, 37 (2010), 189–245.

24 On sex ratio and the transatlantic trade, see Jennifer L. Morgan, *Reckoning with Slavery: Gender, Kinship, and Capitalism in the Early Black Atlantic* (Durham and London: Duke University Press, 2021), 29–54. For East Africa, see Elisabeth McMahon, 'Trafficking and Re-enslavement: Social Vulnerability of Women and Children in Nineteenth Century East Africa' in Benjamin Lawrance and Richard Roberts (eds.), *Trafficking in Slavery's Wake: Law and the Experience of Women and Children in Africa* (Athens: Ohio University Press, 2012), 29–44. For gender and slave trading across the Indian Ocean, see Gwyn Campbell, 'Introduction: Slavery and Other Forms of Unfree Labour in the Indian Ocean World' in Gwyn Campbell (ed.), *The Structure of Slavery in Indian Ocean Africa and Asia* (London: Frank Cass, 2004), vii–xxxii.

25 Robin Law, *The Oyo Empire c.1600–c.1836: A West African Imperialism in the Era of the Atlantic Slave Trade* (Oxford: Clarendon Press, 1977); Toyin Falola and Matt D. Childs (eds.) *The Yoruba Diaspora in the Atlantic World* (Bloomington: Indiana University Press, 2004); Paul Lovejoy, *Jihād in West Africa during the Age of Revolutions* (Athens: Ohio University Press, 2016).

26 Edward Alpers, *Ivory and Slaves: Changing Patterns of International Trade in East Central Africa to the Later Nineteenth Century* (Berkeley and Los Angeles: University of California Press, 1975).

27 See Mariana P. Candido, 'The Expansion of Slavery in Benguela during the Nineteenth Century', *International Review of Social History*, 65:Special Issue S28 (2020), 67–92.

28 Anonymous [Samuel Ajayi Crowther, Thomas Harding, and john Attarra], 'Narratives of Three Liberated Negroes', *Church Missionary Record*, VIII:10 (October 1837), 217–26. Crowther's narrative is easily recognizable and corresponds to his written account of 22 February 1837. The article listed the other two unidentified authors as CMS catechists whose accounts were dated 1 March and 3 March 1837. The first of these is the account of Matthew Thomas Harding, written in a letter of that date. Matthew Thomas Harding, Letter to Mission, 1 March 1837, CA1/O112/12. The second of these is from John Attarra in his letter of 3 March 1837, CA1/O33/3.

29 The earliest known published testimony of a Liberated African is W. A. B. Johnson's recording of the life history of Josiah Yamsey. Published in 1821 it did not receive the same attention as Crowther's later account. See 'Account of a Liberated Negro: Illustrative of the Oppressive Influence of the Slave Trade' in *Proceedings of the Church Missionary Society for Africa and the East, Twenty-First Year, 1820–1821* (London: R. Watts, 1821), 236–41.

30 It was at this time that the first Liberated Africans began returning to the coastal Bight of Benin, as traders who purchased captured slave vessels and proceeded to Badagry, Lagos and Ouidah. This emerging bilateral connection, which was soon to prompt the CMS and MMS to instigate missions to the region, may have also been an impetus for writing a narrative. Interestingly, most of these accounts are dated after the abolition of slavery in the British Empire which may, in part, explain why some did not receive a wider circulation while others were not published at all. The period of October 1838 to June 1839 also coincided with the premature repeal of the post-emancipation apprenticeship system in the British Caribbean and the founding of the British Anti-slavery Society.

31　On conversion narratives and the importance of conversion to missionary discourse, see Gareth Griffiths, '"Trained to Tell the Truth": Missionaries, Converts, and Narration' in Norman Etherington (ed.), *Missions and Empire* (Oxford: Oxford University Press, 2005), 153–72; D. W. Bebbington, *Evangelicalism in Modern Britain: A History from the 1730s to the 1980s* (London: Routledge, 1989), 3–7; Susan Thorne, '"The Conversion of Englishmen and the Conversion of the World Inseparable": Missionary Imperialism and the Language of Class in Early Industrial Britain' in Frederick Cooper and Ann Laura Stoler (eds.), *Tensions of Empire: Colonial Cultures in a Bourgeois World* (Berkeley: University of California Press, 1997), 238–62; Anna Johnston, *Missionary Writing and Empire, 1800–1860* (Cambridge: Cambridge University Press, 2003).

32　W. A. B. Johnson, 24 March 1820, CA1/O126/121.

33　Many of the narrators conducted services in both African languages and English. In Bathurst, John Cupidon and John Gum gave evening services in Wolof. In Sierra Leone, Joseph Wright and Joseph Boston May were among the CMS and MMS members who preached in Yoruba. Martha T. Frederiks, *We Have Toiled All Night: Christianity in The Gambia, 1456–2000* (Zoetermeer: Boekencentrum, 2003), 200; Richard Anderson, *Abolition in Sierra Leone: Re-building Lives and Identities in Nineteenth-Century West Africa* (Cambridge: Cambridge University Press, 2020), 201.

34　See Karen Halttunen, 'Humanitarianism and the Pornography of Pain in Anglo-American Culture', *The American Historical Review*, 100:2 (1995), 303–34; Richard Ashby Wilson and Richard D. Brown (eds.) *Humanitarianism and Suffering: The Mobilization of Empathy* (Cambridge: Cambridge University Press, 2008); Margaret Abruzzo, *Polemical Pain: Slavery, Cruelty, and the Rise of Humanitarianism* (Baltimore: The Johns Hopkins University Press, 2011). Missionaries could go so far as to construct fictional accounts. See, for example, the short story *Dazee, or the Re-captured Negro*, published in 1822 by the hugely popular evangelical children's author Mary Martha Sherwood. Moira Ferguson, 'Fictional Constructions of Liberated Africans: Mary Butt Sherwood' in Tim Fulford and Peter J. Kitson (eds.), *Romanticism and Colonialism: Writing and Empire, 1780–1830* (Cambridge: Cambridge University Press, 1998), 148–64.

35　Greene, *West African Narratives*, 3.

36　Greene, *West African Narratives*, 2. Stephan Palmié points out that while the voice of the formerly enslaved was often presented as an 'unvarnished' truth, editorial interventions made the published slave narrative 'irredeemably composite'. Stephan Palmié, 'Slavery, Historicism, and the Poverty of Memorialisation' in Susannah Radstone and Bill Schwarz (eds.), *Memory: Histories, Theories, Debates* (New York: Fordham University Press, 2010), 363–75.

37　For example, another formerly enslaved person at Freretown named Mbotela related to his son the details of his capture and servitude through a series of conversations and storytelling sessions. His son, James Jumba Mbotela, subsequently published these with a high degree of embellishment. See James Juma Mbotela, *The Freeing of the Slaves in East Africa* (London: Evans

Brothers Limited, 1956) which is translated from the original Swahili version found in Mbotela, *Uhuru wa watumwa* (London and Nairobi: Sheldon Press, CMS Bookshop, 1934).

38 Griffiths, 'Trained to Tell the Truth', 155.

39 See, for an example of such reunification tales in missionary propaganda, A.F. Childe *Good Out of Evil; or, The History of Adjai, the African Slave-Boy* (London: Wertheim and Macintosh, 1852), 90–2.

40 Additionally, Joseph Boston May was named after the European missionary Edmund Boston who ran a school at Bathurst village, Sierra Leone, which Joseph attended. Spitzer, *Lives in Between*, 61.

41 'The Life and Experience of Joseph Boston May', October 1838, MMS, Sierra Leone Correspondence, fiche box 25, box no. 280, 'Sierra Leone Odds papers', fiche no. 1879, #3.

42 Paul Lovejoy, 'The Children of Slavery – the Transatlantic Phase', *Slavery & Abolition*, 27:2 (August 2006), 208. See also Olatunji Ojo 'Child Slaves in Pre-colonial Nigeria', *Slavery & Abolition*, 33:3 (September 2012), 417–34.

43 See Edward A. Alpers, 'Children in the Indian Ocean' in Vanicléia Silva Santos (ed.), *UNESCO General History of Africa, vol. X: Africa and Its Diasporas* (Paris: United Nations Educational, Scientific and Cultural Organization, 2023), 829–35; Richard B. Allen, 'Children and European Slave Trading in the Indian Ocean during the Eighteenth and Nineteenth Centuries', in Gwyn Campbell, Suzanne Miers and Joseph C. Miller (eds.), *Children in Slavery through the Ages*, 35–54. See also Audra Diptee, 'Notions of African Childhood in Abolitionist Discourses: Colonial and Post-colonial Humanitarianism in the Fight against Child Slavery' in Anna Mae Duane (ed.), *Child Slavery before & after Emancipation* (New York: Cambridge University Press, 2017), 208–30; Robin Phylisia Chapdelaine, *The Persistence of Slavery: An Economic History of Child Trafficking in Nigeria* (Amherst: University of Massachusetts Press, 2021); Bernard Moitt, *Child Slavery and Guardianship in Colonial Senegal* (Cambridge: Cambridge University Press, 2024).

44 Eliza Wilson, 'A Brief Memoir of the Late Peter Wilson', 1860, CA1/O6/53.

45 The *Avizo* was a Bahian slave vessel whose crew purchased 467 slaves at Badagry. Wilson's identification of HMS *Maidstone* under Charles Bullen (rather than Buller) corresponds with the register of the Sierra Leone Slave Trade Commission, FO 315/31. Unfortunately, it is difficult to find a registered Liberated African whose recorded name is phonetically similar to 'Lai-guan-dai' despite the narrative specifying that Wilson provides.

46 For the calculation of these estimates see Anderson, *Abolition in Sierra Leone*, 30–5.

47 Maeve Ryan, '"A Most Promising Field for Future Usefulness": The Church Missionary Society and the Liberated Africans of Sierra Leone' in William Mulligan and Maurice Bric (eds.), *A Global History of Anti-slavery Politics in the Nineteenth Century* (Houndmills, Basingstoke, Hampshire: Palgrave Macmillan, 2013), 37–58.

48 The ability of many Liberated Africans to return perhaps explains why this corpus of narratives usually contains more on their lives prior to enslavement

when compared to narratives from North America and the British Caribbean, which 'tend to focus on slaves' lives in the Americas, effacing former experiences of bondage within Africa'. Jerome S. Handler, 'Survivors of the Middle Passage: Life Histories of Enslaved Africans in British America', *Slavery and Abolition*, 23:1 (2002), 25–56.

49 'Horrible Notions of the Africans Respecting the Slave-Trade', *Church Missionary Gleaner*, 2 (1842), 51–2. Also see James Frederick Schön and Samuel Crowther, *Journals of the Rev. James Frederick Schön and Mr. Samuel Crowther Who, with the Sanction of Her Majesty's Government, Accompanied the Expedition Up the Niger, in 1841, in Behalf of the Church Missionary Society* (London: Hatchard and Son, 1842), 143–5, 355.

50 Dr Edward George Irving, 'Journal of a Visit to the Ijebu Country in the Months of December, 1854 and January 1855' (CA2/O52/18) published in *Church Missionary Intelligencer*, vol. vii, 1856.

51 King had been an earlier participant in the Niger Expedition during 1841–42 before returning to Freetown as a native pastor.

52 Jean Herskovits Kopytoff, *A Preface to Modern Nigeria: The 'Sierra Leonians' in Yoruba, 1830–1890* (Madison: University of Wisconsin Press, 1965), 291.

53 'Journal of William Allen, Igbein, 1865', CA2/O18/18; *Church Missionary Society Register of Missionaries* (Church Missionary Society: Printed for private circulation, 1905), 313; Kopytoff, *A Preface to Modern Nigeria*, 283.

54 Law, 'Chronology of Yoruba Wars', 211–22; Law, 'The Owu War', 141–7; Law, *The Oyo Empire*. See also Henry B. Lovejoy, 'Mapping Uncertainty: The Collapse of Oyo and the Transatlantic Slave Trade, 1816–1836', *Journal of Global Slavery*, 4:2 (June 2019), 127–61.

55 MMS, Sierra Leone Correspondence, fiche box 25, box no. 280, 'Sierra Leone Odds Papers', fiche no. 1880, #6.

56 Ann O'Hear, 'The Enslavement of Yoruba', in Falola and Childs (eds.), *The Yoruba Diaspora in the Atlantic World*, 61.

57 David Eltis, 'The Slave Trade in Nineteenth-Century Nigeria' in Toyin Falola and Ann O'Hear (eds.), *Studies in the Nineteenth-Century Economic History of Nigeria* (Madison: African Studies Program, University of Wisconsin, 1998), 89.

58 Francine Shields has drawn upon the CMS Yoruba Mission archive to analyse the history of enslaved women in the nineteenth century. Francine Shields, 'Those Who Remained Behind: Women Slaves in Nineteenth-Century Yorubaland' in Paul E. Lovejoy (ed.) *Identity in the Shadow of Slavery* (London and New York: Continuum, 2000), 183–201.

59 Matthew Thomas Harding, Letter, Gloucester Village, 1 March 1837, CA1/O112/2. Governor Charles Maxwell served as governor from July 1811 to July 1815, though he returned to England in July 1814 leaving in charge Charles MacCarthy, the Lieutenant-Governor at Senegal.

60 John Christian Müller, 1 January 1849, CA2/O72/8. See also 'The Sufferings and Deliverance of James Gerber, a Twice-Liberated African', *Church Missionary Gleaner* 1 (1850–51), 20–3.

61 Letter from Captain Grant to Governor Charles MacCarthy, 24 June 1816, quoted in Lamin Manneh, 'Island Citizens: Environment, Infrastructure, and

Belonging in Colonial Gambia, 1816–1965' (unpublished PhD dissertation, University of Michigan, 2023), 59.

62 For a recent historical and historiographical overview of this history, see Bala Saho, 'The Gambia', in the *Oxford Research Encyclopedia of African History* (2019). On Gambian history more generally, see the foundational work of Florence K. Omolara Mahoney, including *Stories of Senegambia* (Banjul: Government Printer, 1982) and *Creole Saga: The Gambia's Liberated African Community in the Nineteenth Century* (Banjul: Baobab Printers, 2006). See also Frederiks, *We Have Toiled*, 207–13, for a series of short profiles of African Assistant Missionaries in the book, including John Cupidon and John Gum.

63 Frederiks, *We Have Toiled*, 197–200; Florence Mahoney, 'Notes on Mulattoes of The Gambia before the Mid-nineteenth Century', *Transactions of the Historical Society of Ghana* 8 (1965), 128.

64 On slavery and emancipation in The Gambia, see Alice Bellagamba, 'Slavery and Emancipation in the Colonial Archives: British Officials, Slave-Owners, and Slaves in the Protectorate of The Gambia (1890–1936)', *Canadian Journal of African Studies / Revue canadienne des études africaines*, 39:1(2005), 5–41; Liza Gijanto, 'Serving Status on The Gambia River before and after Abolition', *Current Anthropology*, 61:S22 (October 2020), S260–S275.

65 Journal of William Fox, entry 24 April 1835, MMS, box 293, mf. 839.

66 Frederiks, *We Have Toiled*, 199.

67 See Philip D. Curtin, *Economic Change in Precolonial Africa: Senegambia in the Era of the Slave Trade* (Madison: University of Wisconsin Press, 1975), 137–38; Hilary Jones, *The Métis of Senegal: Urban Life and politics in French West Africa* (Bloomington: Indiana University Press, 2013).

68 James F. Searing, *West African Slavery and Atlantic Commerce: The Senegal River Valley, 1700–1860* (Cambridge: Cambridge University Press, 1993), 94, 187. For details of individual merchants see Mahoney, *Stories of Senegambia*, 64–5, 69–70, 85–6; and Mahoney 'Notes on Mulattoes of The Gambia', 120–9.

69 On Gorée from as early as 1819, enslaved people could purchase their freedom and that of their families though this was an option few could afford. Bernard Moitt, 'Slavery, Flight and Redemption in Senegal, 1819–1905', *Slavery and Abolition*, 14:2 (1993), 71. Searing notes that on Gorée between 1830 and 1841, 261 enslaved persons purchased their own freedom for an average of 750 francs. Searing, *West African Slavery and Atlantic Commerce*, 181.

70 Frederiks, *We Have Toiled*, 199.

71 William Fox, *A Brief History of the Wesleyan Missions on the West Coast of Africa* (London: Aylott and Jones, 1851), 359.

72 Florence Mahoney, 'Government and Opinion in The Gambia' (unpublished PhD dissertation, School of Oriental and African Studies, 1963), 148–9.

73 Fox, *Brief History of the Wesleyan Missions*, 359.

74 See J. F. Ade Ajayi, *Christian Missions in Nigeria, 1841–1891: The Making of a New Elite* (London: Longmans, 1965); E. A. Ayandele, *The Missionary Impact on Modern Nigeria, 1842–1914: A Political and Social Analysis* (London: Longman, 1966); Falola, 'Missionaries and Domestic Slavery', 181–92.

75 See Mann, *Slavery and the Birth of an African City*, 185; Toyin Falola, 'Politics, Slavery, Servitude, and the Construction of Yoruba Identity' in Falola, *The African Diaspora: Slavery, Modernity, and Globalization* (Rochester, NY: University of Rochester Press, 2013), 163–86; Olatunji Ojo, 'The Yoruba Church Missionary Society Slavery Conference 1880', *African Economic History*, 49:1 (2021), 73–103.

76 Estimates derived from Matthew S. Hopper, 'Liberated Africans in the Indian Ocean World', in Anderson and Lovejoy (eds.), *Liberated Africans*, 271–94.

77 For the larger history, see Matthew S. Hopper, *Slaves of One Master: Globalization and Slavery in Arabia in the Age of Empire* (New Haven: Yale University Press, 2015) and Lindsay Doulton, 'The Royal Navy's Anti-slavery Campaign in the Western Indian Ocean, c. 1860–1890: Race, Empire and Identity' (unpublished PhD dissertation, University of Hull, 2010).

78 See Robert Harms, 'Introduction: Indian Ocean Slavery in the Age of Abolition' and Lindsay Doulton, '"The Flag That Sets Us Free": Antislavery, Africans, and the Royal Navy in the Indian Ocean World', in Robert Harms, Bearnard K. Freamon and David W. Blight (eds.), *Indian Ocean Slavery in the Age of Abolition* (New Haven: Yale University Press, 2013), 1–22, 101–19.

79 For a recent overview of the history of Bombay Africans, see Clifford Pereira, 'Returnee Africans of the Indian Ocean: The Bombay Africans', in Santos (ed.) *UNESCO General History of Africa, vol. X*, 753–64. See also Joseph E. Harris, *Repatriates and Refugees in a Colonial Society: The Case of Kenya* (Washington, DC: Howard University Press, 1987).

80 For the education of Liberated Africans in India, and David, Semler and Jones in particular, see Colin Reed, *Pastors, Partners and Paternalists: African Church Leaders and Western Missionaries in the Anglican Church in Kenya, 1850–1900* (Leiden: Brill, 1997), especially chapter 2.

81 Fred Morton, *Children of Ham: Freed Slaves and Fugitive Slaves on the Kenya Coast, 1873–1907* (Boulder: Westview Press, 1990), 52–76.

82 Philip Howard Colomb, *Slave-Catching in the Indian Ocean: A Record of Naval Experiences* (London: Longman, Green, and Co., 1873), 101.

83 Pereira, 'Returnee Africans of the Indian Ocean', 753.

84 Doulton 'The Royal Navy's Anti-slavery Campaign in the Western Indian Ocean', 39; Hopper 'Liberated Africans in the Indian Ocean World', 271–94.

85 Morton, 'Small Change', 55–70.

86 Wright, *Strategies of Slaves & Women*; Alpers, 'The Story of Swema', 185–219; Edward A. Alpers and Matthew S. Hopper. 'Speaking for Themselves? Understanding African Freed Slave Testimonies from the Western Indian Ocean, 1850s–1930s', *Journal of Indian Ocean World Studies*, 1 (2017), 60–88.

87 Alpers and Hopper, 'Speaking for Themselves?', 64. For an example of brief accounts recorded by naval officers, see Columb, *Slave-Catching in the Indian Ocean*, 28–30. For testimonies of enslavement from Dutch East India court records, see Matthias van Rossum, Alexander Geelen, Bram van den Hout and Merve Tosun, *Testimonies of Enslavement: Sources on Slavery from the Indian Ocean World* (London: Bloomsbury, 2020).

88 The two lengthiest UMCA accounts are Percy L. Jones-Bateman (ed.) *The Autobiography of an African Slave Boy* (London: Universities' Mission to Central Africa, 1891); Petro Kilekwa, *Slave Boy to Priest: The Autobiography of Padre Petro Kilekwa* (Westminster: UMCA, 1937). Twelve shorter accounts are found in Arthur C. Madan (trs. and ed.) *Kiungani; Or, Story and History from Central Africa* (London: George Bell and Sons, 1887). Kiungani was the main UMCA school for boys on Zanzibar. The UMCA accounts have been discussed in Alpers, 'Representations of Children in the East African Slave Trade', *Slavery & Abolition*, 30:1 (2009), 27; and Alpers, 'The Other Middle Passage: The African Slave Trade in the Indian Ocean' in Emma Christopher, Cassandra Pybus and Marcus Rediker (eds.), *Many Middle Passages: Forced Migration and the Making of the Modern World* (Berkeley, Los Angeles, London: University of California Press, 2007), 20–38; Morgan J. Robinson, 'Binding Words: Student Biographical Narratives and Religious Conversion' in Klaas van Walraven (ed.), *The Individual in African History: The Importance of Biography in African Historical Studies* (Brill: Leiden and Boston, 2020), 197–218.

89 Alpers, 'The Story of Swema'; Alpers, 'The Other Middle Passage'.

90 Robinson, 'Binding Words', 197–218.

91 Morton, 'Small Change', 55.

92 Alpers, *Ivory and Slaves*, 241. Morton, 'Small Change', 57.

93 Autobiographies: William Jones and Ishmael Semler, 1861, C I3/038/65D.

94 See Richard Huzzey, *Freedom Burning: Anti-slavery and Empire in Victorian Britain* (Ithaca: Cornell University Press, 2012); Joanna Lewis, *Empire of Sentiment: The Death of Livingstone and the Myth of Victorian Imperialism* (Cambridge: Cambridge University Press, 2018).

CASE 1

1 His surname is included in some sources, including the University of Birmingham's CMS Archive catalogue, as 'Yansey'.

2 *Church Missionary Society Register of Missionaries*, 6.

3 Adam Jones, 'Receptive Nations: Evidence Concerning the Demographic Impact of the Atlantic Slave Trade in the Early Nineteenth Century', *Slavery & Abolition*, 11:1 (1990), 42–57.

4 Of thirty-eight vessels captured by the Royal Navy and brought to Freetown in the period 1814–16, fifteen visited the Bight of Biafra. Nine of these departed from Brazil. Most visited the port of Old Calabar and the *General*

Silveira and the *Dido* were the only Portuguese vessels that visited the Cameroon coast in this period. The *Dido* is more likely given its voyage dates and the presence of an adolescent named Yamsey on board. *Dido* [Voyage ID 7645] *Voyages* database http://slavevoyages.org/voyage/7645/variables.

5   Vessels, cargoes and slaves proceeded against in the court of the vice-admiralty at Sierra Leone between June 1808 and March 1817, HCA49/97.

6   Liberated African Department Register 6289–8528, Sierra Leone Public Archives (hereafter SLPA). See also information on the African Origins Project. The project database suggests that Yamsey may be a corruption of Nyamsi in Chamba Leko language spoken across the northern Nigerian–Cameroonian border. http://www.african-origins.org/african-data/detail/107169.

7   Possibly a reference to 'red water' a regional form of 'trial by ordeal' administered through ingesting the poisonous Malabar bean.

8   Word unclear. Appears closest to 'sold' but could be 'salt' in this context.

9   A peak on the Sierra Leone peninsula behind Freetown rising 548 metres above sea level.

10 This word is unclear and likely refers to an as-yet-unidentified foodstuff. The published 1820s *Proceedings of the CMS* transcribed the word as 'cocoa'. This is unlikely, beyond the fact that Johnson's handwriting is clearly two identical words (either 'cou cou' or 'coi coi'). Yamsey's account is written too early for cocoa production in the interior of the Bight of Biafra.

11 Thomas Hirst was a Wesleyan Methodist Missionary who was in Sierra Leone from 1811 to *c.* 1817.

CASE 2

1   Robert Bostock was born in Liverpool, the son of a slave trader of the same name. He co-owned slave-trading factories at the Gallinas and St. Paul River on the Upper Guinea Coast. In 1813, he was arrested, convicted of illegal slave dealing, and sentenced to fourteen years in Australia. He became a free settler of Tasmania after his conviction was overturned. Charles Mason was an American slave trader and co-owner with Bostock of the Gallinas and St. Paul factories. At the time of the raid in which David Noah was captured, Mason was away in either Charleston or Havana. Emma Christopher, *Freedom in Black and White: A Lost Story of the Illegal Slave Trade and Its Global Legacy* (Madison: University of Wisconsin Press, 2018), ix–xi.

2   See Padraic X. Scanlan, *Freedom's Debtors: British Antislavery in Sierra Leone in the Age of Revolution* (New Haven, CT: Yale University Press, 2017); Robin Law, 'Abolition and Imperialism: International Law and the British Suppression of the Atlantic Slave Trade' in Derek R. Peterson (ed.), *Abolitionism and Imperialism in Britain, Africa, and the Atlantic* (Athens: Ohio University Press, 2010), 150–74.

3   Christopher, *Freedom in Black and White*, 91–4.

4   John Peterson, *Province of Freedom: A History of Sierra Leone, 1787–1870* (London: Faber and Faber, 1969), 93, 108.

5   *Proceedings of the CMS 1816–1817*, 175.

6   David Noah, 'Journal of David Noah on a Visit to His Native Country, Bassa', February–March 1829, CA1/O165/19.

CASE 3

1   'Narratives of Three Liberated Negroes', *Church Missionary Record*, vol. VIII, No. 10, October 1837.

2   Apprenticeship was the main form of settlement or 'disposal', especially for children, as written into the 1807 Abolition Act. On the apprenticeship system in Sierra Leone see Maeve Ryan *Humanitarian Governance and the British Anti-slavery World System* (New Haven: Yale University Press, 2022), especially 165–95; Richard Anderson, 'Abolition's Adolescence: Apprenticeship as "Liberation" in Sierra Leone, 1808–1848', *English Historical Review*, 137:585 (June 2022), 763–93.

CASE 4

1   Letters from Mrs. Jane Attarra after death of husband in 1866, CA1/O33/21-23.

2   John Attarra first provided a short account of his enslavement in a 3 March 1837 letter (CA1/O33/3) which was subsequently published anonymously in 'Narratives of Three Liberated Negroes'. Roughly eight years later he wrote a lengthier, undated account in two identical letters to mission headquarters (CA1/O33/4 and CA1/O33/5). This version of his life history was published anonymously in two parts as 'A Liberated African's Account of His Slavery, and Subsequent Course', *Church Missionary Gleaner*, VI:2, (February 1846), 16–18 and No.3, Vol. VI, March 1846, 27–8.

3   John Attarra, Letter, Wellington, 8 March 1857, CA1/O33/8.

4   John Attarra, Journal August-September 1836, CA1/O33/37.

5   Fyfe, *A History of Sierra Leone*, 170. As of yet, I have been unable to find mention of Attarra's Mende origins within his original papers.

6   Like many Liberated African converts at Regent, John Attarra sent a letter to Johnson in England during his absence. Attarra to Johnson, 29 April 1823, CA1/O126/96.

CASE 5

1   Even though this document was written in The Gambia it appears in the 'odd paper' series of the Sierra Leone Methodist archive rather than the collection for The Gambia mission.

2   See Kyle Prochnow, '"Perpetual Expatriation:" Forced Migration and Liberated African Apprenticeship in The Gambia' in Anderson and Lovejoy

(eds.), *Liberated Africans*, 347–64; Richard Anderson, 'The Diaspora of Sierra Leone's Liberated Africans: Enlistment, Forced Migration, and "Liberation" at Freetown, 1808–1863', *African Economic History*, 41 (2013), 101–38.

3   Liberated African Register volume 15,114–19,888, Sierra Leone Public Archives. *Bom Jesus dos Navegantes*, Voyage ID 2952, *Voyages* database, www.slavevoyages.org/voyage/2952/variables.

4   The alleged death of the captain and mate does not fit the case of the *Bom Jesus dos Navegantes*, nor does it fit the description of court record for other intercepted ships whose captives were sent to The Gambia.

5   Likely Captain A. M. Fraser of the Royal African Colonial Corps. The Gambia did not have a governor until 1829 when Alexander Findlay was appointed lieutenant-governor, subordinate to the governor of Sierra Leone.

6   Campbell's account is one of many from The Gambia which mentions Charles Grant, an early timber trader who reached Bathurst in 1819. Grant returned to Scotland in the early 1840s, leaving a large Anglo-African family. George E. Brooks, *Western Africa and Cabo Verde, 1790s–1830s: Symbiosis of Slave and Legitimate Trades* (Bloomington, IN: Authorhouse, 2010), 154; Mahoney, 'Government and Opinion in The Gambia', 43; Curtin, *Economic Change in Precolonial Africa*, 137.

CASE 6

1   Smith, *Kingdoms of the Yoruba*, 151.

2   J. F. Ade Ajayi suggested dates of roughly 1820–25, while Curtin suggested a date for Owu's fall in 1825 or early 1826. J. F. Ade Ajayi 'The Aftermath of the Fall of Old Oyo' in J. F. A Ajayi and Michael Crowder (eds.), *History of West Africa, Volume Two* (New York: Columbia University Press, 1973), 129–66; Curtin (ed.) *Africa Remembered*, 318. Robin Law places the onset of the siege as *c*. 1816/7, and the fall of Owu as late 1821 or early 1822. Law, *Oyo Empire*, 275; Law, 'Chronology of the Yoruba Wars', 211–22; Law, 'The Owu War', 142–3. This concluding date is agreed upon by Falola and Oguntomísín. Toyin Falola and G. O. Oguntomísín, *Yoruba Warlords of the 19th Century* (Trenton, NJ: Africa World Press, 2001), 5.

3   Law, 'The Owu War', 142.

4   This includes Dr E.G. Irving's 'Journal of a Visit to the Ijebu Country in the Months of December 1854 and January 1855', CA2/O52/18; and John Raban, *A Vocabulary of the Eyo, or Aku*, Vol. III (London: CMS Bookshop, 1832), 10.

5   Marie Armand Pascal d'Avezac-Macaya, 'Notice sur le Pays et le Peuple des Yébous en Afrique', *Mémories de la Société Ethnologique*, 2:2 (1845), 37; Translated and annotated in Curtin, *Africa Remembered*, 247.

6   Peter Wilson, whose account appears in this volume, was also a Liberated African from Owu. However, Wilson did not describe any aspects of the Owu war or his enslavement.

7   It is not possible to positively identify the slave vessel Harding was on, due in part to poor recordkeeping regarding the 'disposal' of Liberated Africans in 1822. The most likely vessel is the *Gomba*, a Bahian vessel which departed Lagos in 1822 with 324 Africans below deck.

CASE 7

1   Condemned slave vessels were sold at public auctions in Freetown. Vessels could be purchased by slave traders, speculators, legitimate traders or entrepreneurial Liberated Africans. See George E. Brooks, *Western Africa and Cabo Verde, 1790s–1830s: Symbiosis of Slave and Legitimate Trades* (Bloomington, IN: Authorhouse, 2010), 92.
2   Alexander Findlay to R. W. Hay, 4 August 1830, CO 267/103.
3   It is unclear which captured vessel Thompson was on board. There is also no record of Liberated Africans being sent to The Gambia in 1823, though he may have been brought there as an apprentice.

CASE 8

1   William Fox provides a short account of Will's life history based on a speech Will gave at the Wesleyan chapel on Jewin Street, London, while visiting the capital with the missionary Henry Badger in 1848. Fox misidentifies James Will as Joseph Will though the other elements of his life that Fox presents from his speech – including the role of the missionaries Crosby and Wise in his conversion – are identical. Fox, *Brief History of the Wesleyan Missions*, 594–5.
2   The narrative of James Will appears in two parts which appear in distinct sections of the Methodist Archive. It is unclear why the two sections are separated and if they were recorded at the same time. Both parts are written on bound paper, the first appearing to be a small notebook. The first half of Will's narrative appears in a collection of papers catalogued as 'Anti-Slavery Papers 1774–1891' in the Biographical Special Series of the archive. The narrative itself is found within a memo book, dated 1840, belonging to W. Fergusson. James Will – part 1 – MMS/SpecialSeries/VariousPapers/FBN44 (ref mms/17/03/01/58).
3   *Veloz Pasajera* (1830), Voyage ID 2423, *Voyages* database.
4   Liberated African Register 37430–43537, SLPA.
5   Personal correspondence with Olatunji Ojo.
6   Liberated African Register volume 37,430–43,537, SLPA, SL ID #37,732; 'Spanish Ship "La Veloz Passagera" Register of Slaves, Natives of Africa, captured on board', FO 84/116, FO id #22,723. http://www.african-origins.org/african-data/detail/22723.
7   Findlay and Smith, 18 October 1830: Report of the case of the Spanish ship 'Veloz Pasagera', FO 84/104.

8   Other sources place the interception on 7 September 1830 at latitude 5° 8' North longitude 4° 17' East. Findlay and Smith to Earl of Aberdeen, 18 October 1830, FO 84/104.
9   Findlay to Murray, 8 October 1830. CO 267/105.
10 Presumably coconuts.
11 'The lake' may refer to either Lake Ahémé or Lake Nokoueé, to the west and east of Ouidah, respectively. It may alternatively be a reference to Lagos lagoon. Will may simply be using 'lake' to describe the lagoon running along much of the coastline or the Atlantic Ocean itself. As such, it is unclear whether the 'town that is in the lake side' is Ouidah, Lagos, Badagry, Porto Novo or another small coastal trading town.
12 The mention of thunder worship likely refers to the Yoruba deity Ṣàngó, believed to control the forces of thunder and lightning. The worship of snakes, on the other hand, is chiefly associated with the kingdom of Dahomey to the west. The worship of iron may be a reference to the deity Ògún, identified much like Ṣàngó as a pan-Yoruba deity, albeit one whose cult is especially strong in eastern Yorubaland.
13 Will is here providing one of the earliest written descriptions of Ifa divination among the Yoruba. Ifa divination is based upon the manipulation of sixteen (eerindinlogun) palm nuts. Will mentions the use of thirty-two palm nuts, a multiple of sixteen. William Bascom, *Ifa Divination: Communication between Gods and Men in West Africa* (Bloomington: Indiana University Press, 1969), 3.
14 Likely Calabash.
15 Perhaps a metaphor referring to 'possession' by Ṣàngó.
16 Perhaps 'evil doer'.
17 MMS Archive, Biographical, West Africa, MMS/17/02/03 [H-2723 Box 593].
18 This may be a reference to either the Ogun or Ouémé Rivers. Alternatively, and perhaps more likely, Will may be describing travel along the coastal lagoon, a fluvial system running parallel to the beach along much of West Africa's 'Slave Coast'. Will is possibly stating that they 'leave' the canoes at night, that is, spent the nights on shore.
19 Likely Jakin.
20 possibly Godomey-Plage.
21 Lieutenant-Governor Alexander Findlay was promoted from The Gambia to Sierra Leone in April 1830. By this time the policy established in the 1810s and 1820s of sending Liberated African children to Church Missionary Society schools had largely collapsed, hence Will's description of 'no more school in the colony'. The less costly policy of apprenticeship remained the main means of resettling children. The period of indenture was determined by estimated age at arrival.
22 Thomas Will was himself Liberated African, though it is not known exactly when he landed in the colony. By 1830 Thomas was a highly successful trader located on Freetown's Pademba Road.
23 Likely the author's phonetic rendering of the Yoruba *onile* ('owner of the earth', presumably referring to the earth-god Soponna) *gba mi* ('save me').

24 Benjamin Crosby came to Sierra Leone from England in late 1834. He died in the colony in April 1837 after contracting yellow fever. Marke, *Origin of Wesleyan Methodism*, 47–51. Fox, *Brief History of the Wesleyan Missions*, 419–21.

CASE 9

1 Joseph's eldest son Claudius published a posthumous account of his father's life based largely on oral accounts. Claudius May, *A Brief Sketch of the Life of the Rev. Joseph May, Native of the Yoruba Country, and Late Wesleyan Minister of the Colony of Sierra Leone, Read at the Service of Song in Zion Church, Freetown, on Sunday, 25 October 1896* (Freetown, 1896).

2 *Dois Amigos*, Voyage ID: 2970, *Voyages* database, http://slavevoyages.org/voyage/2970/variables.

3 These details of May's life are drawn from Leo Spitzer's excellent biography of Joseph May in Spitzer, *Lives in Between*, 40–72. See also Spitzer, 'A Name Given, a Name Taken: Camouflaging, Resistance, and Diasporic Social Identity', *Comparative Studies of South Asia, Africa and the Middle East* (Volume 30, Number 1, 2010), 21–31.

4 The account here differs from his Son Claudius's later account which states that only his sister was captured. Claudius May, *A Brief Sketch of the Life of the Rev. Joseph May*.

5 Ifacayeh was the second oldest of four children. His mother, Manlawa, was the second of Loncola's three wives. Loncola intended to redeem all of his captured family but fell short of resources after redeeming his wife and Ifacayeh's siblings. Spitzer, *Lives in Between*, 45–8.

6 St. George's is an Anglican church in central Freetown, built between 1817 and 1828. It was made a cathedral in 1852 with the arrival of Emeric Vidal as bishop.

7 Charles Marke, *Origin of Wesleyan Methodism in Sierra Leone and History of Its Missions: Interspersed with Brief Notices of Other Missionary Societies in the Colony* (London: Charles H. Kelly, 1913), facing 189.

CASE 10

1 This date range is based on the observation of his colleague Joseph Boston May that Wright was enslaved when he 'was then about ten or twelve years of age'. Memoir of the Rev. Joseph Wright by the Rev. Joseph May, 192–3.

2 The Rev. John Beecham was a secretary of the Wesleyan Missionary Society. Beecham's volume was compiled from various travel accounts and published by the Wesleyans as a sketch of the 'superstitions of the inhabitants of those countries'. Beecham acquired Wright's narrative from the missionary Thomas Edwards after his return from Sierra Leone. The narrative was included as an

appendix entitled 'Descriptions of a Slave War'. Beecham, *Ashantee and the Gold Coast*, 349–58. William Fox also used extracts of Wright's account in his *Brief History of the Wesleyan Missions*.

3 It is likely that Christopher Fyfe – the authority on sources pertaining to nineteenth-century Sierra Leone – was aware of all these accounts and suggested Joseph Wright's because of its comparative level of detail.

4 Thomas Dove to the general secretaries, 19 April 1842, MMS Correspondence.

5 Wright in Curtin (ed.), *Africa Remembered*, 331, fn. 33.

6 FO 84/66. This date of recapture changes Curtin's calculation for the fall of Oba and of Wright's enslavement. Curtin concluded, 'If the conjectural date of Wright's recapture on 17 March is correct, this would be about 12 March 1827. Wright spent two months in Lagos awaiting shipment, having arrived there perhaps two weeks to one month after the fall of Oba. This would place the fall of Oba in January 1827 or December 1826, a dating which accords with other calculations.' Curtin (ed.), *Africa Remembered*, 330, n.32. The capture of the *Henriqueta* on 6 September 1827 suggests Wright was enslaved in July-August 1827.

7 Wright in Curtin (ed.), *Africa Remembered*, 321.

8 Joseph Wright, 1 July 1844, MMS.

9 Wright in Curtin (ed.), *Africa Remembered*, 322.

10 'Death of the Rev. Joseph Wright', *The Wesleyan Missionary Notices, Relating Principally to the Foreign Missions under the Direction of the Methodist Conference*, Third Series, Volume II, September 1855, 164.

11 'Memoir of the Rev. Joseph Wright by the Rev. Joseph May', *The Wesleyan Missionary Notices,* November 1855, 192–3.

12 'The Dying African's Letter to His Son', *The Wesleyan Missionary Notices*, October 1855, 171–2. Wright's son was at this time studying at Westminster Training College.

13 'Memoir of the Rev. Joseph Wright by the Rev. Joseph May', 193.

14 The 'council' is a reference to the Ògbóni society, an initiation society which during the precolonial period functioned as a town council and civic court. Ògbóni dominated the government of Egba towns before their destruction in the 1820s. See Toyin Falola and Akintunde Akinyemi (eds.) *Encyclopedia of the Yoruba* (Bloomington: Indiana University Press, 2016), 40–1, 165; Saburi O. Biobaku, *The Egba and Their Neighbours, 1842–1872* (Oxford: Clarendon Press, 1957), especially chapter 1.

15 The 'space of about seven years' likely refers to the period between the initial siege of Owu in *c.* 1816–17 and the westward move of the victorious alliance of Ife, Ijebu and refugee Oyo forces from Owu into Egba territories. See Law, 'Chronology of Yoruba Wars', 211–22.

16 Egba religious ceremonies often took place outside of town walls. This was particularly true for the worship of the *orişa* Orò, which among the Egba was held to be 'a secret between man and man'. See J. D. Y. Peel, 'Gender in Yoruba Religious Change', *Journal of Religion in Africa*, 32, Fasc. 2, The Politics of Mission (May, 2002), 146, 154.

17 Korowa, the deity of the town of Oba.
18 Indigenous deities (*oriṣa*) lacked gender as a fixed or intrinsic attribute. But there was a strong inclination to project gender on to them and regard *oriṣa* as either male or female. See Oyeronke Oyewumi, *The Invention of Women: Making an African Sense of Western Gender Discourses* (Minneapolis: University of Minnesota Press, 1997), 140–1; Peel, 'Gender in Yoruba Religious Change', 139–41.
19 Abore Oro, the chief priest of Òrò.
20 Peel describes Òrò as 'enforcers of a patriarchal-gerontocratic order' especially when Òrò 'came out' in town on occasions from chiefs' funerals, assemblies to decide issues of war and peace, consultations of Ifa on affairs of state, to major public sacrifices. During such occasions, women had to stay indoors, under pain of death. Peel 'Gender in Yoruba Religious Change', 144.
21 The *Henriqueta* reached Freetown twenty-three days after leaving Lagos, in keeping with Wright's estimate of 'about a month'.

CASE 12

1 James Gerber was likely named after the Swiss missionary John Gerber, who was in Sierra Leone from 1823 to 1833 and was based at Hastings in 1829–30.
2 The *Church Missionary Gleaner* version of the narrative incorrectly transcribes the account, saying that 'an Ibu man, pitying his wretched condition, bought him for six heads of cowries. He was then carried to the Jebu country'. 'Ibu' [Igbo] is highly unlikely in this region, and both renderings of 'Jebu' [Ijebu] are identical. 'The Sufferings and Deliverance of James Gerber, A Twice-Liberated African', 22.

CASE 13

1 'The Rev. Thomas King of Abbeokuta', *Church Missionary Gleaner*, January 1863, 6–7.
2 *Iberia* [Voyage ID 2368] *Voyages* database, http://slavevoyages.org/voyage/2368/variables.
3 Kopytoff, *A Preface to Modern Nigeria*, 291.
4 The manuscript shows the editorial intervention of CMS officials in London refining King's text for publication.
5 Andrew Wilhelm was an Egba Liberated African from the town of Kesi and one of the earlier returnees to Abeokuta in 1843.
6 William Marsh was a 'native catechist' from Sierra Leone who worked with the mission at Badagry and Abeokuta.

CASE 14

1. Law, 'Chronology of the Yoruba Wars', 220–1.

CASE 15

1. FO 315/31; *Aviso* [voyage ID 2946] *Voyages* database, http://slavevoyages.org/voyage/2946/variables.
2. FO84/38; http://www.african-origins.org/african-data/detail/4987.
3. Personal correspondence with Olatunji Ojo.
4. Michael Melville's service in Sierra Leone formed the basis of a memoir published by his wife, Elizabeth Helen Melville, in 1849. Of Peter Wilson she wrote, 'The history of this individual presents a favourable picture of a liberated African rising to respectability and comparative wealth by his own honest industry. Originally rescued from a slave-ship and emancipated here when a boy, he served an apprenticeship where he learnt, amongst other things, the womanly occupations of sewing, washing, and ironing. On becoming free, in a manner, again, he entered M – 's service, where he was taught, although then a grown-up man, writing and arithmetic … The country name of this man was "Petah" now civilized into "Peter," and his own people, the Akus, pay him due honour for the circumstance of his being a native chief's son.' Elizabeth Helen Melville, *A Residence at Sierra Leone: Described from a Journal Kept on the Spot, and Letters Written to Friends at Home* (London: John Murray, 1849), 23.

CASE 16

1. I would like to thank Olatunji Ojo for assistance in identifying Faulkner as the most likely author. See also 'Estimate for Completing Ebute Metta House Presented by Mr. Faulkner to Finance Committee 1875', CA2/O14.
2. Koelle, *Polyglotta Africana*, 5.
3. Joseph Weeks, Report of Bathurst Schools for the quarter ending 25 September 1833, CMS CA1/O219/52; Strickrodt, 'African Girls' Samplers', 220.
4. Page, *The Black Bishop*, 41.
5. 'Joseph Bola of Igbore' in CMS Z/30 'Biographical Accounts of Nigerian Converts to Christianity Early-Mid Nineteenth Century', 8–25.
6. See Kopytoff, *A Preface to Modern Nigeria*.
7. The King's Yard (or Queen's Yard from 1837 onward) or Liberated African yard was a large, walled compound on the waterfront where Liberated Africans were detained prior to their resettlement or 'disposal'.
8. Moses Forster was catechist of Iseyin church in the 1870s and 1880s.

CASE 17

1. These two men might also be Kru who voluntarily joined naval service, though it is not clear how they would have been able to communicate with Doherty. On Liberated African enlistment into the navy see Anderson, 'The Diaspora of Sierra Leone's Liberated Africans', 101–38; Kyle Prochnow, '"Saving an extraordinary expense to the nation": African recruitment for the West India Regiments in the British Atlantic world', *Atlantic Studies*, 18:2 (2021), 149–71.
2. After 1844, the West Africa Station counted upon seven steamers, increasing the speed, range and success of patrols north of the equator. Leslie Bethell, *The Abolition of the Brazilian Slave Trade: Britain, Brazil, and the Slave Trade Question, 1807–1869* (Cambridge: Cambridge University Press, 1970), 199; Christopher Lloyd, *The Navy and the Slave Trade: The Suppression of the African Slave Trade in the Nineteenth Century* (London: Cass, 1949). According to Richard Robert Madden, the first steamer incorporated into the squadron was the *Pluto* which arrived on the African coast in early 1841. Dr Madden's report on Sierra Leone, CO 267/172.
3. *The CMS Juvenile Instructor, 1873–1879*, 157.
4. Kọla Fọlayan, 'The Career of Thomas Tickel in the Western District of Lagos, 1854–1886', *Journal of the Historical Society of Nigeria*, 5:1 (December 1969), 27–46. See also S. Pearse to Venn, 3 October 1867, CA2/076; S. W. Doherty, Journal of Expedition to Ouidah and Dahomey to obtain the release of prisoners held by the Dahomians December 1866-August 1867, CA2/035/6.
5. This reference is to Jer. 31:15: 'A voice is heard in Ramah, mourning and great weeping, Rachel weeping for her children and refusing to be comforted, because they are no more.'

CASE 18

1. See Kopytoff, *A Preface to Modern Nigeria*, 117–20, 297.
2. James Campbell, *Middle Passages: African American Journeys to Africa, 1787–2005* (New York: Penguin, 2006), 85.
3. See Shields, 'Those Who Remained Behind', 183–201; Marjorie Keniston McIntosh, *Yoruba Women, Work, and Social Change* (Bloomington: Indiana University Press, 2009); Ademide Adelusi-Adeluyi, 'To be Female & Free: Mapping Mobility & Emancipation in Lagos, Badagry & Abẹokuta 1853–1865' in Mariana P. Candido and Adam Jones (eds.), *African Women in the Atlantic World: Property, Vulnerability & Mobility, 1660–1880* (Woodbridge, Suffolk: James Currey, 2019), 131–47.
4. Oroge, 'The Fugitive Slave Question in Anglo-Egba Relations', 61–80.
5. See Kristin Mann and Richard L. Roberts, (eds.) *Law in Colonial Africa* (Portsmouth, NH and London: James Currey, 1991); Trevor R. Getz, *Abina and the Important Men*, 2nd edition (Oxford: Oxford University Press, 2015);

Getz and Lindsay Ehrisman. 'The Marriages of Abina Mansah: Escaping the Boundaries of "Slavery" as a Category in Historical Analysis', *Journal of West African History*, 1:1 (Spring 2015), 93–117.

6. For a discussion of how litigants in different historical contexts utilized testimony and story-telling to persuade sceptical court officials, see Nataline Zemon Davis, *Fiction in the Archives: Pardon Tales and Their Tellers in Sixteenth-Century France* (Stanford: Stanford University Press, 1987); Kimberly M. Welch, *Black Litigants in the Antebellum American South* (Chapel Hill: The University of North Carolina Press, 2018).
7. Glover to Russell, 7 November 1865 and Glover to Russell 6 December 1865, FO 84/1250.
8. Oke Odan, north of Badagry.

CASE 19

1. A verbatim account appears at the British National Archives in the FO 84 series of Foreign Office Correspondence on the slave trade. See 'Deposition of Daniel Dopemu, a Christian Convert at Abbeokuta', Enclosure No. 1 in Slave Trade No. 23, 7 November 1865, FO 84/1250.

CASE 20

1. In 1785, the island's estimated population of 1,840 comprised 70 to 80 Europeans, 116 Eurafrican and free African property holders and their families, 522 free Africans without property, 1,044 domestic slaves and approximately 200 slaves held in transit. Brooks, *Western Africa and Cabo Verde*, 26.
2. William Fox to Lord Glenelg, 14 April 1836, MMS, Gambia Correspondence, Fiche Box 25, Box No. 294.
3. Brooks, *Western Africa and Cabo Verde*, 154.
4. Many European mission societies in Africa engaged in forms of redemption through the purchase of enslaved people near mission stations. The CMS in Sierra Leone adopted and abandoned a policy of redemption at mission stations outside the colony including Canofee and Bashia. Katrina Keefer, *Children, Education and Empire in Early Sierra Leone: Left in Our Hands* (London and New York: Routledge, 2019). See also William G. Clarence-Smith, 'The Redemption of Child Slaves by Christian Missionaries in Central Africa, 1878–1914' in Gwyn Campbell, Joseph C. Miller and Suzanne Miers (eds.), *Child Slaves in the Modern World* (Athens, OH: Ohio University Press, 2011), 173–90; David Maxwell, 'Freed Slaves, Missionaries, and Respectability: The Expansion of the Christian Frontier from Angola to Belgian Congo', *The Journal of African History*, 54 (2013), 79–102. For a comprehensive survey of ransoming and redemption practices, see Jennifer

Lofkrantz and Olatunji Ojo (eds.) *Ransoming, Captivity & Piracy in Africa and the Mediterranean* (Trenton, NJ: Africa World Press, 2016).

5   William Fox to Lord Glenelg, 14 April 1836, MMS, Gambia Correspondence, Fiche Box 25, Box No. 294.
6   Ganjool, inland and south of Saint Louis.
7   Ndakourroo, renamed Dakar by the French, was the Lebou name for the town on the Cape Verde peninsula.
8   Lt. Col. John Fraser, the British commander at Gorée, served on the west coast of Africa in 1801–4.
9   Richard Lloyd was British commander of Gorée from 1804 to 1808. His brother, Edward Lloyd, was captain in the Royal African Corps stationed at Gorée.
10 Possibly Pierre Buadin, a Franco-African négociant from Gorée.
11 The Reverend John Morgan arrived in The Gambia in April of 1821.
12 Here Macubma is likely referring to the Reverend R. Hawkins, who arrived in The Gambia in 1824.
13 S. Dawson arrived in The Gambia in 1826 or 1827.
14 Richard Marshall arrived in The Gambia in 1828. He was stationed at Bathurst until he died in 1830.
15 William Fox arrived in The Gambia in 1833.

CASE 21

1   Cupidon to Townley, 28 August 1831, MMS, Gambia Correspondence, Fiche Box 25, Box No. 293.
2   Brooks, *Western Africa and Cabo Verde*, 150.
3   David Perfect, *Historical Dictionary of The Gambia*, 5th edition (Lanham, MD: Rowman & Littlefield, 2016), 107.
4   John Morgan, *Reminiscences of the Founding of a Christian Mission on The Gambia* (London: Wesleyan Missionary House, 1864), 66.
5   William Moister, *Memorials of Missionary Labours in Africa and the West Indies: With Historical and Descriptive Observations* (London: John Mason, 1850), 66–7; Moister, *Missionary Stories: Narratives, Scenes, and Incidents* (London: Wesleyan Conference Office, 1877), 168.
6   See Brooks, *Western Africa and Cabo Verde*, 174; Martha Frederiks 'John Cupidon', *Dictionary of African Christian Biography*, https://dacb.org/stories/gambia/cupidon-john/, accessed 2 August 2021. Frederiks, *We Have Toiled*, 207–10.
7   Robert Maxwell MacBrair, *Sketches of Missionary's Travels in Egypt, Syria, Western African, &c., &c.* (London: Simpson, Marshall, and Company, 1839).
8   The Wesleyan Missionaries began work on MaCarthy's Island around 1830.
9   Blue Book 1832, CO 90/6; Blue Book 1836, CO 90/10.

10 Fox, *Brief History of the Wesleyan Missions*, 447.
11 Perfect, *Historical Dictionary*, 107.
12 That is, the time at daybreak when a cock characteristically crows.
13 Cupidon is describing his purchase by a signaré, one of the multilingual French-African business women of Gorée and Saint-Louis. See George E. Brooks, 'The Signares of St. Louis and Gorée: Women Entrepreneurs in Eighteenth-Century Senegal' in Nancy J. Hafkin and Edna Bay (eds.), *Women in Africa: Studies in Social and Economic Change* (Stanford, CA: Stanford University Press, 1976), 19–44; Brooks, *Eurafricans in Western Africa: Commerce, Social Status, Gender, and Religious Observance from the Sixteenth to the Eighteenth Century* (Athens, OH: Ohio University Press, 2003); Martin A. Klein, 'Urban Slavery in West and West Central Africa during the Transatlantic Slave Trade', *Journal of African Diaspora Archaeology and Heritage*, 10:1–2 (2021), 46–65.
14 John Morgan arrived in The Gambia in April of 1821 and headed the establishment of the MMS Gambia mission. For additional information, see Morgan, *Reminiscences of the Founding of a Christian Mission*.
15 Here Cupidon is referring to the Barra War of 1831–2. British and French forces assaulted Barra Point and Fort Bullen on the north bank of The Gambia River, directly across from St Mary's Island, and defeated the forces of the Barra kingdom. For additional information, see Donald R. Wright, *The World and a Very Small Place in Africa* (Armonk, NY: M. E. Sharp, 1997), 148–51. Paul Mmegha Mbaeyi, *British Military and Naval Forces in West African History 1807–1874* (London: NOK publishers, 1978), 72–8.

CASE 22

1 Searing, *West African Slavery and Atlantic Commerce*, 103, 105, 116–17.
2 Searing, *West African Slavery and Atlantic Commerce*, 104.
3 Mbaeyi, *British Military and Naval Forces in West African History,* 15.
4 Mahoney, 'Notes on Mulattoes of The Gambia', 125.
5 See Bronwen Everill, '"All the baubles that they needed": "Industriousness" and Slavery in Saint-Louis and Gorée', *Early American Studies: An Interdisciplinary Journal*, 15:4 (2017), 714–39; Hilary Jones, 'Women, Family and Daily Life in Senegal's Nineteenth-century Atlantic Towns', in Candido and Jones (eds.), *African Women in the Atlantic World*, 233–47.
6 Pierre Sallah was an emancipated African of Wolof parentage. He was born free in Senegal but captured as a child and sold as a slave to a signaré. He was one of a number of enslaved Africans who were 'redeemed' from slavery by the Methodists through an appeal to congregations in Britain. He was later educated by William Moister at St. Mary's, where he was appointed an assistance missionary to the Methodist Church. A brief account of his enslavement is found in Moister, *Missionary Stories,* 172–5.

CASE 23

1. In 1859 a colleague described Gum as '[o]ld he truly is in years ... [and] has lost his natural eyesight' having retired due to blindness in 1848. Frederiks, *We Have Toiled*, 212.

2. Makodu was the name of several leaders beginning with Makodu Kumba Jaring (1766–77), the Geej king who conquered Kajoor from Bawol. The reference to famine is not surprising, as a period of decreasing rainfall after 1747 led to frequent drought accompanied by famine and social crisis. See Searing, *West African Slavery and Atlantic Commerce*, 132–44.

3. Captain Alexander Grant left Gorée for The Gambia in March of 1816 with two officers, fifty members of the Royal African Corps, and twenty-four artisans. John Gum writes that Grant 'brought my master and I' on the journey. The purpose of this voyage was to rebuild the fort on James Island in order to protect British merchants trading on The Gambia River and to patrol the river for illegal slave ships. Finding James Fort in deplorable condition, the party instead began constructing a new settlement on Banjul. See Arnold Hughes and David Perfect, *Historical Dictionary of The Gambia*, 4th edition (Lanham, MD: Scarecrow Press, Inc., 2008), xxxiv, 90.

4. Fox, *A Brief History of the Wesleyan Missions*, 360.

5. William Fox to Lord Glenelg, 14 April 1836, MMS, Gambia Correspondence, Fiche Box 25, Box No. 294.

6. Fort James was an earlier island fortification, seized by English forces from the Dutch in 1661 and administered by the Royal Adventurers in Africa Company, Royal African Company, and the Company of Merchants Trading to Africa. John Gum is therefore not referring here to the construction of the fort but likely to the erection of a six-gun battery in 1816. See Kunta Kinteh Island and Related Sites, *UNESCO World Heritage Convention*, https://whc.unesco.org/en/list/761.

7. Here Gum is referring to Alexander Findlay, Lieutenant-Governor of The Gambia from 1829 to 1830.

8. Richard Marshall was among the first Methodist missionaries at The Gambia. By 1829 he had compiled a dictionary of about 2,000 Wolof words and translated a few chapters of the gospel of John. Frederiks, *We Have Toiled*, 47.

9. William Fox arrived in The Gambia in 1833. See Fox, *Brief History of the Wesleyan Missions*.

10. George Rendall served as lieutenant-governor of The Gambia from 1830 to 1837.

11. John Hughes was the son of the British merchant Thomas Hughes who had operated at Gorée for many years. John undertook a brief period of education in Britain before his father's death forced his return to Gorée. Here he worked as a clerk to the wealthy merchant John Finden. Mahoney, 'Notes on Mulattoes of The Gambia', 125.

CASE 24

1. Alpers, *Ivory and Slaves*, 236–7.
2. Marina Carter, Vishwanaden Govinden and Satyendra Peerthum, *The Last Slaves: Liberated Africans in Nineteenth Century Mauritius* (Port Louis: Centre for Research on Indian Ocean Societies, 2003), 23.
3. Hopper, *Slaves of One Master*, 25–6.
4. Hopper, 'Liberated Africans in the Indian Ocean World', 283.
5. Morton, *Children of Ham*, 52–8.
6. Robert W. Strayer, *The Making of Mission Communities in East Africa: Anglicans and Africans in Colonial Kenya, 1875–1935* (London: Heinemann, 1978), 14–19.
7. Lamb to Wright, 4 November 1876, CA5/O17.
8. Holmwood to Streeter, 6 July 1881, FO 541/49; Memorandum of Bombay Africans to the CMS, 28 February 1881, G3 A5 O/1881/30.
9. *Church Missionary Gleaner*, December 1884, Vol. XI, No 132, 140.
10. The *Constance* was a schooner of the Indian Navy (formerly Bombay Marine) launched in 1838. Charles Rathbone Low, *History of the Indian Navy (1613–1863), Vol. II* (London: Richard Bentley and Son, 1877), 105.
11. Rev. John Gottfried Deimler was a CMS missionary based at Bombay from 1855 to 1857. See C I3/O25.
12. Charles William Isenberg (also referred to in documents as Karl or Carl) was a German-born CMS missionary and linguist in Ethiopia and then Western India. See Charles William Isenberg, Letters and Papers, East Africa (Kenya) Mission (1842–3) C/A5/O13 and (1845–64) C I3/O38/1–76.

CASE 25

1. On the Yao see Alpers, *Ivory and Slaves*, 15.
2. Megan Vaughan, *Creating the Creole Island: Slavery in Eighteenth Century Mauritius* (Durham: Duke University Press, 2005), 119.
3. Reed, *Pastors, Partners, and Paternalists*, 186.
4. Morton, 'Small Change', 63.
5. Reed, *Pastors, Partners, and Pastoralists*, 18, 27. *Church Missionary Society Register of Missionaries*, List III, 'Native Clergy', entry 339, unpaginated.
6. Harris, *Repatriates and Refugees*, 13.
7. Quoted in Strayer, *The Making of Mission Communities in East Africa*, 26.
8. *CMS Intelligencer*, September 1904, 693. Reed, *Pastors, Partners, and Paternalists*, 1, 3.
9. Pereira, 'Returnee Africans of the Indian Ocean', 757, 761.

10 George Candy was an officer of the Bombay Army who joined the Society for the Propagation of the Gospel and took charge of the Indo-British Mission. *Church Missionary Society Register of Missionaries*, List I, 'Clerical and Lay Missionaries', entry 411, unpaginated. Theodore Zorn was a German merchant who, along with his wife and George Candy, established the first African Asylum at Bombay. Morton, *Children of Ham*, 53n6.

11 The Zorns had established the first Asylum for African boys at their residence on Waverly Hill. Morton, *Children of Ham*, 100.

12 The transcription of William Henry Jones' account in the *Church Missionary Gleaner* (Vol. XII, 1862, 8) transcribes Cromacunda as 'Asinacunda', though the former spelling is clear in the manuscript source. Cromacunda is not easily identified as a location within Yaoland. The term may relate to Chikunda, a language spoken in the area far inland west of Kilwa. If so, K(c)roma is probably a locative. The spelling of Asinacunda may be a combination of the prefix Asina ('there isno (none)') on the root (c)kunda. This may be a localism with some historic reference. Fred Morton – who kindly assisted with this interpretation – notes that both interpretations are speculative.

13 Kilwa.

CASE 26

1 Based on Isenberg's observation below that Semler was 'of about the same age as W.J [William Jones]'.

2 Semler's narrative below describes periods of enslavement totalling roughly eight years. If accurate, and if Semler arrived at Bombay in 1850 as published missionary sources indicate, then he was very young at the time of his enslavement.

3 Morton, 'Small Change', 63; *Church Missionary Society, Register of Missionaries and Native Clergy* (1904), List III, 'Native Clergy', entry 340, unpaginated.

4 Reed, *Pastors, Partners, and Pastoralists*, 18.

5 Reed, *Pastors, Partners, and Paternalists*, 2.

6 Brahmin, a varna (class) in Hinduism.

7 Inhambane in southern Mozambique.

CASE 27

1 Morton, 'Small Change', 64.

2 Raymond Howell, *The Royal Navy and the Slave Trade* (London and Sydney: Croom Helm, 1987), 104–7.

3 UK/HC/PP, 'Precis of Case of Moma Dhow', inclosure in No.121, 29 November 1875, Slave Trade No. 2 (1877), Correspondence with British

Representatives and Agents Abroad, and Reports from Naval Officers relating to Slave Trade, C.1829, LXXVIII.511, 76.

4 Hopper, *Slaves of One Master*, 169–80.

5 See Klara Boyer-Rossol, 'Makua Life Histories: Testimonies on Slavery and the Slave Trade in the 19th Century in Madagascar' in A. Bellagamba, S. E. Greene, and M. Klein (eds.), *African Voices, Vol. 1*, 466–80; Boyer-Rossol, 'The "Masombika" or "Makoa" in Madagascar', in Santos (ed.), *UNESCO General History of Africa, vol. X*, 345–54.

6 Likely Liberated Africans who had earlier been enlisted into the Navy.

BIBLIOGRAPHY

Manuscripts

Church Missionary Society Archives, University of Birmingham (CMS)
Sierra Leone Mission
Early Correspondence, CA1/E5-E8
Mission Books (Incoming), CA1/M1-M22
Original Papers (Incoming), CA1/O1-O235
Yoruba Mission
Original Papers (Incoming), CA2/O1-O99
East Africa (Kenya) Mission
Original Papers (Incoming, 1841–1880) CA5/O1-O27
Original Papers (Incoming, 1880–1934), G3 A5 O
Mission Books (Incoming), CA5/M1-M6
Western India Mission
Original Papers (Incoming), C/I3/O1-O85
Miscellaneous papers and artefacts for which the provenance is unknown
'Biographical accounts of Nigerian converts to Christianity early-mid 19th century', CMS Z/30

Methodist Missionary Society Archives, School of Oriental and African Studies (MMS)
  Sierra Leone/Gambia Correspondence
  Special Series: Biographical

The National Archives, Kew (TNA)
  Admiralty Papers
  Master's Logs, ADM 52
  Colonial Office Papers
  Gambia, Miscellanea, CO 90
  Lagos Original Correspondence, CO 147
  Sierra Leone Original Correspondence, CO 267
  Foreign Office Papers
  Slave Trade Department and Successors: General Correspondence FO 84

Archives of Sierra Leone Slave Trade Commission, FO 315
  Confidential Print Slave Trade, FO 541
  High Court of Admiralty
  Vice-Admiralty Court: Proceedings, HCA 49

Sierra Leone Public Archives, Fourah Bay College, Freetown
Liberated African Registers and Duplicate Registers (20 volumes)

Published Contemporary Sources

Anti-Slavery Reporter
Church Missionary Society
  Annual Reports
  Church Missionary Gleaner
  Church Missionary Intelligencer
  Church Missionary Record
  The CMS Juvenile Instructor
  Proceedings of the Church Missionary Society for Africa and the East
  Register of Missionaries (clerical, lay, & female), and Native Clergy, from 1804–1904
House of Commons, Parliamentary Papers
  Correspondence with British Representatives and Agents Abroad, and Reports from Naval Officers relating to Slave Trade
The Wesleyan Missionary Notices, Relating Principally to the Foreign Missions under the Direction of the Methodist Conference
d'Avezac de Castera-Macaya, Marie-Armand. *Notice sur le Pays et le Peuple des Yébous en Afrique*. Paris: Vve Dondey-Dupré, 1845.
Beecham, John. *Ashantee and the Gold Coast*. London: John Mason, 1841.
Childe, A. F. *Good out of Evil; Or, the History of Adjai, the African Slave-Boy*. London: Wertheim and Macintosh, 1852.
Columb, Philip Howard. *Slave-Catching in the Indian Ocean: A Record of Naval Experiences*. London: Longmans, Green and co., 1873.
Fox, William. *A Brief History of the Wesleyan Missions on the West Coast of Africa*. London: Aylott and Jones, 1851.
Jones-Bateman, Percy L. (ed.). *The Autobiography of an African Slave Boy*. London: Universities' Mission to Central Africa, 1891.
Kilekwa, Petro. *Slave Boy to Priest: The Autobiography of Padre Petro Kilekwa*. Westminster: Universities' Mission to Central Africa, 1937.
Koelle, Sigismund Wilhelm. *African Native Literature: Or Proverbs, Tales, Fables & Historical Fragments in the Kanuri or Bornu Language*. London: Church Missionary House, 1854.
Koelle, Sigismund Wilhelm. *Polyglotta Africana: or a Comparative Vocabulary of Nearly Three Hundred Words and Phrases in More than One Hundred Distinct African Languages*. London: Church Missionary House, 1854.
Low, Charles Rathbone. *History of the Indian Navy (1613–1863), Vol. II*. London: Richard Bentley and Son, 1877.
MacBrair, Robert Maxwell. *Sketches of Missionary's Travels in Egypt, Syria, Western African, &c., &c*. London: Simpson, Marshall, and Company, 1839.
Madan, Arthur C. (trs. and ed.). *Kiungani; or, Story and History from Central Africa*. London: George Bell and Sons, 1887.
Marke, Charles. *Origin of Wesleyan Methodism in Sierra Leone and History of Its Missions: Interspersed with Brief Notices of Other Missionary Societies in the Colony*. London: Charles H. Kelly, 1913.

May, J. Claudius. *A Brief Sketch of the Life of the Rev. Joseph May, Native of the Yoruba Country, and Late Wesleyan Minister of the Colony of Sierra Leone, Read at the Service of Song in Zion Church, Freetown, on Sunday, 25 October 1896*. Freetown, 1896.

Mbotela, James Juma. *The Freeing of the Slaves in East Africa*. London: Evans Brothers Limited, 1956.

Melville, Helen Elizabeth. *A Residence at Sierra Leone: Described from a Journal Kept on the Spot, and Letters Written to Friends at Home*. London: John Murray, 1849.

Moister, William. *Memorials of Missionary Labours in Africa and the West Indies: With Historical and Descriptive Observations*. London: John Mason, 1850.

Moister, William. *Memorials of Missionary Labours in Western Africa, the West Indies, and at the Cape of Good Hope*. 3rd edition. London: W. Nichols, 1866.

Moister, William. *Missionary Stories: Narratives, Scenes, and Incidents*. London: Wesleyan Conference Office, 1877.

Morgan, John. *Reminiscences of the Founding of a Christian Mission on The Gambia*. London: Wesleyan Missionary House, 1864.

Page, Jesse. *The Black Bishop: Samuel Adjai Crowther*. London: Hodder and Stoughton, 1908.

Price, William Salter. *My Third Campaign in East Africa: A Story of Missionary Life in Troubled Times*. London: W. Hunt & Co., 1891.

Raban, John. *A Vocabulary of the Eyo, or Aku*. Vol. III. London: CMS Bookshop, 1832.

Schön, James Frederick and Samuel Crowther. *Journals of the Rev. James Frederick Schön and Mr. Samuel Crowther Who, with the Sanction of Her Majesty's Government, Accompanied the Expedition up the Niger, in 1841, in Behalf of the Church Missionary Society*. London: Hatchard and Son, 1842.

Seeley, Robert B. (ed.). *A Memoir of the Rev. W.A.B. Johnson, Missionary of the Church Missionary Society, in Regent's Town, Sierra Leone, Africa*. New York: Robert Carter & Brothers, 1853.

Sherwood, Mrs. [Mary Martha]. *Dazee, or the Re-captured Negro*. Newburyport, MA: W. & J. Gilman, 1822.

Secondary Sources

Abruzzo, Margaret. *Polemical Pain: Slavery, Cruelty, and the Rise of Humanitarianism*. Baltimore: The Johns Hopkins University Press, 2011.

Ajayi, J. F. Ade. *Christian Missions in Nigeria, 1841–1891: The Making of a New Elite*. London: Longmans, 1965.

Ajayi, J. F. Ade. 'The Aftermath of the Fall of Old Oyo'. In J. F. Ade Ajayi and Michael Crowder, (eds.) *History of West Africa, Volume Two*. New York: Columbia University Press, 1973, 129–66.

Alpers, Edward A. *Ivory and Slaves: Changing Pattern of International Trade in East Central Africa to the Later Nineteenth Century*. Berkeley and Los Angeles: University of California Press, 1975.

Alpers, Edward A. 'The Story of Swema: Female Vulnerability in Nineteenth-Century East Africa'. In Claire Robertson and Martin A. Klein, (eds.) *Women and Slavery in Africa*. Madison: University of Wisconsin Press, 1983, 185–219.

Alpers, Edward A. 'The Other Middle Passage: The African Slave Trade in the Indian Ocean'. In Emma Christopher, Cassandra Pybus and Marcus Rediker, (eds.) *Many Middle Passages: Forced Migration and the Making of the Modern World*. Berkeley/Los Angeles/London: University of California Press, 2007, 20–38.

Alpers, Edward A. 'Representations of Children in the East African Slave Trade', *Slavery & Abolition* 30, no. 1 (2009): 27–40.

Alpers, Edward A. and Matthew S. Hopper. 'Speaking for Themselves? Understanding African Freed Slave Testimonies from the Western Indian Ocean, 1850s–1930s', *Journal of Indian Ocean World Studies* 1 (2017): 60–88.

Anderson, Richard. 'The Diaspora of Sierra Leone's Liberated Africans: Enlistment, Forced Migration, and "Liberation" at Freetown, 1808–1863', *African Economic History* 41 (2013): 103–40.

Anderson, Richard. 'Uncovering Testimonies of Slavery and the Slave Trade in Missionary Sources: The SHADD Biographies Project and the CMS and MMS Archives for Sierra Leone, Nigeria, and The Gambia', *Slavery & Abolition* 38, no. 3 (2017): 620–44.

Anderson, Richard. *Abolition in Sierra Leone: Re-building Lives and Identities in Nineteenth-Century West Africa*. Cambridge: Cambridge University Press, 2020.

Anderson, Richard. 'Liberated Africans', In *The Oxford Research Encyclopedia of African History*. Oxford: Oxford University Press, 2021. https://doi.org/10.1093/acrefore/9780190277734.013.741

Anderson, Richard. ''Alī Eisami Gazirmabe'. In *The Oxford Research Encyclopedia of African History*. Oxford: Oxford University Press, 2022. https://doi.org/10.1093/acrefore/9780190277734.013.961

Anderson, Richard. 'Abolition's Adolescence: Apprenticeship as "Liberation" in Sierra Leone, 1808–1848', *English Historical Review* 137, no. 585 (2022): 763–93.

Anderson, Richard and Henry B. Lovejoy (eds.). *Liberated Africans and the Abolition of the Slave Trade, 1807–1896*. Rochester: Rochester University Press, 2020.

Ayandele, E. A. *The Missionary Impact on Modern Nigeria, 1842–1914: A Political and Social Analysis*. London: Longman, 1966.

Bailey, Anne C. *African Voices of the Atlantic Slave Trade: Beyond the Silence and the Shame*. Boston: Beacon Press, 2005.

Bascom, William. *Ifa Divination: Communication between Gods and Men in West Africa*. Bloomington: Indiana University Press, 1969.

Bebbington, David William. *Evangelicalism in Modern Britain: A History from the 1730s to the 1980s*. London: Routledge, 1989.

Bellagamba, Alice. 'Slavery and Emancipation in the Colonial Archives: British Officials, Slave-Owners, and Slaves in the Protectorate of The Gambia (1890–1936)', *Canadian Journal of African Studies/Revue canadienne des études africaines* 39, no. 1 (2005): 5–41.

Bellagamba, Alice, Sandra E. Greene and Martin Klein (eds.). *African Voices on Slavery and the Slave Trade: Vol. 1*. Cambridge: University of Cambridge Press, 2013.

Bellagamba, Alice, Sandra E. Greene and Martin Klein (eds.). *African Voices on Slavery and the Slave Trade: Vol. 2: Essays on Sources and Methods*. Cambridge: University of Cambridge Press, 2016.

Bethell, Leslie. *The Abolition of the Brazilian Slave Trade: Britain, Brazil, and the Slave Trade Question, 1807–1869*. Cambridge: Cambridge University Press, 1970.

Biobaku, Saburi O. *The Egba and Their Neighbours, 1842–1872*. Oxford: Clarendon Press, 1957.
Blassingame, John W. (ed.). *Slave Testimony: Two Centuries of Letters, Speeches, Interviews, and Autobiographies*. Baton Rouge: Louisiana State University Press, 1977.
Brooks, George E. 'The Signares of St. Louis and Gorée: Women Entrepreneurs in Eighteenth-Century Senegal'. In Nancy J. Hafkin and Edna Bay, (eds.) *Women in Africa: Studies in Social and Economic Change*. Stanford, CA: Stanford University Press, 1976, 19–44.
Brooks, George E. *Eurafricans in Western Africa: Commerce, Social Status, Gender, and Religious Observance from the Sixteenth to the Eighteenth Century*. Athens: Ohio University Press, 2003.
Brooks, George E. *Western Africa and Cabo Verde, 1790s–1830s: Symbiosis of Slave and Legitimate Trades*. Bloomington, IN: Authorhouse, 2010.
Campbell, Gwyn (ed.). *The Structure of Slavery in Indian Ocean Africa and Asia*. London: Frank Cass, 2004.
Campbell, Gwyn, Suzanne Miers and Joseph C. Miller (eds.). *Children in Slavery through the Ages*. Athens, OH: Ohio University Press, 2009.
Campbell, James. *Middle Passages: African American Journeys to Africa, 1787–2005*. New York: Penguin, 2006.
Candido, Mariana P. 'The Expansion of Slavery in Benguela during the Nineteenth Century', *International Review of Social History* 65, Special Issue S28 (2020): 67–92.
Candido, Mariana P. and Adam Jones (eds.). *African Women in the Atlantic World: Property, Vulnerability & Mobility, 1660–1880*. Woodbridge: James Currey, 2019.
Carter, Marina, Vishwanaden Govinden and Satyendra Peerthum. *The Last Slaves: Liberated Africans in Nineteenth Century Mauritius*. Port Louis: Centre for Research on Indian Ocean Societies, 2003.
Chapdelaine, Robin Phylisia. *The Persistence of Slavery: An Economic History of Child Trafficking in Nigeria*. Amherst: University of Massachusetts Press, 2021.
Christopher, Emma. *Freedom in Black and White: A Lost Story of the Illegal Slave Trade and Its Global Legacy*. Madison: University of Wisconsin Press, 2018.
Clarence-Smith, William G. 'The Redemption of Child Slaves by Christian Missionaries in Central Africa, 1878–1914'. In Gwyn Campbell, Joseph C. Miller and Suzanne Miers, (eds.) *Child Slaves in the Modern World*. Athens, OH: Ohio University Press, 2011, 173–90.
Curtin, Philip D. (ed.). *Africa Remembered: Narratives by West Africans from the Era of the Slave Trade*. Madison: University of Wisconsin Press, 1967.
Curtin, Philip D. *Economic Change in Precolonial Africa: Senegambia in the Era of the Slave Trade*. Madison: University of Wisconsin Press, 1975.
Davis, Charles T. and Henry Louis Gates, Jr. (eds.). *The Slave's Narrative*. Oxford: Oxford University Press, 1991.
Davis, Natalie Zemon. *Fiction in the Archives: Pardon Tales and Their Tellers in Sixteenth-Century France*. Cambridge: Polity Press, 1987.
Diptee, Audra. 'Notions of African Childhood in Abolitionist Discourses: Colonial and Post-Colonial Humanitarianism in the Fight against Child Slavery'. In Anna Mae Duane, (ed.) *Child Slavery before & after Emancipation*. New York: Cambridge University Press, 2017, 208–30.

Domingues da Silva, Daniel B., David Eltis, Philip Misevich and Olatunji Ojo. 'The Diaspora of Africans Liberated from Slave Ships in the Nineteenth Century', *Journal of African History* 55, no. 3 (2014): 347–69.
Doulton, Lindsay. 'The Royal Navy's Anti-slavery Campaign in the Western Indian Ocean, *c.* 1860–1890: Race, Empire and Identity', unpublished PhD dissertation, University of Hull, 2010.
Eltis, David. 'The Slave Trade in Nineteenth-Century Nigeria'. In Toyin Falola and Ann O'Hear, (eds.) *Studies in the Nineteenth-Century Economic History of Nigeria*. Madison: African Studies Program, University of Wisconsin, 1998, 85–96.
Ernest, John (ed.). *The Oxford Handbook of the African American Slave Narrative*. Oxford: Oxford University Press, 2014.
Everill, Bronwen. '"All the Baubles That They Needed": "Industriousness" and Slavery in Saint-Louis and Gorée', *Early American Studies: An Interdisciplinary Journal* 15, no. 4 (2017): 714–39.
Falola, Toyin. 'Missionaries and Domestic Slavery in Yorubaland in the Nineteenth Century', *Journal of Religious History* 14, no. 2 (1986): 181–92.
Falola, Toyin. *The African Diaspora: Slavery, Modernity, and Globalization*. Rochester, NY: University of Rochester Press, 2013.
Falola, Toyin and Akintunde Akinyemi (eds.). *Encyclopedia of the Yoruba*. Bloomington: Indiana University Press, 2016.
Falola, Toyin and G. O. Oguntomísín. *Yoruba Warlords of the 19th Century*. Trenton, NJ: Africa World Press, 2001.
Falola, Toyin and Matt D. Childs (eds.). *The Yoruba Diaspora in the Atlantic World*. Bloomington: Indiana University Press, 2004.
Ferguson, Moira. 'Fictional Constructions of Liberated Africans: Mary Butt Sherwood'. In Tim Fulford and Peter J. Kitson, (eds.) *Romanticism and Colonialism: Writing and Empire, 1780–1830*. Cambridge: Cambridge University Press, 1998, 148–64.
Ferreira, Roquinaldo. *Cross-cultural Exchange in the Atlantic World: Angola and Brazil during the Era of the Slave Trade*. Cambridge: Cambridge University Press, 2012.
Fogleman, Aaron Spencer and Robert Hanserd (eds.). *Five Hundred African Voices: A Catalog of Published Accounts by Africans Enslaved in the Transatlantic Slave Trade, 1586–1936*. Philadelphia, PA: American Philosophical Society, 2022.
Fọlayan, Kọla. 'The Career of Thomas Tickel in the Western District of Lagos, 1854–1886', *Journal of the Historical Society of Nigeria* 5, no. 1 (1969): 27–46.
Frederiks, Martha T. *We Have Toiled All Night: Christianity in The Gambia, 1456–2000*. Zoetermeer: Boekencentrum, 2003.
Fuentes, Marisa J. *Dispossessed Lives: Enslaved Women, Violence, and the Archive*. Philadelphia: University of Pennsylvania Press, 2018.
Fyfe, Christopher. 'Four Sierra Leone Receptives', *Journal of African History* 2, no. 1 (1961): 77–85.
Fyfe, Christopher. *A History of Sierra Leone*. London: Oxford University Press, 1962.
Getz, Trevor R. *Abina and the Important Men*. 2nd edition. Oxford: Oxford University Press, 2015.
Getz, Trevor R. and Lindsay Ehrisman. 'The Marriages of Abina Mansah: Escaping the Boundaries of "Slavery" as a Category in Historical Analysis', *Journal of West African History* 1, no. 1 (Spring 2015): 93–117.

Gijanto, Liza. 'Serving Status on The Gambia River before and after Abolition', *Current Anthropology* 61, no. S22 (2020): S260–S275.
Gray, John Milner. *A History of The Gambia*. Cambridge: Cambridge University Press, 1940.
Greene, Sandra. *West African Narratives of Slavery: Texts from Late Nineteenth- and Early Twentieth-Century Ghana*. Bloomington: Indiana University Press, 2011.
Griffiths, Gareth. '"Trained to Tell the Truth": Missionaries, Converts, and Narration'. In Norman Etherington, (ed.) *Missions and Empire*. Oxford: Oxford University Press, 2005, 153–72.
Hair, P. E. H. 'The Enslavement of Koelle's Informants', *Journal of African History* 6, no. 2 (1965): 193–203.
Halttunen, Karen. 'Humanitarianism and the Pornography of Pain in Anglo-American Culture', *The American Historical Review* 100, no. 2 (1995): 303–34.
Handler, Jerome. 'Survivors of the Middle Passage: Life Histories of Enslaved Africans in British America', *Slavery & Abolition* 23, no. 1 (2002): 25–56.
Harms, Robert, Bernard K. Freamon and David W. Blight (eds.). *Indian Ocean Slavery in the Age of Abolition*. New Haven: Yale University Press, 2013.
Harris, Joseph E. *Repatriates and Refugees in a Colonial Society: The Case of Kenya*. Washington, DC: Howard University Press, 1987.
Hopper, Matthew S. *Slaves of One Master: Globalization and Slavery in Arabia in the Age of Empire*. New Haven: Yale University Press, 2015.
Howell, Raymond. *The Royal Navy and the Slave Trade*. London and Sydney: Croom Helm, 1987.
Huzzey, Richard. *Freedom Burning: Anti-slavery and Empire in Victorian Britain*. Ithaca: Cornell University Press, 2012.
Johnston, Anna. *Missionary Writing and Empire, 1800–1860*. Cambridge: Cambridge University Press, 2003.
Jones, Adam. 'Recaptive Nations: Evidence Concerning the Demographic Impact of the Atlantic Slave Trade in the Early Nineteenth Century', *Slavery & Abolition* 11, no. 1 (1990): 42–57.
Jones, Hilary. *The Métis of Senegal: Urban Life and Politics in French West Africa*. Bloomington: Indiana University Press, 2013.
Keefer, Katrina. *Children, Education and Empire in Early Sierra Leone: Left in Our Hands*. London and New York: Routledge, 2019.
Klein, Martin A. 'Urban Slavery in West and West Central Africa during the Transatlantic Slave Trade', *Journal of African Diaspora Archaeology and Heritage* 10, no. 1–2 (2021): 46–65.
Kopytoff, Jean Herskovits. *A Preface to Modern Nigeria: The 'Sierra Leonians' in Yoruba, 1830–1890*. Madison: University of Wisconsin Press, 1965.
La Rue, George Michael. 'Seeking Freedom in Multiple Contexts', *Journal of Global Slavery* 2, no. 1–2 (2017): 11–43.
Larson, Pier M. 'Horrid Journeying: Narratives of Enslavement and the Global African Diaspora', *Journal of World History* 19, no. 4 (2008): 25–56.
Law, Robin. 'The Chronology of the Yoruba Wars of the Early Nineteenth Century: A Reconsideration', *Journal of the Historical Society of Nigeria* 2 (1970): 211–22.
Law, Robin. 'The Owu War in Yoruba History', *Journal of the Historical Society of Nigeria* 7, no. 1 (1973): 141–7.

Law, Robin. *The Oyo Empire c.1600–c.1836: A West African Imperialism in the Era of the Atlantic Slave Trade*. Oxford: Clarendon Press, 1977.
Law, Robin. 'Abolition and Imperialism: International Law and the British Suppression of the Atlantic Slave Trade'. In Derek R. Peterson, (ed.) *Abolitionism and Imperialism in Britain, Africa, and the Atlantic*. Athens: Ohio University Press, 2010, 150–74.
Law, Robin and Paul E. Lovejoy (eds.). *The Biography of Mahommah Gardo Baquaqua: His Passage from Slavery to Freedom in Africa*. Princeton: Marcus Wiener, 2001.
Lewis, Joanna. *Empire of Sentiment: The Death of Livingstone and the Myth of Victorian Imperialism*. Cambridge: Cambridge University Press, 2018.
Lindsay, Lisa. *Atlantic Bonds: A Nineteenth-Century Odyssey from America to Africa*. Chapel Hill: University of North Carolina Press, 2017.
Lindsay, Lisa A. and John Wood Sweet (eds.). *Biography and the Black Atlantic*. Philadelphia: University of Pennsylvania Press, 2014.
Lloyd, Christopher. *The Navy and the Slave Trade: The Suppression of the African Slave Trade in the Nineteenth Century*. London: Cass, 1949.
Lofkrantz, Jennifer and Olatunji Ojo (eds.). *Ransoming, Captivity & Piracy in Africa and the Mediterranean*. Trenton, NJ: Africa World Press, 2016.
Lovejoy, Henry B. 'Mapping Uncertainty: The Collapse of Oyo and the Trans-Atlantic Slave Trade, 1816–1836', *Journal of Global Slavery* 4, no. 2 (2019): 127–61.
Lovejoy, Paul E. 'Biography as Source Material: Towards a Biographical Archive of Enslaved Africans'. In Robin Law and Douglas Chambers, (ed.) *Source Material for Studying the Slave Trade and the African Diaspora: Papers from a Conference of the Centre of Commonwealth Studies, University of Stirling, April 1996*. Stirling: University of Stirling, 1997, 119–40.
Lovejoy, Paul E. 'The Children of Slavery – the Transatlantic Phase', *Slavery & Abolition* 27, no. 2 (2006): 197–217.
Lovejoy, Paul E. '"Freedom Narratives" of Transatlantic Slavery', *Slavery & Abolition* 32, no. 1 (2011): 91–107.
Lovejoy, Paul E. *Jihād in West Africa during the Age of Revolutions*. Athens: Ohio University Press, 2016.
Mahoney, Florence K. Omolara. 'Government and Opinion in The Gambia', unpublished PhD dissertation, School of Oriental and African Studies, 1963.
Mahoney, Florence K. Omolara. 'Notes on Mulattoes of The Gambia before the Mid-Nineteenth Century', *Transactions of the Historical Society of Ghana* 8 (1965): 120–29.
Mahoney, Florence K. Omolara. *Stories of Senegambia*. Banjul: Government Printer, 1982.
Mahoney, Florence K. Omolara. *Creole Saga: The Gambia's Liberated African Community in the Nineteenth Century*. Banjul: Baobab Printers, 2006.
Mann, Kristin. *Slavery and the Birth of an African City: Lagos, 1760–1900*. Bloomington: Indiana University Press, 2007.
Mann, Kristin and Richard L. Roberts (eds.). *Law in Colonial Africa*. Portsmouth, NH and London: James Currey, 1991.
Manneh, Lamin. 'Island Citizens: Environment, Infrastructure, and Belonging in Colonial Gambia, 1816–1965', unpublished PhD dissertation, University of Michigan, 2023.

Maxwell, David. 'Freed Slaves, Missionaries, and Respectability: The Expansion of the Christian Frontier from Angola to Belgian Congo', *The Journal of African History* 54 (2013): 79–102.
Mbaeyi, Paul Mmegha. *British Military and Naval Forces in West African History 1807–1874*. London: NOK publishers, 1978.
McIntosh, Marjorie Keniston. *Yoruba Women, Work, and Social Change*. Bloomington: Indiana University Press, 2009.
McMahon, Elisabeth. 'Trafficking and Re-enslavement: Social Vulnerability of Women and Children in Nineteenth Century East Africa'. In Benjamin Lawrance and Richard Roberts, (eds.) *Trafficking in Slavery's Wake: Law and the Experience of Women and Children in Africa*. Athens: Ohio University Press, 2012, 29–44.
Moitt, Bernard. 'Slavery, Flight and Redemption in Senegal, 1819–1905', *Slavery and Abolition* 14, no. 2 (1993): 70–86.
Moitt, Bernard. *Child Slavery and Guardianship in Colonial Senegal*. Cambridge: Cambridge University Press, 2024.
Morgan, Jennifer L. *Reckoning with Slavery: Gender, Kinship, and Capitalism in the Early Black Atlantic*. Durham and London: Duke University Press, 2021.
Morton, Fred. *Children of Ham: Freed Slaves and Fugitive Slaves on the Kenya Coast, 1873–1907*. Boulder: Westview Press, 1990.
O'Hear, Ann. 'The Enslavement of Yoruba'. In Toyin Falola and Matt D. Childs, (eds.) *The Yoruba Diaspora in the Atlantic World*. Bloomington: Indiana University Press, 2004, 56–73.
Ojo, Olatunji. 'Child Slaves in Pre-colonial Nigeria', *Slavery & Abolition* 33, no. 3 (2012): 417–34.
Ojo, Olatunji. 'The Yoruba Church Missionary Society Slavery Conference 1880', *African Economic History* 49, no. 1 (2021): 73–103.
Olney, James. '"I Was Born": Slave Narratives, Their Status as Autobiography and as Literature', *Callaloo* 20 (Winter 1984): 46–73.
Oroge, E. Adeniyi. 'The Fugitive Slave Crisis of 1859: A Factor in the Growth of Anti-British Feelings among the Yoruba', *Odu* 12 (1975): 40–53.
Oroge, E. Adeniyi. 'The Fugitive Slave Question in Anglo-Egba Relations, 1861–1886', *Journal of the Historical Society of Nigeria* 8 (1975): 61–80.
Oyewumi, Oyeronke. *The Invention of Women: Making an African Sense of Western Gender Discourses*. Minneapolis: University of Minnesota Press, 1997.
Palmié, Stephan. 'Slavery, Historicism, and the Poverty of Memorialisation'. In Susannah Radstone and Bill Schwarz, (eds.) *Memory: Histories, Theories, Debates*. New York: Fordham University Press, 2010, 363–75.
Peel, J. D. Y. 'Gender in Yoruba Religious Change', *Journal of Religion in Africa* 32, Fasc. 2, The Politics of Mission (2002): 136–66.
Peel, J. D. Y. *Religious Encounter and the Making of the Yoruba*. Bloomington: Indiana University Press, 2000.
Perfect, David. *Historical Dictionary of The Gambia*. 5th ed. Lanham, MD: Rowman & Littlefield, 2016.
Peterson, John. *Province of Freedom: A History of Sierra Leone, 1787–1870*. London: Faber and Faber, 1969.
Prochnow, Kyle. '"Saving an Extraordinary Expense to the Nation": African Recruitment for the West India Regiments in the British Atlantic World', *Atlantic Studies* 18, no. 2 (2021): 149–71.

Reed, Colin. *Pastors, Partners and Paternalists: African Church Leaders and Western Missionaries in the Anglican Church in Kenya, 1850–1900*. Leiden: Brill, 1997.

Reis, João José. *Divining Slavery and Freedom: The Story of Domingos Sodré, an African Priest in Nineteenth-Century Brazil*. New York: Cambridge University Press, 2015.

Reis, João José, Flávio dos Santos Gomes and Marcus J. M. de Carvalho. *The Story of Rufino: Slavery, Freedom, and Islam in the Black Atlantic*. Oxford: Oxford University Press, 2019.

Robinson, Morgan J. 'Binding Words: Student Biographical Narratives and Religious Conversion'. In Klaas van Walraven, (ed.) *The Individual in African History: The Importance of Biography in African Historical Studies*. Brill: Leiden and Boston, 2020, 197–218.

Ryan, Maeve. '"A Most Promising Field for Future Usefulness": The Church Missionary Society and the Liberated Africans of Sierra Leone'. In William Mulligan and Maurice Bric, (eds.) *A Global History of Anti-slavery Politics in the Nineteenth Century*. Houndmills, Basingstoke and Hampshire: Palgrave Macmillan, 2013, 37–58.

Ryan, Maeve. *Humanitarian Governance and the British Anti-slavery World System*. New Haven: Yale University Press, 2022.

Saho, Bala. 'The Gambia'. In *the Oxford Research Encyclopedia of African History*, 2019. https://doi.org/10.1093/acrefore/9780190277734.013.623

Santos, Vaniclêia Silva (ed.). *UNESCO General History of Africa, vol. X: Africa and Its Diasporas*. Paris: United Nations Educational, Scientific and Cultural Organization, 2023.

Scanlan, Padraic X. *Freedom's Debtors: British Antislavery in Sierra Leone in the Age of Revolution*. New Haven, CT: Yale University Press, 2017.

Searing, James F. *West African Slavery and Atlantic Commerce: The Senegal River Valley, 1700–1860*. Cambridge: Cambridge University Press, 1993.

Shields, Francine. 'Those Who Remained Behind: Women Slaves in Nineteenth-Century Yorubaland'. In Paul E. Lovejoy, (ed.) *Identity in the Shadow of Slavery*. London: Continuum, 2000, 183–201.

Smith, Robert. *The Kingdoms of the Yoruba*. Third Edition. Madison: University of Wisconsin Press, 1988.

Sparks, Randy J. *The Two Princes of Calabar: An Eighteenth-Century Atlantic Odyssey*. Cambridge, MA: Harvard University Press, 2004.

Spitzer, Leo. *Lives in Between: Assimilation and Marginality in Austria, Brazil, and West Africa, 1780–1945*. Cambridge: Cambridge University Press, 1989.

Spitzer, Leo. 'A Name Given, a Name Taken: Camouflaging, Resistance, and Diasporic Social Identity', *Comparative Studies of South Asia, Africa and the Middle East* 30, no. 1 (2010): 21–31.

Strayer, Robert W. *The Making of Mission Communities in East Africa: Anglicans and Africans in Colonial Kenya, 1875–1935*. London: Heinemann, 1978.

Strickrodt, Silke. 'African Girls' Samplers from Mission Schools in Sierra Leone (1820s to 1840s)', *History in Africa: A Journal of Method* 37 (2010): 189–245.

Sweet, James H. *Domingos Álvares, African Healing, and the Intellectual History of the Atlantic World*. Chapel Hill: University of North Carolina Press, 2011.

Thorne, Susan. '"The Conversion of Englishmen and the Conversion of the World Inseparable": Missionary Imperialism and the Language of Class in Early

Industrial Britain'. In Frederick Cooper and Ann Laura Stoler, (eds.) *Tensions of Empire: Colonial Cultures in a Bourgeois World*. Berkeley: University of California Press, 1997, 238–62.

Van Rossum, Matthias, Alexander Geelen, Bram van den Hout and Merve Tosun. *Testimonies of Enslavement: Sources on Slavery from the Indian Ocean World*. London: Bloomsbury, 2020.

Vaughan, Megan. *Creating the Creole Island: Slavery in Eighteenth Century Mauritius*. Durham: Duke University Press, 2005.

Welch, Kimberly M. *Black Litigants in the Antebellum American South*. Chapel Hill: The University of North Carolina Press, 2018.

White, Sophie and Trevor Burnard (eds.). *Hearing Enslaved Voices: African and Indian Testimony in British and French America, 1700–1848*. Abingdon: Routledge, 2020.

Wilson, Richard Ashby and Richard D. Brown (eds.). *Humanitarianism and Suffering: The Mobilization of Empathy*. Cambridge: Cambridge University Press, 2008.

Wright, Donald R. *The World and a Very Small Place in Africa*. Armonk, NY: M. E. Sharp, 1997.

Wright, Marcia. *Strategies of Slaves & Women: Life Stories from East/Central Africa*. New York: Lilian Barber Press, 1993.

INDEX

Abeokuta 12–13, 18, 44, 83, 95, 100, 103, 114, 118, 125–6, 129, 193 nn.5–6
Act for the Abolition of Slavery (1833) 134
Act for the Abolition of Slave Trade (1807) 35, 187 n.2
African Asylum 20, 162, 201 nn.10–11
Africa Remembered (Curtin) 1, 81–2, 175 n.3
Ajayi, J. F. Ade 18, 53, 188 n.2
Akinlu/Akinyalu 64
Aku 9, 44, 65, 83
Allen, William 12–13
Alpers, Edward A. 20–1, 176 n.6, 179 n.26, 185 n.89
amanuensis 6, 8, 21, 113, 117
anti-slavery squadron 20
apprenticeship 64–5, 187 n.2, 190 n.21, 194 n.4
Arab slave trade 18, 23, 155, 162
Attarra, John 7–8, 40, 187 n.2, 187 n.6
   life history 43–4
   statement of 44–8
autobiographical narratives 5–6
Avizo 10, 108, 181 n.45
Awa 6, 13, 18
   deposition of 127–8
   Dopemu, Daniel 126
   Robbin, Henry 125–6
   testimony of 126
Ayandele, E. A. 18

Badagry 12, 16, 64, 76, 95, 100, 108, 179 n.30, 181 n.45, 193 n.6
Bambah 28–9
Banjul 16, 199 n.3
Bann 114
Barber, James 11, 13, 103–5

Bassa (Liberia) 15, 35–6
Bathurst 16–17, 57, 114, 133–4, 137–8, 144, 180 n.33, 188 n.6
Beecham, John 191 n.2
Bight of Benin 2, 6, 10–11, 13–14, 16, 64, 114, 125–6, 179 n.30
Bight of Biafra 10, 185 n.3, 186 n.10
Bola, Joseph 113–14
Bola, Susannah
   birth name (Karunwi) 114
   Crowther, Susan 114
   Doherty, William 113–14
   enslavement 114
   life history 115
Bombay Africans 20–1, 155–6, 168, 178 n.22, 184 n.79, 200 n.8
Bom Jesus dos Navegantes 49, 188 nn.3–4
Bostock, Robert 35–6, 186 n.1
Brenn, Lewis 172
A Brief Memoir of the Late Peter Wilson (Eliza) 108–11, 181 n.44

Cameroon grasslands 15
Campbell, John 9, 195 n.2
   life history 49
   statement of 50–1
Candido, Mariana P. 179 n.27
Candy, George 201 n.10
Chikunda 201 n.12
Church Missionary Society (CMS) 1–2, 15, 18, 169–70, 177 nn.12–13, 178 n.19
   Awa 126
   Bola, Susannah 114
   David, George 155–6
   Doherty, William 117–18
   Gerber, James 95
   Industrial Mission 20

Isenberg, Charles William 200 n. 12
Jones, William Henry 162
journal extracts 3
King, Thomas 99–100
'native agents' 11–12
Noah, David 35
Semler, Ishmael 167
 in Sierra Leone 196 n.4
Townsend, Henry 114
Yoruba mission 3, 11–12, 182 n.58
CMS. *See* Church Missionary Society (CMS)
cocoa 186 n.9
Cole, Thomas 114
Colomb, Philip Howard 184 n.82
composition process 8
Constance 200 n.10
conversion 2, 17–18, 82–3, 118, 156, 176 n.6, 189 n.1
 Awa 126
 importance of 180 n.31
 spiritual 7–8
 statements 7
 Yoruba 117
Cromacunda 201 n.12
Crosby, Benjamin 191 n.24
Crowther, Samuel 12, 22, 82, 178 n.18, 179 n.28
 barracoon 4
 'Narratives of Three Liberated Negroes' (Article) 7, 39–40
 worked with King, Thomas 100
 Yoruba wars 13
Crowther, Susan 114
Cupidon, John 16, 198 n.13, 198 n.15
 birth of 138
 career 137
 death of 138
 enslavement 137–8
 MacCarthy's Island 138
 statement of 139–41
Curtin, Philip 1–2, 81–3, 175 n.3, 178 n.22, 192 n.6

David, George 20–1, 162
 biography 157–60
 birth of 155
 at Bombay 156
 education and marriage 156

Lamb, James Abner 156
Streeter, John 156
 at Zanzibar, Arab traders 155–6
Deimler, James 21, 170–1
Deimler, Paul 171
Dido 28, 186 n.3
Doherty, William 114, 117
 captured by Dahomean forces 118
 enslavement 118
 life history 118–22
Dois Amigos 76, 191 n.2
domestic slavery 17–18, 76, 138, 196 n.1
Dopemu, Daniel 13, 18, 129
 Awa 125–6
 deposition of 130–1
 Robbin, Henry 129
Doulton, Lindsay 184 n.84, 184 nn.77–8
Dove, Thomas 7, 82, 192 n.4

East Africa, enslavement in 19–23
Ebute Metta 113
Egba 11–12, 14–15, 82, 99, 103–4, 114, 126, 192 n.14, 192 n.16, 193 n.5
Egba Alake 82
Egbado 117–18
Egypt 5, 178 n.20
Eltis, David 14, 182 n.57
emancipation 4, 11–12, 18, 49, 100, 103, 108, 162, 183 n.64, 198 n.6
enslavement 1–2, 4, 176 n.5, 181 n.48, 183 n.69, 187 n.2, 192 n.6, 196 n.4, 198 n.6, 201 n.2.
 See also Liberated Africans
 in East Africa 19–23
 geographies and chronologies 10–16
 missionary sources 178 n.20
 in West Africa 16–19
Ethiopia 20, 200 n.12

Faulkner, Valentine 113, 194 n.1
Findlay, Alexander 188 n.5, 189 n.2, 189 n.7, 190 n.21
Fọlayan, Kọla 195 n.4
Fox, William 17–18, 54, 138, 183 n.71, 196 n.2, 197 n.5, 199 n.5

Act for the Abolition of Slavery (1833) 134
Gum, John 147
Will, James 189 n.1
Freetown 3, 10–12, 16, 28, 36, 39, 44, 57–8, 63–4, 82, 92, 100, 103, 114, 118, 177 n.9, 185 n.3, 189 n.1, 191 n.6, 193 n.21
Frere, Bartle 20
Frere Town 20, 156, 162, 168–70, 180 n.37
Fyfe, Christopher 44, 177 n.12, 187 n.5, 192 n.3

Gambia, The 2, 7, 49, 54, 76, 92, 183 n.62, 187 n.1, 188 nn.4–6, 197 nn.11–15, 198 n.14, 199 nn.8–11
  Cupidon, John 137–8
  enslavement 16–19
  Findlay, Alexander 190 n.21
  Gay, Mary Ann 143–4
  Grant, Alexander 199 n.3
  Gum, John 147–8
  Harding, Charles 13, 54
  Macumba, Jack 133–4
  slavery and emancipation 183 n.64
  Thompson, George 57
Gay, Mary Ann 6
  life history 143–4
  statement of 144–6
Gerber, James 16, 193 n.1
  life history 95
  statement of 96–7
Glover, John Hawley 126–7
Godman, Matthew 138
Gorée 16–18, 133–4, 137–8, 143–4, 147, 183 n.69, 197 n.9, 198 n.13, 199 n.11
Grant, Alexander 16, 182 n.61, 199 n.3
Grant, Charles 134, 138, 188 n.6
Greene, Sandra E. 8, 180 n.36
Griffiths, Gareth 8
Gum, John 199 n.1, 199 n.3, 199 n.6
  life history 147–8
  statement of 148–51

Hamerton, Atkins 19
Handler, Jerome S. 182 n.48
Harding, Charles 13
  life history 53–4
  Owu War 53–4
  statement of 54–5
Harding, Matthew Thomas 15–16, 179 n.28, 182 n.59
  life history 39–40
  statement of 40–1
Henriqueta 82, 192 n.6, 193 n.21
HMS *Brisk* 28
HMS *Esk* 76
HMS *Maidstone* 82, 108, 181 n.45
HMS *Primrose* 64
HMS *Thetis* 170, 170
homelands 9, 170
Hopper, Matthew S. 20, 184 n.76
'How Thomas King Became a Slave' (Article) 4–5, 178 n.18
Hughes, John 199 n.11

Ibadan 11, 16, 103–4
Iberia 12, 100
Ifacayeh. *See* May, Joseph Boston
Ijemo 11, 103
Ikereku Idan 13, 104
Ikotto 75
Indian Ocean 9, 19–21, 177 n.9
indigenous deities 193 n.18
Irving, Edward George 11, 182 n.50, 188 n.4
  Barber's testimony 103–5
  statement of 104–5
Isenberg, Charles William 20, 22, 156, 162, 167, 200 n.12, 201 n.1
Iwarreh/Iware 75

James Island 16, 199 n.3
Janjanbureh 17
Johnson, Samuel 53
Johnson, William Augustin Bernard 3, 8, 44, 177 n.13, 179 n.29
  Proceedings of the Church Missionary Society for Africa and the East 27–8
  and Yamsey, Josiah 27–33
Jones, Adam 185 n.2
Jones, William Henry 20–1, 165, 201 n.12
  autobiography of 163
  birth of 161

death of 162
East Africa, CMS mission in 162
self history 163–4
at Sharanpur 162
at Zanzibar 162
journal extract system 3

Kealoo 64
Kenya 2–3, 5, 19–21, 23, 156, 162
Kilwa 19, 22, 155, 162, 201 n.12
Kilwa Kisiwani 155
the King's Yard 114, 194 n.7
King, Thomas 4, 9, 12–13
  education 100
  enslavement 99–100
  statement of 100–2
Koelle, Sigismund Wilhelm 2, 114, 176 n.8
Kopytoff, Jean Herskovits 182 n.52

Lagos 2, 10, 12–13, 15–16, 18, 49, 76, 82–3, 100, 114, 118, 125–6, 129, 190 n.11, 192 n.6
Lake Ahémé 190 n.11
Lake Malawi (Lake Nyasa) 21–2, 161, 170
Lamb, James Abner 156
Law, Robin 4, 13, 53–4, 177 n.15, 179 n.25
Lemain Island 16
Liberated Africans 2, 14–15, 83, 108, 114, 179 nn.29–30, 181 n.45, 181 n.48, 188 n.6, 190 n.21, 194 n.7, 195 n.1. *See also* enslavement
  Allen, William 12
  Attarra, John 43–8
  Barber, James 11, 103–5
  Campbell, John 49–51
  Doherty, William 117–22
  education of 184 n.80
  Gerber, James 16, 95–7
  Harding, Charles 53–5
  Harding, Matthew Thomas 39–41
  homelands, reminiscences of 9
  Jones, William Henry 161–5
  King, Thomas 99–102
  May, Joseph Boston 75–9
  movement of 10–11
  Noah, David 35–8

'returnees' 3
Semler, Ishmael 167–8
Thompson, George 57–61
Wilhelm, Andrew 193 n.5
Will, James 63–74
Will, Thomas 64–5, 190 n.22
Wilson, Peter 10
Wright, Joseph 82–3
Yorubaland 13
Lloyd, Edward 143–4
Lloyd, Richard 143–4, 197 n.9
Loreto 57
Lovejoy, Paul 9, 181 n.42

Mabruki, Cecil 173
MacBrair, Robert Maxwell 138
MacCarthy, Charles 11, 16–17, 182 n.60
MacCarthy's Island 16–17, 54, 138
Macumba, Jack
  enslavement 133–4
  Fox, William 134
  Grant, Charles 134
  manumission 134
  statement of 134–6
Mahoney, Florence 18, 183 n.63
Mahoney, Frances 144
Makodu 199 n.2
Makua 21, 161, 170
manumission 18, 134
Marke, Charles 191 n.7
Marshall, Richard 54, 197 n.14, 199 n.8
Marsh, William 193 n.5
Martin, John 57–8
Mason, Charles 35–6, 186 n.1
Mauritius 19
Maxwell, Charles 28, 39, 182 n.59
May, Claudius 191 n.1, 191 n.4
May, Joseph Boston 7, 9, 79, 181 n.40, 191 n.1
  birth of 75
  domestic slavery 76
  the life and experience of 77–8
  statement of 76–7
  teaching profession 76
Mbotela, James Jumba 180–1 n.37
Melville, Michael 194 n.4
Methodist Missionary Society (MMS) 1–2, 4, 11, 15, 23, 81, 133–4,

137, 147–8, 176 n.7, 179 n.30, 198 n.14
Mill, John Sterling 36
mission agents 2–3, 6, 178 n.19
missionary publications 4, 7, 21
mission stations 2, 20, 126, 156, 168, 170, 196 n.4
MMS. *See* Methodist Missionary Society (MMS)
Moister, William 137–8, 197 n.5
Moitt, Bernard 183 n.69
Morgan, John 138, 197 n.11, 198 n.14
Morton, Fred 4, 20, 162, 178 n.17, 184 n.81, 201 n.12
Mozambique 20–1, 161, 167, 170
Müller, John Christian 16, 95, 182 n.60

narratives 1, 17, 23–4. *See also* Liberated Africans
  autobiographical 5–6
  homelands 9
  improbable and poetic 8–9
  structure and arc 6
'Narratives of Three Liberated Negroes' (Article) 7, 39–40
Ndakourroo 197 n.7
Ngindo 155
Nigeria 2, 10, 13–14, 23, 113
Noah, David 186 n.1, 187 n.6
  Mason and Bostock 35–6
  Mill's slave factory 36
  Sierra Leone, arrival in 36
  statement of 37–8

Oba 82–3, 192 n.6, 193 n.17
Ògbóni 192 n.14
Ògún 190 n.12
Ogun River 75, 190 n.18
O'Hear, Ann 182 n.56
Olney, James 178 n.21
Oroge, E. Adeniyi 195 n.4
Owu War 13, 53–4, 64, 107
Oyo Empire 4, 6, 10–11, 13–14, 53, 75, 99, 107

Page, Jesse 178 n.18
Palmié, Stephan 180 n.36

Peel, J. D. Y. 3, 177 nn.11–12, 193 n.20
Pemba 21, 155
Peterson, John 36, 186 n.4
Pierre, Antoine 134
Polyglotta Africana (Koelle) 2, 176 n.8
Price, William Salter 20, 156
Primitive Methodist Missionary Society (PMMS) 176 n.7
Princess Charlotte 35–6
Principe 64
Proceedings of the Church Missionary Society for Africa and the East (Johnson) 27–8

Rebmann, David 172–3
Rebmann, Johannes 162, 168
redemption 17, 134, 196 n.4
red water 186 n.6
Rendall, George 18, 134, 148, 199 n.10
Republic of Benin 14
Right, Joseph 91
  Crowther, Samuel 91
  Gambia and Sierra Leone mission fields 92
  statement of 92–3
River Gambia 16–17
Robbin, Henry 18, 125–6
  cotton production 126
  deposition of Awa 127–8
Robinson, Morgan J. 21
Ryan, Maeve 181 n.47

Saint-Louis 17, 138, 143, 198 n.13
Sallah, Pierre 198 n.6
Schön, James Frederick 11
Searing, James F. 183 nn.68–9
Semler, Ishmael 9, 20, 156, 201 n.2
  life history 167–8
Senegal 133, 138, 143, 182 n.59, 198 n.6
Seychelles 19
Sharanpur 20, 156, 162
Shields, Francine 182 n.58
Sierra Leone 2, 7, 9, 20, 23, 32, 92, 108, 114, 170, 180 n.33, 190 n.21, 192 n.3, 196 n.4

African mission agents 3
Attarra, John 43–5
Barber, James 13, 103–4
Campbell, John 49
Doherty, William 118
Gerber, James 16, 95, 193 n.1
Harding, Charles 54
Harding, Thomas 15, 39–40
interpreters and CMS 'native agents' 11
King, Thomas 99
Marke, Charles 191 n.7
May, Joseph Boston 75–6
Melville, Michael 194 n.4
Noah, David 35–6
Robbin, Henry 125–6
Thompson, George 57–61
Wright, Joseph 82–3
Sierra Leone Public Archives (SLPA) 186 n.5
slave ships 10, 12, 19, 28, 57, 76, 100, 108, 199 n.3
slave trade
 Arab 18, 23, 155, 162
 Brazilian 64, 83
 East African 6, 20, 155, 170
 European 99
 Havana 100
 nineteenth-century 6, 9
 Portuguese 15–16, 76
 transatlantic 6, 10, 14–15
 Zanzibar 155
spiritual biography 7–8
Spitzer, Leo 4, 178 n.16, 191 n.3
St. Mary's Island 16–17, 54, 92, 147
Streeter, John 156
Sudan 5, 178 n.20

Tanzania 5, 19, 155–6, 162
Thompson, George
 journal of 58–61
 life history 57–8
Townsend, Henry 114
transatlantic slave trades 6, 10, 14–15
translation 8, 11, 100, 117, 138, 169, 181 n.37, 199 n.8
Treaty of Paris (1814) 16

Uganda 5, 156
United Methodist Missionary Society (UMMS) 176 n.7
Universities' Mission to Central Africa (UMCA) 21, 185 n.88

Vaughan, Megan 161
Velas 82
Veloz Pasajera 64
Venn, Henry 3

Wesleyan Methodist Missionary Society (WMMS) 49, 54, 176 n.7
West Africa, enslavement in 16–19
West Central Africa 14
Wilhelm, Andrew 193 n.5
William, Duiah 173–4
Will, James 189 n.2, 190 n.13
 apprenticeships 64
 birth of 63–4
 escaping from enemy 69
 fears of returning home 69–70
 food and clothing 65–6
 HMS *Primrose* 64
 Kealoo 64
 loss of family members, punishment 70–1
 men's trade 66–7
 praying to god 72–4
 Veloz Pasajera 64
 war and slavery 68–9
 Will, Thomas 64–5
 worship 67–8
Will, Thomas 64–5, 190 n.22
Wilson, Eliza 181 n.44
Wilson, Peter 10, 188 n.6, 194 n.4
 Avizo 108, 181 n.45
 birth name ('Lai-guan-dai') 108
 birth of 107
 A Brief Memoir of the Late Peter Wilson (Eliza) 108–11
 HMS *Maidstone* 108, 181 n.45
 life history 107–8
 Owu War 107
Wolof 17, 138, 180 n.33, 198 n.6
Wright, Joseph 9, 91–2
 birth of 82
 Curtin, Philip 81–2

death of 83
  enslavement 192 n.6
  funeral 83
  life of 84–9
  May, Joseph Boston 83, 180 n.33, 191 n.1
  in Sierra Leone 82–3
  visit to Britain 82
Wright, Marcia 20, 176 n.6

Yamsey, Josiah 8, 15
  Dido 28
  HMS *Brisk* 28
  life history 27–8, 179 n.29
  Proceedings of the Church Missionary Society for Africa and the East (Johnson) 27–8
  statement of 28–33

Yao 21–2, 161, 167
Yoruba 7, 9, 92, 117, 180 n.33, 182 n.58, 190 n.12, 190 n.23
  CMS 'native agents' 12
  language 82
  Liberated African 9, 49, 57, 75
  mission 3, 11–13, 43, 99–100
  Owu War 53–4, 107
  slave trade 6
  Townsend, Henry 114
  wars 4, 6, 11, 13–14, 21, 103–4
Yorubaland 13, 53–4, 99, 114, 190 n.12

Zanzibar 19–21, 155–6, 162, 170, 185 n.88
Zorn, Theodore 201 nn.10–11

www.ingramcontent.com/pod-product-compliance
Lightning Source LLC
Chambersburg PA
CBHW071838230426
43671CB00012B/1998